I, GOLDSTEIN

I, GOLDSTEIN

My Screwed Life

BY AL GOLDSTEIN
AND JOSH ALAN FRIEDMAN

THUNDER'S MOUTH PRESS • NEW YORK

I, Goldstein: *My Screwed Life*

Published by
Thunder's Mouth Press
An Imprint of Avalon Publishing Group, Inc.
245 West 17th Street, 11th floor
New York, NY 10011
www.thundersmouth.com

AVALON
publishing group incorporated

First printing, October 2006

Library of Congress Cataloging-in-Publication Data is available.

ISBN: 1-56025-868-3
ISBN-13: 978-1-56025-868-1

9 8 7 6 5 4 3 2 1

Interior book design by Maria E. Torres

Printed in the United States of America
Distributed by Publishers Group West

For No One

Contents

Special thanks to Richard Jaccoma, who helped in every editorial capacity throughout the preparation of this book

There is no man so good who, were he to submit all his thoughts and actions to the laws, would not deserve hanging ten times in his life.

—Michel de Montaigne, French philosopher

Prologue

STATEN ISLAND FERRY, 2005

I went into the toilet. From $11 million to nothing. I feel like nothing. A deposed porn king, exiled to Staten Island. Holding a shopping bag of prescriptions, I wait on line for the ferry at the bottom of Manhattan. The people shuffling in with me at South Ferry are failures and losers who can't afford the big city. They should have zeros on their foreheads, like Auschwitz, where the Jews had tattoos. I'd like to put up an Auschwitz sign at the entrance with showers to hose everyone down. I feel no inspiration looking out the unwashed windows of the ferry at the Statue of Liberty each morning on my way to be examined at Bellevue mental hospital, along with the poor, huddled masses. I'm poor and huddled. Bellevue has served the immigrant poor since 1736. I'm now a poor immigrant. I wait on line four hours for a blood test, to see how my lithium is interacting with a dozen other medications.

Norman Podhoretz said, "One of the longest journeys in the world is the journey from Brooklyn to Manhattan." I say, the most pathetic journey in the world is the journey from Manhattan to Staten Island.

CHAPTER 1

The Great Pornographer: A Day in the Life

PRIME OF GOLDSTEIN, CIRCA 1980

On a typical restless night without sex, I hear a dozen cuckoo clocks go off at once in my head. But I know I'm not nuts. They're like internal cuckoo clocks, each alarm representing a perceived slight, an enemy real or imagined, a score to be settled. So I did what I always do, no matter how late—dial the dictaphones of my four secretaries and reign abuse into their answering machines. My abusive calls—dumping on an employee paid to take it—would then be soberly typed up as office minutes. *Oh, that Al.* All in a morning's work for the secretaries. It might be a rant about the corner dry cleaner that ruined a shirt, an airline that lost my luggage, or a defect in, say, my new Mercedes Benz. I might blast the New York Health & Racquet Club for their membership scams, or a clerk at Forty-seventh Street Camera who yawned and turned his head when asked a shopping question.

While average Joes shriveled under the daily indignities of life, frozen in a silent scream—like my own father—something set me far apart from the Little Man, with whom I've sided my entire life. I published the most notorious, uproarious and influential porno-graphic newspaper in the world: *Screw*.

What motivates me is not love, but hatred. Without my many enemies, I would not be able to get up in the morning. I have never turned the other cheek. *Screw* was always fueled by anger. Unlike others who reach success, I was not warmed or tempered by it. I remained angry and only got crazier. I got up every morning to face my enemies. And I loved it.

In the case of the Mercedes, I hollered into Bobbi's dictaphone for ten minutes, blaming her fat ass, her dead mother's fat ass, and the CEO of Mercedes Benz for the unrepaired defect in my car. I wasn't concerned that some arrogant CEO wouldn't know me from a rat's ass—or the repair schedule of my local dealership. And I didn't even know if Bobbi had a dead mother with a fat ass—she was my coked-up, bottom-bitch secretary who screened my calls and made appointments. But I yelled until I was hoarse. I'd arrange mock Mercedes ads in *Screw* and on my cable TV show, *Midnight Blue*. I'd dredge up a forty-year-old history about Mercedes's prodigious involvement in Hitler's Third Reich war machine. Buy a Benz—Kill a Jew! I'd paste their CEO's head on an SS uniform, goose-stepping his autoworkers through the Mercedes assembly line. Unless they made good on the warranty and fixed the defect in my new Benz. They were fucking with Citizen Goldstein, the Hebrew Pit Bull, the wrong customer. And that's why I'm cheered by cops, firemen, cab, truck and bus drivers, mailmen, Chinese waiters, and even sanitation workers hanging from garbage trucks, whenever I'm seen on the streets of New York.

With this off my chest, I go back to sleep like a satiated baby.

Morning in Manhattan. I can't wait to get to work. Step out of my oversized silk pajamas that stretch around my girth. *I feel pretty, oh so pretty, oh so witty and flitty and gay!* Never time for breakfast. I want to get to the office. Dinner is the special meal. The office is where I'm king of the mountain. Kiss the wife, who teaches high school English, get the kid off to private school, nod to his nanny, ring for my limo. Wave to good neighbor Bill Cosby, whose townhouse adjoins mine at 247 East Sixty-first Street, as we both leave for work. He's a lovely man. I'm ready to leave this sheltered environment—a demilitarized zone away from the world I would now enter.

Morning pickup by John Flynn, my debonair chauffeur and armed bodyguard. Flynn is a retired NYPD vice cop who once busted blind news dealers for selling *Screw*. Whenever we go to Times Square, the older hookers still remember him. "Hey, John Flynn!" they heckle, "What'cha doin', John Flynn, you hot, John Flynn. Suck yo' dick tonight, Officer Flynn?"

Milky Way Productions, 114 West Fourteenth Street, is head-quarters of the Goldstein empire. We ride up to the fourth floor, the business offices. The editorial and art departments are on the eleventh. We buzz through the metal door where my four secretaries are manning phones and typewriters. Flynn takes a seat, pours a coffee, cracks open his *Daily News*. I enter my private office. My message machine is filled with anonymous death threats. The death threats don't faze me at all. But after two chocolate chip cookies, I feel like jumping out the window. Probably gained some weight, reminds me of the fat days. I have Bobbi book another appointment at the fat farm in Durham, North Carolina.

Sitting on my desk are today's *Times, News, Wall Street Journal* and a new pile of mail-order catalogs. The first order of the day is to rifle through the catalogs like a greedy, spoiled infant, circling *chatchkas* by the dozen from Sharper Image, Hammacher Schlemmer, Neiman Marcus, you name it. I had money to burn. The back-page advertising in *Screw* alone brought in fifty grand a week. I had several money losing conceits, like *Cigar*, the first publication for tobacco connoisseurs. Bill Cosby read it. I never pressed him to be in *Screw*, but he graciously sampled cigars for *Cigar*. In my newsletter, *Gadget*, I road-tested electronics, mostly freebies, and could write off my manic-compulsive mail orders. Once a year I went to the Consumer Electronics Show for five days on a buying splurge.

Bobbi is head secretary, whose thousand-dollar-a-week freebase habit I tacitly help support. I have an extra bachelor apartment at 215 West Thirteeth Street, where Bobbi gets stoned when she isn't seeing her husband. I took Bobbi to Europe on the Concord. She's a hot piece of ass, my "Gal Friday," as Walter Winchell would have said. Donna Berg is another secretary/girlfriend; Terri is another; Els Price is an efficient secretary, but I didn't fuck her. So I feel deprived. I always want more. These four women are like my slaves. Three of them basically fulfill daily catalog mail orders and returns—that's how much crap I acquire. Bobbi handles my appointments, takes my calls, the den mother.

Porn star/publisher Gloria Leonard, of *High Society*, is another girlfriend. We toyed with getting married. She's smart, a good friend and a great lay. We went to the Concord Hotel in upstate New York with my son Jordon, who spent four days at a magic camp. As with everyone I've known, I got into a fight with Gloria. She got mad when she found out I wanted to fuck her grown daughter. I'm unforgiving and inflexible—you're either my friend or enemy. I will eventually lose valuable long-term friendships with Hugh Hefner, Larry Flynt, Dennis Hoff . . . the list goes on and on.

But there are many people who love and admire me. I pick up lavish dinner checks every week for a wide circle of friends, male and female, high and low. I'm bosom buddies with a small fraternity of cocksmen who make porn movies, like Harry Reems, Marc Stevens, and Jaimie Gillis, the best actor in the biz; *Deep Throat/Devil in Miss Jones* director Gerard Damiano; *Penthouse* publisher Bob Guccione; Fred Lincoln, Tiffany Clark, and Bobby Hollander, who was Gloria Leonard's boyfriend and the Svengali of doomed young porn starlet Shauna Grant, who would shoot herself to death. I also count many luminaries from the real world as friends—journalists, novelists, artists, stars of stage and screen, comedians, business tycoons and most important of all, delicatessen and restaurant owners.

"Al, you have a blowjob from Seka scheduled at ten thirty," comes Bobbi, matter-of-factly, checking my calendar. "That gives you two left after today." Formally speaking, I have a *Midnight Blue* interview with her first. Seka recently lost a bet. She owes me five blowjobs, to be administered wherever and to whomever I decide. I've already used up two. I could bestow one upon visiting business dignitaries to sweeten the negotiations for, say, the distributors of a Japanese *Screw* deal I'm brokering. On second thought, I'll keep Seka's blowjobs for myself.

But the most underrated of my daily enjoyments is just about due. The sensation of a healthy shit topped off with super-plush toilet paper in my private stall is a marvelously sensual thing that makes life far better than death. Last night I dined at the Palace restaurant; a six-hour, twelve-course dinner. The swordfish was truly fresh, broiled perfectly. The turds that graduate from the Great Pornographer's bowels are wonders to behold and represent the finest in cuisine New York has to offer. After dinner, I enjoy smoking a double Corona smuggled in from Switzerland.

Several pounds lighter, I saunter into the *Midnight Blue* studios on the same floor. My show began in 1975 as *Screw's* TV counterpart, and has remained the most popular program on Manhattan cable TV since. It also beams into Honolulu, but don't ask me how. *Midnight Blue* has two full-time overworked technicians. Bearded cameraman Albert Jaccoma, for years the picture of blue-collar propriety, suddenly started sporting a dress to work each day. In the offices of *Screw*, nobody seems to notice. Second cameraman Irwin Friman is Albert's foil. Albert tortures Irwin. "All this man ever talks or thinks about is *shit!*" cries Albert in mock exasperation to guests in the studio. "It's shit in the morning, shit in the afternoon, shit in the evening. Shit, shit, shit!" And then he hoists his dress and thrusts out his derrière. "Stare into the *abyss*, Irwin!" he orders, spreading his buttocks while describing an imaginary "grape-like cluster of hemorrhoids."

Dorky Irwin approaches the girls after a lesbian shoot, his Adam's apple bobbing up and down: "Umm . . . did ya, did ya really come? Really?"

These are the type of individuals I have to work with, the kind of unlaid losers on my payroll. We're on standby for my interview with Seka, who arrives at the studio with her husband Ken. Albert and Irwin train their cameras, the red lights glow and we're rolling:

AL: You know I respect you like crazy. Have you read Spinoza lately, or Aristotle?

SEKA: No.

Al: Sit on my face anyway. I don't give a shit. How many fuck films have you made in the past and what films are projected for the future?

SEKA: I have done approximately thirty full-length feature films; I've lost count of my 8 mm loops, there are so many of them. I took some time off for myself. I needed to reju-venate and put it all back together. There are many surprises in the future, so you'll see Seka like you've never seen her before.

AL: Hopefully on my face.

SEKA: That we can do anytime.

AL: Again and again, until I get it right. As you now, our readers hardly ever have a real woman in front of them. What is your sexual life in reality?

SEKA: This is not a cartoon character for me. I enjoy fucking and sucking or I couldn't do it on screen. I don't do anything on screen that I don't enjoy in my private life.

AL: What about cocksucking. Is that something you enjoy doing?

SEKA: Of course. I have been named *the* cocksucker of pornography.

AL: What about Women Against Porn, who would say that you are being used and abused? Are you being forced to do what you're doing? Are there guns at your head? Do you enjoy what you're doing or do you feel you're being exploited?

SEKA: *Exploitation* is a large word. It doesn't deal only with pornography. You can be exploited in any field you're in; it does not matter what you do. I don't feel I'm being exploited at all. I'm doing what I want to do. There's not a machine gun at my back if I sit here with Al Goldstein.

I feel that members of Women Against Pornography probably never had orgasms in their lives and probably never will. They say that women are being misused and abused in the adult entertainment industry. There are men in this industry, too, and if women are being exploited and their bodies are making money for other people, then they should also jump on the bandwagon for men, because men are there, too; they're being exploited, they're being used, their bodies are making money just like women's.

AL: Would you go down on a woman who looked like most of the Women Against Porn?

SEKA: If I felt they would enjoy it and it was something I wanted to do, yes. I don't always take someone's looks into account. That's bad sexually.

AL: How did you feel when you first saw Johnny Holmes's cock? How long ago was that?

SEKA: Six years ago. And I had seen many of John's movies and magazines and had always fantasized about seeing that cock because how often do you see a thirteen-and-a-half-inch cock? When he dropped his pants, I dropped my jaw. I couldn't believe that there was that much cock in the world.

AL: How much did you get down your throat?

SEKA: Not a lot of it. He's big around.

AL: When John Holmes was fucking you, how much of his cock did he get into you?

SEKA: I'd say that about four inches were left over.

AL: About as much as most guys are! You must have felt him at the end of your pussy. Was that when it became painful and you said that there's no more room?

SEKA: It didn't feel painful. It felt fantastic.

AL: What would happen if he forced the other four inches in?

SEKA: We could probably do it, but I would have to just totally relax.

AL: You really felt stuffed but you never felt full? Did you feel like a turkey with Christmas stuffing in it?

SEKA: I felt . . . packed.

AL: You once said John Holmes is the best pussy-eater you've ever experienced. Which seems amazing because I think he'd be so narcissistic and self-centered, he would not care about your pleasure.

SEKA: As soon as he started eating my pussy he knew exactly where to go and exactly what to do. He didn't waste any time getting there.

AL: You're dressed up, I feel like I'm with a nun. Can you get this fucking stuff off? I'd like to see your tits.

SEKA: I'm dressed too demure? Is that better? [removes one tit]

AL: That's lovely. I forgot the next question! Okay, where are fuck films going? [*Al mouths tit*]

SEKA: Look what you're doing to me. My nipple is getting hard. I've never seen my nipple get this hard before.

AL: I've never seen my dick get this hard before . . . Seka, I respect you like crazy. Okay, while I'm playing with your tits—and I'm so happy. This is a great joy. I'm in no hurry for this interview to end—let's get the other one out. Why don't you talk about the Gettysburg Address, I don't care what you tell us. . . .

I created the porn star interview and do at least one a week. I always try for some pussy or a blowjob. Sometimes it's a done deal, I don't even have to ask. Other times my groveling Brooklyn charm back-fires and I can barely get an interview subject to fish out a tit. Some porn starlets are screaming prudes in real life. In 1973, *Screw* released its first fuck film, *It Happened in Hollywood*, directed by future horror meister, Wes Craven. I received an onscreen blowjob from a starlet named Katherine. After I came in her mouth, I asked her out to lunch. She declined; it would be "cheating" on her boyfriend.

In the case of ice queen, Annette Haven, I groveled on my knees for a blowjob for years and got nothing. But Seka is a "real trouper," as we respectfully call enthusiastic women in the trade.

Next up is my "Fuck You" taping for *Midnight Blue*. The show saves me thousands in psychiatric bills as I vent my daily frustrations, both petty and profound, into the succoring camera. My former ally Mayor Koch reported with glee the closings of porn shops in Times Square, while violent crimes there were on the rise. The once liberal and progressive Ed Koch won reelection even though I endorsed him. He now bows to the basest interests of Big Real Estate, destroyers of the soul of New York and its ethnic neighborhoods. My open letter to Mayor Koch protested the new "Dear John" policy, whereby the names of convicted "johns," patrons of prostitutes, were being released to the media for publication and broadcast on radio. Koch responded on Office of the Mayor, City of New York letterhead, published as a *Screw* editorial:

Dear Al:

Et tu, Goldstein?

I really wasn't expecting to hear from you the subject of johns and prostitutes. But, since you asked, here's my answer.

I make no moral judgment on the question of prostitution per se. It has been my position that what consenting adults do is no one else's business. However, what happens on the streets and in public places is the legitimate concern of everyone. It has been clearly demonstrated throughout our five boroughs that streetwalkers of either sex do not engage in "victimless" crime. The first victim of hookers who engage in public solicitation is the quality of life on the streets. Sex acts are performed in parks, doorways and parked cars. Crimes such as intimidation, drugs and robbery sharply increase.

Do you really believe in the myth that streetwalking is a "victimless" crime?

The central issue here is a legal one. The State Legislature has determined that prostitution is a crime, and that prostitutes and those who patronize them are equally guilty. My suggestion to release the names of convicted johns to the media was prompted by the injustice of courts, which frequently level penalties against prostitutes while allowing the johns to go unpunished.

I do not share your belief that red-light districts (even if they are renamed "Eros Centers") are the answer to this problem. While at one time I suggested that an adult pleasure zone might be established where Constitutionally protected books and movies could be located, I have never recommended the establishment of a "Combat Zone" where prostitution would be lawful. The negative and sometimes violent results of Boston's "Combat Zone" have served as a warning to other cities.

What happens in public is subject to public approval. Your call for dignity in sexuality can best be realized by keeping it private.

Sincerely,

Edward I. Koch

Mayor

I wholeheartedly disagree, but graciously acknowledged Koch's viewpoint. My wife Gena agreed with him totally. However, I decided to shitlist him anyway, put his head in a toilet, and gave Hizzoner the finger with a resounding "Fuck You" on *Midnight Blue*.

I have now dumped three loads—my morning bowel movement, my invective bile, and my jism in Seka's mouth. I feel light and gay. But it isn't long before I become angry again. I yell at John Kois, *Screw*'s associate publisher, about how to negotiate with major advertisers like Spartacus Leisure Spa and Plato's Retreat. Kois serves as my cold business alter ego, my prick. I hired him to be a prick, to handle all unpleasant matters of running the company—firing and hiring among thirty full-time employees, chasing debts, all the petty dirty work. That way, I can remain Lovable Al, letting everyone bask in the greatness of my grossness. I call him a prick, I introduce him to people as a prick. Everyone agrees: he is a prick.

Though *Screw* had an anniversary ball every November, it is the associate publisher's idea not to invite our many advertisers. This is good business strategy. Kois also discouraged there ever being a separate advertiser's ball for the motley madams, pimps, hookers, parlors, and clubs that make up our back pages. He doesn't want them all to meet at once—and commiserate. We bulldozed open the first advertising venue for getting laid, I went to jail for it. We've since maintained the exclusive loyalty of New York's sex trade for many years.

Kois came to New York from Wisconsin, where the underground paper he edited in the sixties stirred some controversy, which came to my attention. He soon left behind his counterculture roots and became the squirming, toadying, snakelike prick that his job required. Kois is highest paid at Milky Way Productions after myself, and stands to make a killing someday from the company's profit-sharing plan. I always sense, when doomsday arrives and the company goes down in flames, Kois will be poised to climb out of the bowl, like the little Tidy Bowl man, and escape unscathed as the troubled waters of *Screw* go swirling down the toilet. He will eventually embezzle from the company.

I am putting up my townhouse as collateral for $160,000 to keep Plato's Retreat founder Larry Levenson out of jail on a bogus tax rap. It's an obvious frame-up. The City wants to close Plato's, the most successful swing club in America, because it's a sex business. No one's sure whether Levenson is just a frontman, a patsy, maybe even a goombah who changed his name. Except he's too dumb to change his name. I've let Larry slide on the back-page Plato's Retreat ad in *Screw* every week. He owes me fifty grand, which I doubt I'll ever get back, but we're good friends. We often challenge each other—kike to

kike—on bets about losing weight, schtupping broads, and a legendary "Pecker Full of Miracles" contest in which Larry came fifteen
times within twenty-four hours. Who really owns Plato's? I'll tell you
who. Maybe you shouldn't ask too many questions, that's who. When
I testified at Levenson's trial, the judge gave me the dirtiest look I've
ever received in my life. I'm the ultimate trophy he'd like to have
before his sentencing gavel.

Each weekly issue of *Screw* is one more strike against the world. If
I ever lose it all, I'll merely shrug, amazed to have even gotten so far.
Back in my office, I chew out a well-known porn director over the
phone for using a *nom de cinema*, instead of his real name. Am I the
only pornographer who uses his real name? I chew out *Screw*'s comp-
troller, Philip, for not writing off my hookers in Hong Kong as tax
expenses. Philip keeps *Screw*'s books neater than a Torah scroll,
making sure we pay more than we owe. The IRS has a guy in here
every week. The government allows us to run our hooker advertising,
as long as we cut them in on it.

Lawyers love me and I make them rich. I strategize daily with Ken
Norwick, Esq., about my continuing lawsuit against the NYPD for
refusing me a gun permit. The publisher of the *New York Times* is
allowed to carry a gun, and so are sixty-six thousand other permit
holders in New York. I threaten to sue whenever they delay NYPD
press ID cards for my editorial staff. I won't let them set a precedent
this year by denying us the same credentials as the dailies. I fuck
them! Fortunately, I have friends on the other side of the law to keep
things smooth. I take a phone call from a former stripper, Tiffany
Day, who now owns her own club called Playmates in Times Square.
The mob just beat the shit out of her and took over her establishment. She begs me to help her; I rarely refuse someone in trouble. I'll

quietly use my own influence. One properly placed call and I can have Playmates's current management removed and Tiffany reinstated. This becomes a done deal.

I send Flynn to pick up "happy hooker" Xaviera Hollander, who was deported for her chutzpah in trying to liberate prostitution. She's visiting from Amsterdam, and I'll take her to lunch at Pastrami King on Forty-seventh Street, in the Diamond District. The big Irishman, John Flynn, escorts us to our table, surrounded by Hassids and Lubavitcher Yids. I love New York. Xaviera and I are two middle-aged Jews who discuss and devour pastrami, gefilte fish, chopped liver, and a bowl of sour pickles. Neither of us utter so much as a syllable about sex the whole hour. We could care less when there's food on the table.

After lunch is the weekly *Screw* editorial meeting. I take the back service elevator to the eleventh floor. Joe drives me up. He's the fat, Puerto Rican building super, and I offer to comp him a hooker for Christmas. Joe breaks a smile and contemplates my offer with relish: "I'll unzip my pants to my knees, stand back like this and tell her: Go ahead, *enjoy jourself!*"

It's later reported Joe couldn't get erect until he led her back to the service elevator. He draped curtains inside for the occasion and then performed *amore*, elevator-style.

I look out over my staff, a collection of misfits and losers that could only be assembled under the auspices of *Screw*. News items for the week are discussed with *Screw*'s entire art and editorial departments. The succession of editors I have to put up with are all sexually repressed; that's why they work for me. A sorry bunch, but I'll spare you the details. I'm a generous publisher, at least with "petty cash" expenses. We sit on couches and chairs assembled in the managing editor's office with fresh donuts, coffee, and fruit arranged by Sydney, the gorgeous Creole editorial assistant, on the center table. The sky windows are dirty, looking uptown at the city from the eleventh floor over funky Fourteenth Street. Joe doesn't do windows. There are great *cuchifrito* counters downstairs, with Cuban *pernil* sandwiches and strong Puerto Rican café con leche, which fuels my editors. We often have a visitor in attendance quietly observing the weekly editorial meeting. Recent guests include Melvin Van Peebles, Philip Roth, and Abbie Hoffman, who came out of hiding for one afternoon. He was a hero to me. I wanted desperately to be in the Chicago Seven trial, but I was nobody then.

Philip Roth spent three days at the *Screw* offices, declaring my staff "nine-to-five anarchists." I am the ultimate litmus test for anti-Semitism. If you can tolerate my fat, whining presence, you've seen the worst Jews have to offer. I figured prominently in Roth's novel, *The Anatomy Lesson*. Roth's alter ego, Nathan Zuckerman, impersonates the Goldstein persona as a conservative Jew's worst nightmare, absolute anathema to someone like historian Irving Howe or *Commentary*'s Norman Podhoretz. This excerpt reflects my thinking from the early days of *Screw*:

> I want my readers to know that they shouldn't feel self-hatred if they want to get laid. If they jerk off it doesn't make them beneath contempt. And they don't need Sartre to make it legit. . . . You wouldn't know it from *Playboy* . . . but in the back of movie theaters, in the washrooms of bars, outside the diners where the truck drivers stop— most of the blowjobs in America are being given right there. Sex is changing in America—people are swinging, eating pussy, women are fucking more, married men are sucking cocks. . . . What are we supposed to do—lie?

My loyalty is to the common man. My loyalty is to the guys on the street corner I grew up with and the guys I served with in the merchant marine. That's why I'm in this. It's the hypocrisy I can't stand. The sham. The denial of our cocks. The disparity between life as I lived it on the street corner, which was sexual and jerking off and constantly thinking about pussy, and the people who say it shouldn't be like that. How to get it—that was the question.

Gay Talese spent three months interviewing me for his epic history of the sexual revolution, *Thy Neighbor's Wife*. Talese always went for the big picture, and considering he made his bones at the *New York Times*—not necessarily known for its cock-swaggering alumni—Gay was a champion stud. He fucked my wife, Mary Philips. But my marriage was already ending. Mary got upset, told his wife Nan, and it created a furor. I remember having dinner at Gay's house with David Halberstam. I thought ours would be a lifetime friendship. But I failed to realize that every writer betrays his friends. As the saying goes: a writer either betrays his friends or himself. I was merely a subject to Gay Talese and Philip Roth; they examined me like a bug. And I'm guilty of the same thing. Most porn bimbos I interviewed for *Screw* and *Midnight Blue* meant nothing, they're the cunt of the week. I can't have a high and mighty attitude because I'm just as guilty of using people as Gay Talese, Philip Roth, or any other writer.

Though Philip Roth and Buck Henry were silent observers at Plato's Retreat, they would never drop trou. But when Jerzy Kosinski came with me to Plato's, he was off the charts. He came to get laid, he never took any shit, and didn't waste time. Pussy was so accessible at Plato's, even though I rarely got laid. I became desensitized and concentrated on the buffet, which was more exciting. I didn't know such high times would end, and wish I had taken advantage of getting laid more at Plato's. The City shut them down in the early eighties during the AIDS panic.

My own editors are guilty and repressed, and I give them unbridled freedom to vent their own nightmares in print. They've highjacked entire theme issues of *Screw* given over to the subject of diarrhea, the Three Stooges, or a hoax interview with Albert Speer, Hitler's still-living Third Reich architect. The Jewish Defense League thought it was real. I've got to keep these pseudo-intellectual nitwits in line, they think this is a college paper. It is not a college paper, and when my editors think they're getting clever, I'll reprimand them with an iron fist. This is pornography! Keep it porn, goddamit! *Screw* is printed on cheap newspaper stock with smeary ink and coarse, rehashed stock photos of cunts and cocks. We have thousands of eight-by-tens in tall stacks and files that date back to the sixties. I don't want to buy any more. A fuck is a fuck.

We recently had Polish pressmen walk out of the Brooklyn plant. They refused to print that week's issue of *Screw*. It featured the Polish Pope's visit to New York, suggesting his entire tour was of men's public bathrooms. I'm prepared for printer walkouts at all times, and the plant brings in an alternate crew of Puerto Ricans. Or Italians or Slavs or whichever ethnic group is not too offended to handle that week's subject matter. Managing editor Richard Jaccoma reports that the New York Public Library finally has a complete collection of *Screw* and a current subscription. We document a unique aspect of the city's history that future generations may wish to consult. Strangely enough, I have nothing but trouble from the "Public" Library, which never seems to properly archive *Screw* and, I suspect, throws out its issues.

Our *Consumer Reports*–like "Naked City" listings are taken seriously. Mistress Valerie offered the "Naked City" editor, Josh Alan Friedman, an envelope stuffed with twenties as a bribe for an extra cock rating, demanding to be equal with Belle Du Jour (another matronly Jewess with a Brooklyn accent). But it's no-go, of course, and she has her rating lowered instead. More importantly, I discuss the logistics of flying five of my staff members to Havana, where they will return by dinghy to the Miami docks with thousands of smuggled cigars to feed my habit. They're cheaper than using missionaries. They opt to accompany me to Cuba instead, where I will fill their luggage with contraband cigars.

Washed-up nice-guy porn actor Harry Reems stops by the meeting, hoping I can help find some company to name a dildo after him. When he was top cock, he sued companies to take his name *off* of dildos.

MR. NOSEBLEED

I bestow a lifetime *Screw* subscription upon one of our longtime contributors, Norman Jackson. He comes to the editorial meeting with a black eye, battered to hell by a rough dominatrix on behalf of a *Screw* assignment. Norman pursued more two-figure writing assignments from small sex periodicals—fifty-dollar gigs—than any other writer. The smaller the assignment, the smaller the pay, the more he worked like a dog. A fifty-year-old alkie who downed two six-packs of Bud each day, Jackson was dubbed *Screw*'s "Man of a Thousand Feces," a title he cherished. All perversions involving human excrement are his specialty. He conducted *Screw*'s beer survey, in which Annie Sprinkle sampled twenty brands, then pissed in Norman's mouth for a rating. Norman's twenty-nine-year-old son and his elderly father are both Baptist ministers down South. His parents send a portion of their social security pittance to TV evangelist Jimmy Swaggart each month. Norman, in turn, proudly sends copies of his *Screw* articles, which only makes them pray harder for his condemned soul.

We were all touched by Norman's innocent, fairytale vision of the world, full of kitty cats, happy little children, and pornography, all of which he sees as forces for good healthy living. Jackson insisted on having his own "kitty cat" pictured in one of his toilet articles for *Screw*. "That way, the cat will join me in hell," he explained. While writing an article on Asian mail-order brides, Norman decided to order one himself. A young lady flew in from the Philippines and they had a formal wedding at Belle du Jour's S&M establishment, with many guests. Instead of a band, the entertainment consisted of a performer who stood onstage and hammered his own scrotum into a two-by-four board with a dozen carpentry nails. Now, that's entertainment. The guy was available for parties, weddings, bar mitzvahs. Norman's bride, disoriented from the culture shock of arriving in the USA, was led to believe that this was custom at all American weddings. Last I heard, many years later, they were still married.

A "Rainbow Showers" vomit photoshoot, featuring Annie Sprinkle and Norman Jackson, was arranged on a Sunday afternoon on Wall Street. At the finish, the poor, poor man lay in the gutter, like a nose-bleeding derelict covered in vomit. My editors, Jaccoma and Friedman, couldn't allow him in their car for a ride uptown. There were no cabs available. So they wrapped Jackson up among the soiled props in a plastic tarp, and tossed him in a Wall Street dumpster to fend for himself. Jackson was happy as a pig in shit.

Screw follows the *New York Times* style sheet with more precision than the *Times*, and fewer typos. The Neanderthal captions that accompany photographs became legend in the men's field. They presumably reflected, in verse, what the *Screw* reader thought at the brink of orgasm. J. J. Kane, who became the *New York Daily News*'s Phantom of the Movies, handled "Smut From The Past." This column demonstrated that pornography was nothing new. Inevitably, someone saw their grandmother sucking cock, or some seventy-five-year-old showgirl might submit a long forgotten snapshot of herself, from the days when private camera clubs operated in smoky basement dens. Kane was one of *Screw*'s best caption writers, whose stock-in-trade was, as the old Minsky's burly-Q comedians said, the "dubble entender."

Some *Screw* captions, in musical parlance: "Yids Say the Darndest Things," "Pre-Op A Lu La: He-She-It's My Baby," "Bi Bi Love," "Sex and the Sphincter Girl," "Don't Jerk Off on the Piano Player," "Bloke Gets in Her Thighs," "Chancres Away!" "Pooper Troupers," "I Wanna Be a Matzo Man," "A Tale of Two Clitties," "Ejaculatin' Rhythm," "The Lady Is, Uh, Damp," "Just a Spoonful of Booger," "Let's Go Fly a Kike!"

"Fuckbooks" reviewer Michael Perkins was an English professor with a PhD who writes books of serious literary criticism. I could never bring myself to fire him because he's been with me since 1968. I've considered having a contract killing put out on him, since nobody ever stayed with me that long.

Steve Kraus, as a child, escaped Poland in the last caravan to get out alive in 1939. Many European émigrés have claimed the distinction of being "the last one out." But no others ended up writing for *Screw* and hosting *Midnight Blue*. Kraus indulged in swing club orgies, and his continental accent charmed his way into the pants of porno queens. "*Q'uell bouquet!*" he once blubbered, emerging tipsy from underneath Vanessa Del Rio's dress with a half-empty bottle of Bordeaux. I continued my interview:

Al: What's the biggest cock you've ever sucked?

Vanessa: I think Red Baron, this black guy who really had a tremendous cock. It was thin at the tip. I did an anal scene with him, and I couldn't believe it—he was so fat! But, the tip of it was so small.

Al: What about Jews? Are they as inept as we're told by our wives? How do they rate? Hurt us; I don't care. Be honest.

Vanessa: I never really looked at it that way. I never said, "Well, he's Jewish, so let's rate him," or "He's black, let's rate him."

In the final order of business, I reprimand my staff for not insulting me enough in print. They are duty-bound to ridicule my corpulence, my puny cock, to call me a faggot, a penny-pinching mockey. Nowhere am I more ridiculed than in my own newspaper, *Screw*. Insulated by this protective cocoon of insults and degrading cartoons, outsiders have no choice but to compliment me. My own editors have to compliment me behind my back.

That week's "Sex Scene" column in *Screw* announces the lucky "Win a Date with Al Goldstein" winners:

> We're certain there are plenty of women around who fantasize about fucking blind, paraplegic priests. We're also sure there are just as many who yearn to make love to amputee baboons, and others who come in their panties at the mere thought of seducing brain-damaged Dobermans. But only Ginger and Chris of Glendale, Calif., wanted to go out with *Screw* publisher Al Goldstein. . . .

Two giddy college girls go out with me on a lark, but of course, I can't get laid. *Oh, that Al!*

Nighttime in Manhattan. I lead a party of Japanese dignitaries through Times Square with my Naked City editor. They're from a newly christened Japanese edition of *Screw*. They speak almost no English and this is their first time in New York. I remain ten steps ahead of the entourage, a fat Peter Pan on a spree in Live Nude Girl Land. The *Midnight Blue* camera team and staff photographer, Don Demcsik, follow, documenting the tour. Bodyguard John Flynn was not with us.

"Go get 'em, Big Al!" shout strangers on the Broadway traffic island where the pigeon-shat statue of George M. Cohan stands.

I raise my fist to the sky in response. "The night is young!" I yell. "We'll be arrested yet!" Derelicts join the procession, until I feel like the pied piper, skipping through the gutter, a legion of Times Square proletariat following behind.

If anyone ever wondered where old pigeons go to die, my Naked City editor knows. He shows the Japanese the decrepit tarpaper space atop the marquee of the Selwyn Theater on Forty-second Street. It's a pigeon graveyard. The Japanese are duly impressed, taking notes.

Japanese *Screw* will have their own Naked City listings for Tokyo, and my editor shows his Tokyo counterpart the ropes. But they've never seen anything like this in Japan. Blackjack is the name of the roughest peep emporium on Forty-second Street. It's a filthy two-floor rathole that violated every health code on the books, a criminal enclave crawling with pimps, pickpockets, and gutter con-men. The kind of joint where the pumped-up quarter cashiers could be overheard talking about robberies they pulled the night before.

A mobster named Eddie Dolls opened Blackjack in the late 1960s.

Two scarfaced goombahs behind the counter warn customers to pick up magazines with both hands so as not to bend the corners, hurry up and make your choice, this ain't the library. Handwritten signs loom over the store, warning "The management has proven that 'hanging out' is hazardous to your health." The black bouncers seem trigger-ready to pummel any white motherfucker in a three-piece suit that so much as smiled at them. One bouncer shoulders a paying customer against the wall: "I kicked Sugar Ray's ass, I knocked out Norton, I blinded Ben-i-tez and I wiped the floor with Frazier—I'll mess you up so bad you be sorry you was born, bitch!"

Why is it so crowded? There are hot girls by the dozen strutting in the open-window peep upstairs. Any sexual contact physically possible through an open porthole is yours. Blackjack has "coin of the realm" in spades, and that coin is hot pussy for a dollar a grab. New York on one dollar a minute. Plus quarters for the slots. A Big Apple bargain. They're making scumbags full of money here, and nobody shuts them down. Yet.

Such is Times Square, and where the straight world saw only depravity, *Screw* magazine found beauty. Our Japanese guests are in awe. But do the Japanese actually understand the Jewish gestalt of *Screw*? They probably understood better than we'll ever know. But one thing got by them: *Screw* did a soft parody of the Poppin' Fresh doughboy humping the dough girl while she had a yeast infection. Pillsbury hit me with a $50 million lawsuit. When the suit was dismissed, I claimed possession of the doughboy to appear on *Screw's* cover for a year. Japanese *Screw*, franchised at that time, had no familiarity with Pillsbury and assumed Poppin' Fresh was *Screw's* mascot. Throughout the run of Japanese *Screw*, Pillsbury's corporate symbol graced every cover.

• • •

Next on the itinerary is a walk up to Show Follies at 711 Seventh Avenue, part of the Show World empire. My editor was the sentry, going ahead of the group to smooth the way at each establishment. But there was trouble at the gate. A beefy gargoyle of a manager comes out from behind the counter and belligerently blocks the door. He has some bug up his ass about *Screw*. Doesn't like the magazine, it's a piece of shit, and doesn't want any entourage touring the store. My editor reports this back. I send the editor back to tell him Al Goldstein himself requests that he reconsider—we've got Japanese tourists here, they'll probably spend money, and we're all in the same business anyway. But the manager gets nastier, calls over some goons to the door, and said he doesn't give a shit about Al Goldstein, he can go fuck himself.

I walk up to the entrance. The entire porn industry has flourished in the wake of *Screw*, which fought the battles for their right to exist. I haven't fucking survived in this business for twelve years for nothing. I jab my finger at the goons blocking the door, all of them towering over me, as they advance. "I'll see you dead, mother-fuckers!" The rest of our tour backs away, anticipating an attack with baseball bats. I stand alone with righteous anger, my finger cocked at them with supreme confidence and issue one last warning. "I'll see you dead first!"

The goons stop in their tracks. Maybe they have second thoughts. The porn emporium manager chokes up. They all walk back into the store.

Soon after *Screw*'s Mercedes ads ran, I received a notice offering to buy back the car. *And* Mercedes paid me an additional thirty thousand dollars to just drop the whole matter. Corporate targets, as well as hundreds of quality-of-life abusers, received rebuke in public commons they'd *really* prefer not to have been mentioned in—*Screw* and *Midnight Blue*. I also receive a call from Gambino capo, Robert "DiB" DiBernardo, the most powerful Mafia overseer of pornography in the country. He apologizes for the behavior of this scumbag manager at 711 Seventh Avenue, says the guy didn't realize who I was. DiB asks what I would like done with him—do I want him fired, banished from New York, or something worse? Anything I want. I don't have to think twice. I'm gracious about such matters and don't want to take away a man's livelihood, his job. A mere apology will do, and we'll forget about it. A week later, I receive a humble crayon-scrawled apology from the porn emporium gargoyle, thanking me for sparing his job, and welcoming *Screw* anytime; anything we want is on the house.

After the standoff at 711, I've had enough for one day. I want to go the fuck home. I excuse myself and bid everyone goodnight.

I still needed marriage, the trap of the bourgeoisie, to keep me structured enough for *Screw* to come out each week. I have a wife, we go to dinner, I read Dr. Suess to my son. My six-year-old boy loves me. My sanity relies on going home to East Sixty-first Street, reading the *New York Times*, keeping my distance. I know there is a real world out there—not just coked-up secretaries, lunchtime blowjobs, Times Square porn premieres and scumatoriums. There had to be a demarcation, a separation of church and state. There were two worlds. Otherwise, I would have been swallowed up in the quicksand of the porn underworld. Larry Levinson of Plato's Retreat fucked up his life because he got totally swallowed up in the sex underworld. I am not Jaime Gillis, who sniffs soiled panties on airplanes to stay calm, or John Holmes, whose cock is his only meal ticket, or Norman Jackson, who prefers sex in dumpsters, or porno hippo Ron Jeremy. Ron Jeremy *is* what you see. He has no real life, no separation from porn, he's never had a relationship, he fellates himself. If I became like that, I'd fall in a labyrinth of insanity. No, I wasn't *really* part of this world. Or was I?

In an assignment for *Penthouse*, I went "Around the World Without Getting Laid." It was supposed to be an Asian sex tour, but ended up a total bust. I was so hard up on the plane home, I spied a used Kotex in the sanitary-napkin disposal slot of the john. Desperate to grab hold of a stray pubic hair, I angled my hand into the slot and got stuck. The flight attendants had to pry me loose. My head rang out like a cuckoo clock.

STATEN ISLAND FERRY

Maybe I should have ass-kissed more people or taken out an IRA. Destitution was never part of the plan. The million dollars in watches I stashed with my son could've supported me now, but he won't give them back. I lost four homes. All my ex-wives and former employees wound up with property but me. What a sucker I've been. A female attorney helped run my company into the ground, then dumped me when I went broke. But I loved eating her pussy, maybe because she was a lawyer. She was just another broken wedding engagement toward the end of my run at *Screw*—in this case, one who embezzled money and swindled me. Two Japanese girlfriends, sexual hors d'oeuvres on the side, disappeared. Women are so predatory. Men are attracted to beauty, women to money. That's the quid pro quo. It's the animal kingdom.

I didn't even have enough money to file for bankruptcy. There's a $2 million libel judgment against me from a store called BrandsMart in Florida, which I supposedly slandered on radio and libeled in print. They sell cheap Hong Kong knockoffs of your favorite name brands, guaranteed to break before you get them out of the shopping bag. Why wait for a huge cock in your ass? Shop at BrandsMart. Normally, I would have slam-dunked this run-of-the-mill lawsuit, because the store really was a gypsy rip-off operation, and my comments were within the bounds of protected speech. But I was living on the street and couldn't show in court.

CHAPTER 2

A Bed-Wetting Stutterer from Brooklyn

My poor father. He was like Camus' *The Stranger*. He walked around his whole life in mortal fear. Sam Goldstein worked for a syndicate called International News Photos, later bought by United Press. It was on the same floor as the *Daily Mirror*, the paper his photos appeared first. He never received credit, it just said INP Photo. He went out in the radio car to do what they called "commercials," which were commercial assignments. The *Daily Mirror* was a tabloid owned by Hearst, which occupied the forty-fifth floor in a building on Forty-fifth Street. It was created to compete with the *Daily News*, which itself began in 1919 as a sensationalistic tabloid and attained the largest circulation in America. The *Mirror's* management once stated the paper contained 10 percent news and 90 percent entertainment—so it was a forerunner to today's media.

My father's most prized assignment was covering the Brooklyn Dodgers at Ebbets Field for the *Daily Mirror*. He used a Speed-Graphic camera called the Big Bertha. The idea of photographing naked girls would have been unthinkable to my father. But baseball, not sex, was foremost on my mind. When he came back from work at night, he'd bring me eight-by tens prints of the Dodgers. The next day I'd sell the photos for a dollar each in class at Boys High.

Sam Goldstein was a simple man. All he wanted to do was work, and he worked eighty hours a week, running with the news hacks chasing down headlines. This taught me the work ethic. He never had a close friend, never went to a movie, never read a book, never had an original thought. He listened to Walter Winchell on the radio, believed everything that the reactionary right-wing *Daily Mirror* and *Journal-American* said. He believed in Eisenhower. He would say friends aren't important, just protect yourself. He got excited when he met the Pope.

He also picked his nose in public and ate with his mouth open. He had bad grammar. He would yell only at me. I thought he was gross. He was only one generation removed from the world of Russian pogroms, where Cossacks could kill you with impunity. So he walked around frightened. He said sir to elevator operators.

Yet, contrary to all of his passivity, my father exhibited nothing but bravery as a war photographer. He acquired a certain prestige among his peers and won photography awards during his thirty-four years aiming a camera. He stood alongside legendary World War II correspondent Ernie Pyle when Pyle was machine gunned by a Japanese sniper in Okinawa. Sam was on three separate navy boats that got torpedoed. These were not tall tales; he was not one to boast. There were newspaper stories on him, one headlined WHAT MAKES SAMMY RUN? taken from the title of Budd Shulberg's book. Though Sam Goldstein seemed like a fucking nerd, he was a hero of sorts to me and I kept a scrapbook of his war photos.

People called all the time for baseball and basketball tickets. When the *Daily Mirror* folded in 1963, my father's phone went silent. That was a lesson for me in how shitty and opportunistic humans are.

• • •

I was always known as Sammy's son when I tagged along behind the scenes. I learned with a press card you're hot shit. I watched the Louis-Marciano fight up close as my father leaned into the ring angling Big Bertha while I carried his strobe light. I loved it. I was learning a craft. He also had a studio in Williamsburg called Humpty Dumpty Photos, where I learned to develop pictures. He took wedding pictures on the side, which I helped with, too. We went to the Little League World Series and attended boxing matches at the Garden on Friday nights. Accompanying my father, I felt like a member of the press.

But most thrilling was when my father took me into the Dodgers dressing room at Ebbets Field. We ate Sabrett hot dogs in the press room free. I thought they tasted better than the ones sold in the stands. He took a picture of me with Jackie Robinson when I was about twelve. Unfortunately it's lost. There in the dressing room, I saw Pee Wee Reese's and Jackie Robinson's cocks. 1947 was the one and only big season "da bums" beat the despised Yanks in the World Series (WHO'S A BUM!—*Daily News*). Their dangling cocks seemed mightier, swaggering with World Series bravado. Robinson was the first black athlete to break the color line in professional sports and "a credit to his race." By association, one might presume he led the league in cock size. But he sported an average slugger between his legs, the same size as the white ballplayers.

At the dawn of television in New York, I became a regular on an after-game baseball program. *Happy Felton's Knothole Gang*, broadcast from Ebbets Field, had local little leaguers on, usually from St. Bernadette's Little League in Brooklyn. Happy and his sidekick, Bucky. I appeared as Little Alvin Goldstein the baseball expert, their resident tout on statistics. Little Alvin, who would grow up to democratize pornography in America. I read the *Sporting News* religiously and memorized batting averages. There were three other guests. When my turn came, I'd rattle off up-to-the-minute batting averages and breathlessly recount highlights of the game.

But nobody in school saw me, they didn't have TVs yet. In 1948, televisions were only available in places like Irish bars.

Brooklyn was always New York's working-class melting pot, a borough of underdogs. Brooklyn was famous for its inferiority complex, daring Manhattan and the whole world to knock the chip off our shoulder. The mere mention of Brooklyn was once a borscht belt punchline. In the 1940s, there was a Society for the Prevention of Disparaging Remarks about Brooklyn. But the Dodgers were our rallying cry. The Dodgers actually lived in Brooklyn. Gil Hodges and Duke Snyder drank egg creams on stools at neighborhood luncheonettes. Dodger players took off-season jobs as department store Santas. Deli owners waved salamis in the air when the Dodgers won and gave out free slices. When Cal Abrams, a Jewish reserve outfielder once went on a hot streak, the *Brooklyn Eagle* wrote, "Mantle, Schmantle, we got our Abie." Gil Hodges, Roy Campanella, Carl Furillo, "Duke of Flatbush" Snider, Dixie Walker, Ducky Medwick, Dolph Camilli, Casey Stengal, when he was manager—palookas with the kind of names and mugs that don't exist anymore—these were my childhood heroes.

Aside from admitting the first Negro ballplayer, I had no idea whether the Dodgers practiced right-wing politics and could care less if they hated commies. I was a stuttering, bed-wetting kid. Ebbets Field was heaven. The lobby rotunda had a marble floor inlaid with baseball stitches and a huge chandelier in the form of bats and balls. The *H* on the Schaefer Beer scoreboard in right field would light up after a hit and the *E* would light up after an error.

When the Dodgers left Brooklyn I cried. Like everyone else in

Brooklyn, I felt betrayed and heartbroken. I never went to another game. I watched one Yankee game recently and realized it's no longer a sport, just a business. The endless statistics are suffocating. Billy Crystal and all these other respectable Jews talk about Brooklyn and the Dodgers for baseball documentaries, but no one's ever come to me. I'm a pornographer, not considered human.

HARVEY FIERSTEIN

AL: I saw *Torch Song Trilogy* and loved it. But let's talk about growing up in Brooklyn.

FIERSTEIN: When you're in a play like this, all the old friends come back to see you, people you haven't seen since you were six-years-old. I called my mother to say, "You'll never believe who came to see the show." And she asked, "Oh, is he married?" And I said, "Yes, to a nice colored guy." All my childhood friends turned out to be gay. . . . It was definitely something in the water in Brooklyn.

AL: No one's asked how big your cock is. This is *Screw*. Are you going to tell?

FIERSTEIN: Oh, it's Brooklyn-size. Jewish.

AL: I've been to the Anvil and some of the gay clubs—what I remember is hundreds of good-looking, skinny guys, all being beautiful. I was happy they were gay because it meant there were more women for me. But the primary thrust of my perception was the sadness, the waiting.

FIERSTEIN: I believe that is sort of a retarded state of social development, where you cannot make a commitment. A place like the Anvil is a painting of rejection. They are set up not to go home with each other; they listen to this incredibly loud music so they can never say hello and, with drugs, they are not themselves. If they do manage to say hello, with the drinking on top, they'll be sick and can't go home because they would throw up on the other person.

—*Screw*, May 1983

STATEN ISLAND FERRY

I still have my cell phone and receive interview requests every single day. The *International Herald Tribune* calls as I wait for the ferry. The editor says he admires me, I'm a First Amendment hero. I tell him the same thing I tell all reporters: "I'm hurting. Give me a hundred bucks, or at least a fifty-dollars honorarium for an interview." He declines. "Then you're a piece of shit. I have nothing to publicize, why should I do interviews?" I hang up.

As a publisher, I've always considered it unethical to pay or be paid for an interview. The only one who ever demanded payment was black porn actor Johnny Keyes, in the seventies. We passed. But now that I've just recovered from a year homeless on the streets of New York, I've changed my tune.

Penn Jillette, of Penn & Teller, rescued me with a modest apartment on Staten Island. He pays my rent. I'm a kept man. At five A.M. last week, I woke up to the sound of the ceiling caving through over the shower. The living room ceiling has a hundred imprints from my cane, from banging on it to complain of noise above. A few weeks ago I was burglarized, they stole my last remaining jewelry. My young wife suffers from severe Crohn's Disease and lives back with her parents. I've cheated in every marriage but the one I'm currently in, my fifth. I've been monogamous for a year and a half, but not necessarily out of choice. I'm depressed, my diabetes has fucked up my hormones, and because I have no money, women aren't interested.

I fester in my Staten Island apartment where a small pathway gives way through junk and refuse piled four feet high. It resembles the City Island garbage dump. I'm surprised there aren't seagulls hovering above. I once had four secretaries, a full-time bodyguard-chauffeur, a nanny, a maid—and lowliest of all, thirty *Screw* and *Midnight Blue* employees. There's no one to pick up my garbage now and I can't do it myself.

CHAPTER 3

Sodom by the Sea

Brooklyn had one other promised land and that was Coney Island—Sodom by the Sea, on the southern shore. Where roller coasters and hot dogs were invented. Food occupies a hallowed part of my Coney Island memories. They sold knishes on the beach. My favorite were the lobster rolls at Nathan's. At the height of *Screw*, I'd limo back to Nathan's in a fit of gluttonous nostalgia to gorge on hot dogs, french fries, and four lobster rolls at once. I still love the lobster rolls. They were thirty-five cents, now they're four dollars.

By the late sixties, the area around Nathan's became predatory and ominous, and has remained Puerto Rican since. But in the Dodger days of Ducky Medwick and Cookie Lavagetto, you saw the same hot dog guy at the grill your whole childhood, the same guy every year serving those meaty, fat, scalloped french fries. Nathan's had an oxidized grill that cooked the best hot dogs in the world. Added to this was the salt air of Brooklyn by the sea. People in Brooklyn couldn't afford the French Riviera. They went to the Brooklyn Riviera at Coney Island. One year my parents rented a bungalow for the summer.

At the turn of the twentieth century, there were three great amusement parks in Coney Island. Dreamland burned down in 1907. As a
very young pornographer-to-be, I went to Luna Park twice, before it
burned down in 1944. From then on we had only Steeplechase: the
Funny Place. Admission plus any rides cost one dollar. Steeplechase,
which ran from 1897 to 1965, was named after the wooden horse
ride that encircled the seaside pavilion on a track. Dames held tight
to dates on the racing wooden horses, one of many devious dry-
hump entanglements that Steeplechase devised during those prudish
times. The oceanside entrance to the Barrel of Love, a polished
wooden drum, spun strangers into suggestive contact. The Insani-
tarium had dancing card decks, swaying barrels, and heaving floor-
boards. Clowns and dwarves cackled like hyenas as they pulled levers
delivering shocks and airbursts from floor holes. Staircases flattened
into slides. I'd laugh at the sorry schmuck in front of me as he tum-
bled in humiliation—then it was my turn.

The sucker ethic was perfected at Coney, wherein the public is supposed to enjoy being conned out of its cash on the midway. A little bit
like the sex business, a bait-and-switch routine. In the 1940s, a horny
dwarf, Little Angelo, whacked women's fannies with a dingbat as
their skirts blew up from the floorboard airbursts. Then his tiny greedy
hands grabbed at their tits as they lost balance. Little Angelo's disreputable behavior as a carnie molester finally cost him his job.

Watching attentively as Brooklyn girls' skirts blew up, I, Little
Alvin Goldstein, caught my first stolen glimpses of the indentation of
pussy protruding from panty-girdles. I saw the midgets poke them
with an electric stinger. Imagine how politically incorrect this would
be today—midgets blowing up girls' skirts, whacking their *tokhis* with
paddles, and poking them with electric prods. How hot is that? No
wonder Robert Moses's highways bypassed Coney Island on their way

to the antiseptically wholesome Jones Beach. Such was Steeplechase in Coney Island—exotic, horny, decadent, cheap, and magical.

My family life was not so magical. We lived at 482 Bedford Avenue in Williamsburg, Brooklyn. The block before Bedford Avenue became a one-way street. My strangest friend, Joey Berkowitz, also lived in the building. I wanted to *be* Joey Berkowitz. He won class president at PS 16 and read Nietzsche. His mother picked out books for me to read. My own mother knew nothing about books. Joey also wanted to kill people. He became a doctor.

When we were fifteen, Joey planned to leave poisoned food in front of apartment houses, and then hope to read about it in the papers. He taught me how to masturbate at age twelve. I had to be shown and copied what he did. Then I became addicted to masturbation. I whacked off to thirty-two-page Tijuana Bible cartoon books throughout high school. Later, I jerked off to Candy Barr, the blond Texas bombshell sentenced to fifteen years in prison for marijuana possession (she served three-and-a-half years). I saw her live in the 1950s. There was a picture I jerked off to more than a hundred times of Candy Barr with her perky tits, straddling the face of this Mexican.

When we were seventeen, Joey Berkowitz introduced me to mescaline. Mescaline could be bought legally in England then, and since Joey was preparing for medical school, he would capsulize his own mescaline at four hundred milligrams a hit. We tripped fifteen years before the Summer of Love. I read *The Doors of Perception* by Aldous Huxley. I could hear colors and see music. I had four great trips and four psychotic ones, where I felt I was a rodent.

Boys High School in Bedford Stuyvesent was 98 percent black. I was one of only a dozen white guys. Easton was closer, in Williamsburg, but my mother didn't want me to attend the Easton district because there were girls, which she thought would distract me. So at Boys High all we did was talk about pussy. I was painfully shy, could never get a girlfriend. I had but one pathetic brush with romance. The girl, Ruth Tinsky, was much taller than all the boys, but I actually dry-humped her and we played post office on her couch. My friends Davie and Ted would tell me about all the girls they were fucking and I believed them. I was sexually retarded. They were all lies.

Some say if I'd been allowed to pull my pants down in public as a boy, there would never have been *Screw*. I've had relationships revolve around one stolen kiss at night's end, followed by a week's fantasizing. That's because I have the sentimentality of a fifteen-year-old. My façade of amorality and detached sex has always been a cover for being afraid of being hurt. So what else is new. *Screw* was such an antiromantic publication as compensation for that. When I was fifteen and inept, I used to lie awake until the wee hours tormented by some girl's rejection. I sent away for *How to Kiss Girls*, one of the Little Blue Books, an underground press that included atheist writings. I practiced on my hand. That's where I'm still at today. Like every other sexual retard, I wondered how you were supposed to kiss without banging noses. I sent for another book on how to write love letters, a series by an editor named Haldeman. Of course, I had no one to send them to and still don't.

Nobody at Boys High cared if you were smart. Good grades meant less street credibility. I had ten street fights and lost every one. Beaten up and humiliated by blacks. Then I became a photographer for the *Red & Black*, the Boys High newspaper. Like my father, I took pictures of football and basketball games and gave the players prints the next day. My ghetto classmates loved seeing themselves in action. From then on I never got beaten up. I sold eight-by-tens of the Dodgers but gave them away to kids who would've beaten me up. I learned that you trade things off for protection.

Roy Hodges was a great football player at school. I invited him home for dinner one night. My mother was polite during dinner, but upset afterward. She told me that races shouldn't mix together. Yet my parents sent me to all-black Boys High. I was colorblind and had never thought twice about it. My father's best friend, another photographer and moron, argued that blacks smelled just like racehorses. So I went into the gym dressing room the next day and sniffed around. I decided they smelled the same, but their dicks were bigger.

STATEN ISLAND FERRY

The Bowery Mission is perhaps the best homeless shelter in New York. You know who tried to get me in when I was homeless? Cal Thomas, the religious conservative columnist, who I debated several times when I was the King of Porn. He came to visit with a priest, Tom Maharis. They got me into the Bowery Mission from the horrible Harlem one where I was then stationed. But then I got this apartment from the great illusionist, Penn Jillette. Or maybe it was just an illusion. From the left wing nobody did shit, but a right-wing priest came through. I gave up my Star of David. Now a Catholic cross hangs from my chest. I felt doomed as a Jew and would try anything.

I found the Hassidim in Williamsburg far more alien than blacks. They had *payess*, those sidelocks of hair hanging past their ears, and wore black outfits in the middle of the summer. They would block traffic Friday and Saturday during the Sabbath, when Orthodox regulations dictate you can't drive. How dare they! I had a 1949 Ford, one of a few Boys High kids to have a car when I was eighteen. I tried to knock Hassids over in my car. I hated them. The Hassidim were a cult of repressive scumbags, whereas Negroes represented freedom and abandon.

I did, however, like my paternal grandfather. I knew him as

Zaydeh, the Yiddish word for grandfather, and he was a rabbi born in Russia. Today, his name rings out like some comic book super-hero—Zaydeh: Super Rabbi and Defender of Talmudic Law! He'd walk over the Williamsburg Bridge from the Lower East Side to visit us on Saturdays. He spoke mainly Yiddish and brought me *halavah*.

Zaydeh died when I was in high school. He would have never understood *Screw*. He came from a world that was so dark, if it wasn't in the Talmud, he couldn't see it. Everything Jewish, that's it. He lived in another dimension. I think my grandfather would have seen *Screw* no differently than if I published a magazine on coal mining. It would be like looking at hieroglyphics. He would have considered sex no differently than other bodily functions, our intestines, bowel move-ments, it just happens. The deepest drives, like hunger, were foremost to survival, and that's what he dealt with in the old country. Sex is a luxury after we have a full stomach and civilization around us.

My father and mother were not religious, but we attended an orthodox synagogue in Williamsburg. The women were separated upstairs. I was bar mitzvahed there and hated every moment. Rabbi Shinnerman kept throwing me out of Hebrew class because I objected too often. I remain a born atheist. (My son went to the synagogue on Sixty-fifth and Fifth, the most expensive one in the United States.)

Although I became captain of the debating team, I also got thrown out of Boys High. During my last term I hit the civics teacher, Mr. Kraskow. Proving I was macho, I threw a water balloon at him. So I never got my Boys High diploma. But I finally gradu-ated, from Tombstone Union High School near Fort Huachuca, Ari-zona, during my stint in the army. I had to memorize the Arizona constitution. Yet, to this day, I still have trouble reciting the alphabet and can't do multiplication tables.

I received further humiliation when my parents sent my brother

Bob and me to Camp Agouda, an Orthodox Hassidic camp with *tsfillin*, prayer shawls, and Talmudic rhetoric. I had a nervous break-down, and credit Camp Agouda with first bringing forth my manic depression. It was only two weeks, but I didn't belong there. My mother justified it because we had no money. When I first shopped at Forty-seventh Street Camera and told them I went to Camp Agouda, the Hassidic management couldn't believe it, they said we were like brothers. But they never gave me a discount, probably even charged more. Due to the endless headaches I've endured with their policies and broken equipment, Forty-seventh Street Camera became an all-time favorite recurring "ShitList" targets.

Brooklyn parents tried to get their kids the fuck out of the city when it got hot. Another summer escape was the legendary Jewish resort, Grossinger's, in the Catskill Mountains. My father worked gratis for proprietor Jennie Grossinger. Lou Goldstein (no relation) was their big attraction, their morning *tummler*, who did Simon Sez. My father took resort photos for their brochures in exchange for our use of the facilities. One summer my father landed me a job in the kids' dining room. The kids' dining room was for breaking in novice waiters, the minor leagues. Some children had special kosher orders. It wasn't long before I mouthed off to some spoiled Jewish brat and told him to go fuck himself. I was fired.

The Eddie Fisher–Liz Taylor wedding took place that summer, after Fisher dumped Debbie Reynolds. Needless to say, the masti-cating, nose-picking Brooklyn photographer, Sam Goldstein, and his family weren't invited. But I saw Liz Taylor herself walk by me when I was sixteen. She was drop-dead beautiful. I was paralyzed. Eddie Fisher seemed like such a nerdy Jew, but he had those great pipes. I don't care how old she is now—before I die I'd like to have the taste of Liz Taylor's pussy on my lips.

• • •

This exchange occurred with porn star Ron Jeremy, one of my best friends, and his then-girlfriend, Devon Shire:

AL: You are incapable of intimacy. . . . You say you want to be a father, and you say you want a relationship. You have a very stunted relationship with Devon Shire, who is also stunted, so you two make a great combination. Because no one else will have either of you.

JEREMY: Yeah. But I have had sex with her friends. She's had sex with my friends. I meet pretty girls through her. She meets nice guys through me.

AL: Devon, do you ever think of this man as being married, with children, in an intimate relationship of caring and concern?

SHIRE: I don't see him being in one, but if he was, he would be the most wonderful father and husband.

AL: But Ronnie, you're not capable of it. Is that why you're still able to fuck onscreen, because you're crippled and handicapped?

JEREMY: Being separated from being emotional helps, probably.

AL: If you were an integrated, fully feeling human being like I am—

JEREMY: Four wives. Look at this guy!

AL: Yeah, four wives. At least I tried.

JEREMY: This is the guy I gotta listen to, here.

AL: So if you were this feeling human being, you would not be able to come on cue as you do in a porn film.

JEREMY: As Masters and Johnson have said, you can separate your recreational sex from making love.

AL: You're emotionally dead.

JEREMY: I am capable. My whole family has not one divorce in it.

AL: Yeah, but your whole family isn't making fuck films. Look how dysfunctional you are.

JEREMY: That's true, too. They're all doctors, lawyers, teachers.

AL: You are the genetic misfit. I want to share this with people.

JEREMY: Can we say something positive?

AL: Let's talk about some other things wrong with you. Why is it you're always afraid you're going to miss something and stay up all night?

JEREMY: That's accurate. I always like to be at events. Like if you walk into a Hollywood party, you look around. Number one, any good food that I like? Two, is there a phone I can use? Three, is anybody here who can help my career or Devon's career? Any girl I want to fuck, any guy Devon wants to fuck? Any celebrity we can brag that we met? Check those five criteria. If not, we're out of there. Five minutes, that's it.

AL: Okay, let's talk about your bowel movements. Why do you sit on the toilet for two hours? Do you have cancer or something?

SHIRE: He really is reading. He sits there and reads a magazine.

AL: The last question is what do you want your headstone to say? "He came and he conquered?"

JEREMY: Here was a nice guy, who lived the kind of life he wanted and had fun having nookie.

AL: That would cost too much. I would just change it. "He lived the kind of superficial life he wanted . . .

JEREMY: That's all.

AL: . . . and he never had an intimate moment with any member of any gender or species in the whole world."

— *Screw*, September 1995

CHAPTER 4

Blame My Mother

Let's go ahead and blame my mother, the former Gertrude Breslow, for unleashing the world's most notorious pornographer. Why not, everybody else does. She spread her legs and made it all possible. I was a mama's boy. My mother thought I was God and could do no wrong. She was alive, vibrant, had a lot of drive and curiosity. Women didn't have careers then and she held only one job I remember—saleslady at a women's chain called the Rainbow Shop. She was also the daughter of Russian immigrants and stuttered like me. She had me when she was only seventeen.

I was a flabby teenager with a weight problem. When I was fifteen my mother took me to this diet doctor, Harry Stone, MD. He prescribed Dexedrine, those little green pills of legend, a potent amphetamine long since discontinued. It fucked me up and I couldn't sleep. Dr. Stone and I had no particular camaraderie—but I noticed he gradually stopped charging us for visits. Then my mother suddenly received a new Cadillac from him as a gift. It turned out my mother was cheating with my diet doctor. I was utterly confused. Dr. Stone took her on cruises and trips to Europe. My father was sold this bill of goods that the doctor thought of my mother as his daughter. She was still in her thirties, an attractive woman. Stone was twenty years older.

She told me the reason she took on a lover for ten years was because my father was so inadequate. When she was cheating, he was too dumb to know it. I think he had Alzheimer's by his late forties. Though my father was a putz, this established in me a real distrust of women. Like any boy, I wanted my mother to be faithful. Years later I accepted that even my mother was entitled to pleasure. I turned feminist in order to process this.

The Dodgers and their swaggering locker-room cocks were like mythical gladiators in my childhood imagination. But the real model of manhood before me was Sam Goldstein. Meek, frightened, and cuckolded. Years later, my mother was on the Tom Snyder show with me. On national TV, she said, "Your dad's a wham-bam-thank-you-ma'am kind of guy." Then my mother started to disrobe and underneath her blouse she wore a *Screw* tee shirt.

My father was humiliated. And he quietly accepted it. As far as I could determine, my mother's adultery made my father impotent. I never wanted to become cuckolded and impotent like my father. So I cheated all the time on my first four wives. I don't want to go into a semantic debate about the word *cheating*. But my attitude as a man was crippled by the same guilt, the same middle-class, bourgeois double standard that everyone else suffers. Blacks still bear the results of 246 years of slavery, and we all still bear the emotional carnage of the Puritan ethic. With the exception of some African nations like Sudan, Somalia, Eritrea, Mali, and Djibouti—where they practice forced clitoridectomies, or female genital mutilation—America is the most sexually fucked-up country in the world. And that's why I was born.

Tropic of Henry

I traveled three thousand miles in 1970 to interview my top lit-
erary/cunt eating hero, Henry Miller. I was so choked up meeting
him, I choked up. I dropped in on the Los Angeles home of Miller. I
had smuggled Olympia Press Travelers Companion copies of both
Tropic of Capricorn and *Tropic of Cancer* past customs and luxuriated in
his prose for years. I was awash in hero worship and talking with him
only intensified my love for him. I couldn't believe his simple white
home in the suburbs of Los Angeles had no plaque or monument testifying as to who resided inside.

Though I was an unexpected guest, I was thrilled to find a copy of
Screw on his coffee table adjacent to a magazine called *Liberation*. His
first question, which cut through my awe-struck gaze was, "Why do
you use so many four-letter words when you're such a good writer?"

Miller had an entire wall in his house set up where he could write
directly or make sketches and diagrams. On the wall were snatches
from the Bible, foreign phrases or whatever was on his mind. The
handwriting was precise and artistic. He also had photographs of himself on that wall, one with a young attractive Japanese woman who was
his wife, hiding upstairs. As he talked with a soft voice he constantly
reached out and touched my hand or shoulders.

"Twenty-five years ago I wrote a book called *The Air-Conditioned
Nightmare* and predicted exactly what's happening in America. The
falling apart of society, the riots and chaos, and, of course, the violence.
Like Elizabethan times. Today is similar. Violence and irreverence.
The mayhem of old England and the assassinations of Kennedy and
King have frightening similarities to the old period. So often past
times in history are identical to our time.

"I never travel in America, I have Europe around and within
me . . . many times I've wanted to go to Israel. I have a brother-in-law

who lives in Israel but the Israelis I've met I haven't liked because they are too aggressive and arrogant. I enjoy the Mediterranean countries and in particular Spain, Italy and France. The people of those countries are a little bit decadent and a little bit of decadence makes for a good life."

Miller said his favorite writer was Issac Singer, that he and his friends enjoyed *Screw*, and asked that I send him more copies, which he could pass on to his twenty-one-year-old son in Canada.

—*Screw*, May 1970

STATEN ISLAND FERRY

The girl I miss most sexually is movie scream-queen Linnea Quigley. She dumped me when I lost *Screw*, like everyone else. If she came back, I wouldn't even kiss her hello, I'd dive right for her asshole. I've been a pussy eater for half a century but acquired a more sophisticated palate for women's rectums in my dotage.

I'm not entirely broke. I do receive social security. For the legions of followers who miss my weekly "Screw You" editorial in *Screw* and "Fuck You" on *Midnight Blue*, I write a weekly blog for Booble.com. It pays a thousand a month. But this trifling income doesn't make a dent in my debts and liens. Whatever change I can sift out of it pays my cell phone, cable TV and for the cheaper cigars I now must smoke. I asked for a position as host or manager at Scores Cabaret and at the Hustler Club. Both said no. I've applied for minimum wage jobs—Home Depot for $11/hour, Blockbuster for $7.50/hour., and all the Starbucks in Manhattan for $8/hour. None would hire me. My wife said that Starbucks may have been put off by the brown cigar juice that continually drools down my now-toothless jaw in a drug-induced stupor. Doesn't Starbucks want Al Goldstein's brown cigar juice in their cappacino? Friends warned I'd flip off the first impatient customer and be fired in an hour.

Comedian Gilbert Godfried's lovely girlfriend Dara said she'd help me become a dog walker. But I don't like dogs. I don't want to end my life in a minimum wage job. My recurring fantasy is to take 100 milligrams of Valium, get in a warm bath, and cut my wrists. Or better yet, hang myself like an impotent old queer, hoping to cut the rope at the last minute and enjoy one last hard-on.

CHAPTER 5

Alvin Sticks It In

If I had seen a modern day porn video back in the 1940s, when I was a teenager, I would have fainted dead away, out cold. I went through my father's drawer and found what passed for pornography then. The photographers at the *Daily Mirror* got it from the vice squad, who seized it in porno busts. It was so mysterious and exciting. Later, I received 1950s pornography myself from the cops, who handed the contraband out to press photographers instead of destroying it.

In 1952, Mickey Jelke, the fat, little twenty-two-year-old Oleomargarine heir, was ensnared in a sting that scandalized café society. Jelke ran a citywide prostitution ring after being cut off from his trust fund and had pimped out his nineteen-year-old fiancée, Pat Ward. The cops confiscated pictures of Jelke with what seemed like the most beautiful women in the world sucking his dick. I jerked off to one of those photos about 140 times, my record with one photo, even more than Candy Barr. I saw Candy's 1951 smoker, *Smart Aleck*, the best known of all stag films. I saw a few stags shot in the 1930s, the guy wearing black socks and lowered boxer shorts as he sticks it in.

It was so forbidden, and so amateur, which made it hotter. In *A Stone for Danny Fischer*, by Harold Robbins, there was a description of pussy. I jerked off to the words. When I was fifteen, I discovered Henry Miller and jerked off to *Tropic of Cancer* and *Tropic of Capricorn*. He spent four pages describing pussies. My testosterone was galloping. Kids today don't get this. Sex seems too accessible and something's missing. Teenagers don't think a blowjob is sex anymore? That was the only sex we wanted back then. To have a girl *kiss our dick*. The idea of a girl putting my dick in her mouth, that was the sluttiest thing in the world. It seemed unbelievable.

Uncle George was my mother's older brother. He ran a Broadway parking lot and lived at the Hotel Bryant on Fifty-fourth Street. A Manhattan residence was hot shit to a Brooklyn kid. He parked the expensive cars of the Broadway elite. He was the only guy I knew who was divorced. I suspect now he was also pimping one of his girlfriends. Uncle George opened some doors for me. Living two blocks from Birdland, he hung out with jazz musicians and introduced me to marijuana. But most important, he arranged the defining event of my youth: Uncle George got me laid at age sixteen in 1952.

I wore my outgrown bar mitzvah suit for the deflowering, sans yarmulke. I met Uncle George downstairs at the Hotel Bryant above Times Square and we knocked back a couple of drinks. I was nervous and a little drunk. The appointment was for ten P.M. in suite 709. When we entered, George wished me good luck and steered me to his bedroom door, which was half open. Then he sat down to watch a wrestling match on TV.

The lights were out. The first thing I smelled was her perfume as she welcomed me into the dark bedroom. She invited me to undress so I started to remove my bar mitzvah suit. Then she directed my head to a pair of large tits in motherly fashion. As my mouth opened upon this womanly offering—the first time I suckled since infancy—she softly intoned, "Anything you want is all right. Anything a man and woman do together is good."

She sucked my dick and then instructed me to get a rubber waiting on the table. I saw my own teenage erection in the reflection of neon lights streaming in the window from Broadway. I was so excited, speech eluded me. She slipped the rubber on by herself and said, "Put your head between my legs and taste me." Apparently, George had instructed her to do this. It was delicious, better than whitefish, nearly as good as smoked sable. She told me to go slower and where to lick. I had masturbated to such fantasies. I'd read about it in the novels of Frank Harris and Henry Miller. And suddenly, here I have my tongue in the black hole. Then I climbed aboard and stuck it in. Finally, sex—I, Alvin Goldstein, was having it. After I came, I was the happiest I'd ever been in my life. She knew I had school the next morning, so she sent me off with a kiss while she remained in the bed.

I never saw her. The lights had remained out the entire time. Uncle George shook my hand. I was a man. I don't know for sure if she was a hooker. They didn't want me to know her identity because she was a girlfriend of Uncle George. For her it was exciting to be a sixteen-year-old's first piece of ass. Whenever I saw Uncle George with a girlfriend afterward, I'd wonder if she was the one I had sex with.

Like my father, George was never introspective, never went into analysis, which he could have used. Right after I started *Screw*, Uncle George saw my name in the papers and wanted a job from me. I owed him a lot, but didn't have a position at *Screw*—it was still only Buckley, myself and a secretary. He left New York to work as a restaurant inspector in Fort Myers, Florida. Uncle George felt I betrayed him and never spoke to me again.

After that one glorious evening, sex still remained out of reach. The Brooklyn Blowjob—that unmistakable heart-shaped signature in red lipstick around your cock, delivered by a slutty, gum-smacking Brooklyn damsel in a sweater with heavy eyeliner and too much lipstick, talking Brooklynese, the quintessential New York tongue—this cherished myth eluded me, a bed-wetting stutterer from Brooklyn.

STATEN ISLAND FERRY

I don't leave the house except for hospital visits. I'm too fucked up on lithium. My lithium blood count was 8 today and the doctor wants to get it up to 10. I'm also on Prozac for depression, Metaphormin for diabetes, Cozaar for my blood pressure, Lipitor for my cholesterol, Valium and Alphamin to sleep. I'm starting to get arthritis and await more prescriptions. Neither Bellevue, Medicaid, or ElderCare would give me Viagra. Finally, the Veterans Administration allotted me four Viagras per month. Since I served during the Korean War, they figure I'm entitled to four hard-ons a month, but no more.

CHAPTER 6

G.I. Goldstein

I saw Johnny Ray at the Latin Quarter the night before I went into the army. He was like a fag Janis Joplin, all emotion. I didn't have enough money for a table so I sat at the bar. I loved Johnny Ray, who along with Frankie Laine, hit big in the years right before rock 'n' roll.

I went to Tango Palace at Forty-ninth and Broadway in Times Square. There was nothing palatial about it and I never saw anyone do the tango. It was a dime-a-dance hall for sailors on leave, but I frequented this dive before I even joined the service. By the late 1950s, inflation had already set in—they sold their dance tickets for a dollar a pop, with a ten-dance minimum. Rubbing my teenage erection against a "taxi dancer"—so called because you hired them on the clock, like hacks—I'd get off by the second or third dance. I was left with a stain on my boxers and a handful of dance tickets. Tango Parlor didn't give refunds. But that's what guys did. You got what crumbs you could.

I began my two-year hitch in the army at age nineteen. I like to fancy myself a Korean War veteran, but the cold truth is I joined after it ended. I was first assigned to the infantry. But my father went to his *Daily Mirror* photo editor, Mr. Reed, who wielded some influence.

Politicians and the press always fraternized. So my infantry assignment was pulled and I was transferred into the Signal Corps, where
I could be a photographer. Instead of going to Fort Knox, Kentucky,
and following tanks with an M1, I did boot camp at Fort Dix. Then
I reported to Fort Huachuca, Arizona, the Signal Corps. I took pictures of military ceremonies, parades, and once photographed my
sergeant getting a blowjob from a hooker. Military orders. I paid for
my first hooker myself while on leave to Nogales, Mexico, near the
base. The Mexican girl said "Fucky for love. Three dollars for room."
I got syph. It was cured, but there's a syphillis shadow following me
that still registers to this day on my blood test.

A year in the army did little to toughen me up. I was a whining
Jew faggot. When I was on kitchen duty, peeling potatoes and
cleaning pots, I would dream of shooting myself in the leg. I went
back to my father and he got me transferred to Long Island City for
my next year. I was reassigned to the Second Signal Photo Platoon
Army Pictorial Center, where we did propaganda for the military—
now the Kaufman Studios in Astoria, Queens. I got to drive an army
jeep in New York City. Bruce Davidson, who became an award-
winning *Life* magazine photographer, and then an old intellectual
Jew, was my buddy in the photo lab. Guys who worked with chemi-
cals developing pictures were called "hypobenders." We would commiserate in the dark room about how badly we were treated. While
we were in the Corps, Davidson got his first twelve-page photo
spread in *Life* magazine, an incredible achievement. After I started
Screw, he tried to sell *Esquire* an article on me, but it never ran.

I was discharged honorably in December 1956 after a full two years,
and got into Pace University on the G.I. Bill. As a twenty-one-year-
old junior, I became the school's resident beatnik, rebelling against

wearing a suit and tie. I grew a goatee and they nicknamed me "Weird Beard." Pace was an accounting college that had just widened its program and I was in their first wave of English majors. I interviewed Allen Ginsburg and it was the first time the Pace newspaper used the word *fuck*. During a reading in the auditorium at Shapely Hall, Ginsburg mentioned "the stars fucking heaven." I quoted him in my article and got chewed out by some dean. So I began to publish my own modest literary paper called *Skepsis*. I became president of the International Relations Club. I was the worst actor at Pace, appearing in *Hedda Gabler* and *Our Town*. Both roles were the guy who kills himself. They weren't comedies, but I remember the audience snickering at me at the theater in the round.

As captain of the debating team, I overcame the worst of my stuttering. I especially hated the Ivy League debating teams because they seemed born into privilege.

I attacked the Ivy League snobs, arguing that rock 'n' roll was the new music. I listened to Allen Freed on radio, who played music of the street. I went to Allen Freed's Paramount and Brooklyn Fox rock 'n' roll shows, heard Frankie Lymon and the Teenagers and saw Fats Domino shuffle across the stage. I sensed double entendres in R&B lyrics—"goin' downtown" meant going between a girl's legs. I bought my 45s on the Negro side of Flatbush Avenue.

My college experience was helped along by a black girlfriend, Imogene. We were together six months. Imogene was all things nice, wonderful, and authentic. Her pussy tasted like smothered chicken. But mixed couples were despised. I remember stares of hatred when we walked the streets, even in Greenwich Village. These reactions finally wore us down and we broke up.

I also had a white girlfriend while at Pace. A beautiful girl named Althea Schwartz who went to Hunter College. She was a junkie. The only path to her pussy was through the ritual of shooting heroin. Men will do anything. She mainlined me four times. The blood was fearsome coming back up the needle. I only skin-popped afterwards. I heard heroin stopped your sex drive, but Althea was so hot when stoned, I remained just as horny through my deep lethargy. I would have let someone cut a finger off to taste pussy. Why else would I put a needle in my arm, when I was afraid of blood work? When she was bombed out, I put my dick in her mouth, she didn't care. She was a heroin whore, a white girl who knew where to cop in Harlem. Uncle George got pissed when we got caught doing this in his hotel room. Althea died of an overdose in the late fifties. I never did heroin again.

My classes went from nine A.M. to two P.M., then I had extracurricular activities. Seventeen credits, flunking Math One three times. But I often fell asleep in class—I worked a full night shift for the *Daily Mirror*, midnight to 8:30 in the radio car. So I never got that degree, falling six credits short of a BA. In 1960 I was accepted at New York Law School. They would take you without a B.A. But I was tired of school. The G.I. Bill of Rights had just ended. So I didn't go to law school. If I had gotten that BA, I'd probably have become a teacher or lawyer and wouldn't be living in such abject poverty now.

STATEN ISLAND FERRY

A year and a half before I ended up on Staten Island, I hit bottom and the impossible happened. I ended up on the streets. I walked past the townhouse I used to own on East Sixty-first Street and I kept thinking: "That's where I lived. I was a somebody." What happened to my bodyguard, John Flynn? Where was Bobbi? My limo, Rolls Royce, and seven other cars? The hundred Cerruti suits in my closet, custom-tailored for every fluctuation in my girth? My bachelor pad on Thirteenth Street, my apartments in Amsterdam and L.A.? My Pompano Beach manse with a twelve-foot stone statue of a hand flipping the finger to boats on the Intracoastal Waterway? My two-inch thick wad of credit cards?

Now I slept at Bellevue Men's Shelter.

Famed for my weekly "Fuck You" sermons, the final fuck you was on myself. I compulsively burned through my last $11 million, spending forty grand a week on travel, restaurants, endless *chachkas*, gold watches, computers I didn't even know how to turn on. They were merely the accoutrements of a self-loathing lower-middle-class Brooklyn Jew.

Out on the streets, I wanted to kill myself. Al Goldstein was finished, over, washed up. Like one of T. S. Eliot's *The Hollow Men*. I wrote a suicide note. Mostly because my son betrayed me. Jordan did not invite me to his Harvard graduation. He stole a million dollars worth of watches. I've since read much about fathers and sons. Benjamin Franklin did not speak to his son for twenty years because his son supported the English. Alexander the Great killed his father. But I loved my son. I read to him every night, took him to dude ranches, magic camp, gave him five hundred dollars a week and a car. Each year I bought him a ten-thousand-dollar gift, and the last year we were together I gave him a million travel miles from American Express. But money can't buy you love. When he became a Harvard lawyer, he didn't even invite me to graduation. He's suddenly ashamed of me. Of all the shit in my life, from *Screw* going under, four failed marriages, multiple arrests—most of which I'm proud of—my son turning on me is the greatest wound of my life. I wanted to die.

But if I killed myself it would silence me and I couldn't attack him on Howard Stern. Ninety-eight percent of the world abandoned me.

The worst of the scumbags was Dennis Hoff of the Moonlight Bunny ranch cathouse in Nevada. He bought a $70,000 Da Vinci watch from me for $5,000 because he knew I was desperate. He had watch envy, always had his eye on it. I'm practically selling blood in Times Square. I said, gimme a job, let me be the maître d' at a whorehouse. He turned his back. Larry Flynt loaned me $3,500. I gave him $20,000 in watches as collateral. But ultimately, he was not loyal and didn't offer a job.

SAMMY DAVIS, JR.

SCREW: The way you dress onstage turns a lot of people on.

DAVIS: That's groovy. Occasionally I really feel like being raunchy and I don't wear anything under my clothes. But I don't think that's where sex is. I don't think it's the length of your cock. I think sex on stage is attitude. If a cat is small, he's got it made better than a big cat, because he can wear things big guys can't, and if he takes care of himself, if he has any kind of body at all, most chicks can relate to him. (As a matter of fact, I think I'm one of the few guys who turns dykes on. Not that they want to ball me, but my lesbian friends tell me that.)

SCREW: Do you agree with Terry Southern (see Screw #86) that the powers-that-be might use these student rebellions as an excuse to create a repressive police state?

DAVIS: I read a lot of science fiction, and I fantasize that there's probably some rich cat in Texas who would like to spend his money to create a police state. He knows the only way to do this is to cause such anarchy that the Nixon administration would be happy to step in and clamp down. If you wanted to go from here to Rochester, you'd need a pass. I don't feel we have any of the freedoms that we enjoyed, or thought we were going to enjoy, during the Kennedy administration. I get the feeling that if Nixon is reelected in '72, that'll be the end of freedom. He won't stand for smut, and most people who don't live in New York, Chicago, San Francisco, or L.A. could really care less about defending magazines like *Screw* or *X*.

—"What Makes Sammy Come?" *Screw*, January 1971

CHAPTER 7

Winchell

My night-shift job was driving the *Daily Mirror* radio car for Walter Winchell. A photographer and I, a gofer, would pick Winchell up at the Copa after midnight. There were eleven daily newspapers in New York, and eight of them had yet to fold as a result of television's rise. I'd burn rubber racing the *Daily News* and *Journal-American* radio cars to be first at crime scenes.

Winchell (1897–1972), a seminal figure in the history of American media, invented the gossip column. He broke the taboo against exposing private lives of public figures, permanently altering the shape of journalism. "I usually get my stuff from people who promised somebody else that they would keep it a secret," Winchell famously explained. He created a telegraph-style shorthand in his columns, filled with staccato slang and the use of ellipses . . . between news items. He invented the culture of celebrity and was besieged by press agents. In his heyday, he made and broke careers by the hundreds, he could christen a Broadway show a hit or flop, enhance or destroy political careers, including Roosevelt's reelection in 1938. J. Edgar Hoover supplied favors and scoops in exchange for Winchell's backing. A fanatic anticommunist, Winchell's support of McCarthy lost him credibility after McCarthy's downfall. Before I drove Winchell, in 1952, I ran home from Boys High each day, spellbound by the McCarthy hearings on TV. The whole witch-hunting charade was an eerie preview of my own battles in years to come.

Winchell was also the first major commentator to attack Hitler. Fifty million Americans, Sam Goldstein included, hung on every word during his big Sunday night radio broadcast. As a telegraph key stroked urgently in the background, he announced: "Good evening, Mr. and Mrs. America, and all the ships at sea. Let's go to press."

By the time I drove Winchell, his reputation was already in steep decline.

He was exposed as a power-brokering bully in the fictional guise of Ernest Lehman's *Sweet Smell of Success*. He was on a perpetual search for headlines—not stories—along "Baloney Boulevard" (Broadway) and "Hard Times Square." He always had a different nineteen-year-old showgirl with him in the back seat, getting his cock sucked—this great patriotic American who hated commies, loved cops, and carried a gun.

Reporters were instructed not to cover Harlem. When we heard a police call about a burglary or assault occurring far uptown, we would not "roll," which meant speeding to the scene. "The niggers are getting upitty," Winchell would mutter. Negroes were jungle bunnies, not newsworthy for a white, Hearst-run newspaper. The disparity between appearance and reality was startling. There we were, peons in the front seat who didn't exist, while Mr. and Mrs. America and All the Ships at Sea got his nightly blowjob like an arrogant, though diminished, god in his chariot looming over the city. Winchell never ate pussy. It would be un-American.

I'd be up all night, then go to Pace University by day, punchy and exhausted. But it was exciting. Take the night Marylin

Monroe was on Fifty-second and Lexington shooting *The Seven-Year Itch*, the famous picture of her skirt blowing up over the subway grate. I was there with William Randolph Hearst, Jr., himself a photographer at the *Daily Mirror*. His family owned the paper. We were making radio car rounds. He suddenly ran into this beautiful stripper. "Al, you're on your own tonight," said young Hearst, and off they strolled.

I read the mainstream liberal *New York Post*, *P.M.* magazine, and Lyle Stuart's *Independent*. I was a pinko lefty. I listened to Barry Gray on WMCA, who started talk radio. He discussed nudity in European films and New York prostitution, subjects no other commentator touched. Winchell got into a big press battle with Barry Gray, who had begun attacking him on radio. Winchell called Gray "Borey Pink, the disk jerk." Gray was eventually found beaten up, and Winchell thereafter kept a bloodied picture of Gray on his office wall. The Ed "Sullivision"–hating Winchell—Sullivan was once Winchell's lesser rival in the gossip pages, who'd gone on to overshadow him on TV—sometimes ordered lightening to strike his enemies dead. His wishes sometimes came true, like with evangelistic fraud Father Divine. Perhaps these utterances were a predecessor to the Goldstein Curse. I became the Walter Winchell of porn in *Screw*. My own weekly editorial opened on page three of each issue. Laying-low airlines, hotels, restaurants, and politicians, my diatribes were an influential aside to thousands of businessmen each week who scanned *Screw* for hooker ads on trips to New York.

The biggest limo company in New York is Fugazy Continental, a feculent firm that is arrogant, incompetent and in fact a compelling argument for the horse and buggy. Fugazy is totally unresponsive to consumer needs and functions rather like a Nazi Panzer attack. Not to be out-smelled in this loser's sweepstakes is a small but equally incompetent limo company called Zermatt. Its cars are ramshackle recreations of Deep South poverty pockets, its drivers probably drummed out of the Army Canine Corps for being non-housebroken. To hire a Zermatt limo would be more injurious to your health than simply raising your thumb and hitchhiking. . . .

I took with me a photo of a shirt that Barney's had advertised in *GQ*; however, when I tried to buy the shirt, I was told it was "not available." When a retail establishment runs pictures of products it doesn't plan to sell, it is an indication of incompetence and insensitivity to the wasted time of the public.

What's more, I found Barney's to be a cavernous, forbidding store with all the ambiance of a bus depot. Trying to find order in this maze of mayhem is akin to masturbating while your house is burning down. In addition to sleazy salesmen, Barney's prices are absurdly high. . . .

An even bigger festering sore on the face of American capitalism is the New York Health & Racquet Club, one of the Big Apple's most disreputable fitness spas. This joint is nothing more than a razzmatazz con job to separate a naîve public from its earnings. I joined NYHRC over a year ago, when I was in the first flushes of pride at my suddenly svelte body. Working out three times a week since, no one on the staff ever gave me so much as a word of greeting, encouragement, or direction on the Nautilus equipment. The club's constant drumming of its promotions are an unscrupulous rip-off. The after-the-sale-policy of this putrid place is no different than that of a Port Authority Bus Terminal hooker who's given you a dose of the clap. Though the NYHRC is not doing anything illegal, what it does is so shady as to make anyone coming in contact with the club a potential card-carrying, bomb-throwing Trotskyite. The only thing I can wish on the owners of this sleazy joint is that they be forced to work out in their own sterile, vacuous facilities until they croak.

—"Screw You," May 5, 1980

STATEN ISLAND FERRY

I'd just plea-bargained guilty on harassment charges from my ex-wife Gena and received three years probation. In effect, it stipulated I couldn't be in the sex business. The only business I had expertise in. I couldn't relocate to L.A. to accept the few measly offers from the porn industry. They would rather I work the deep frialator at McDonald's. Anyone who wished ill on me felt vindicated because my life turned into a horror. Everyone who hated me could now laugh. I saw myself on newsstands ridiculed in tabloids like *The Globe*: FROM PORN KING TO PENNILESS ran the headline, with a picture of me lying in the street. I became the most famous homeless person in New York. Goldstein sightings became sport. Dispatches regularly appeared in the *New York Times*, *Post*, *Daily News* and were reported on Howard Stern.

The first six months I stayed at Bellevue Men's Shelter. The case workers have no humanity—they're not even Homosapiens, they're members of the animal kingdom; they show contempt for everyone. You'd expect to see the Bellevue staff posing in *National Geographic*. I ran out of diabetic medicine, Prozac, and Cozaar. I kept fainting and collapsing. I saw hot flashes of my family, homes, cars, secretaries, employees, my fiefdom known as Milky Way Productions— now all gone.

I had to get to Bellevue at eight o'clock to sign for a bed. If I didn't get there in time, I slept in Central Park—which happened on six occasions. A homeless guy gave me five dollars. He said, "Don't have pride. Take the money." I slept in a large room with twenty other creatures, most of whom talked to themselves and smelled. Some just ended up here after a divorce or medical emergency. Even successful people are one paycheck away from being homeless. The safety nets have holes and under capitalism we're all vulnerable.

After cursing my enemies for thirty-four years behind the bully pulpit of *Screw* and *Midnight Blue*, I no longer had my soapbox. All I could do was tell my twenty-eight-year-old fifth wife, suffering from Crohn's, that when she's dead I'm going to date her sisters. At least she didn't marry me for my nonexistent wealth. Until her, I thought women were all despicable and vile and I preferred salami any day. If women feel they're sex objects, men are just money objects. I still had to attend fifty hours of anger management on Roosevelt Island for wife beaters. This, due to my ex-wife Gena, for the harassment arrest. I've never hit a woman in my life. But my mouth is a weapon.

CHAPTER 8

Jailed in Cuba

In 1960, I won a thousand-dollar prize for a college short-story contest in the tits 'n' ass magazine *Escapade*. Even bottom-of-the-bin men's mags ran real short stories back then, by famous writers. The story was about a black kid I went to school with. I wouldn't write anything again until I worked for the *National Mirror* eight years later.

But having apprenticed in photography for Hearst papers, I received a 1960 assignment to Cuba. The assignment came from an agency called Pictorial Parade. They'd take 40 percent, I'd get 60 percent for pictures sold. I was not a communist, but I was a lefty, a pinko. I also did photo assignments for Bruce Gibson of the Fair Play for Cuba Committee. It turned out Lee Harvey Oswald was a member. Batista was a scumbag and I was pro-Fidel.

In 1960, I was twenty-four, and not that smart. I was visiting my mother in Deerfield Beach, Florida. I booked a Cubana Airlines flight from Miami to Havana. Upon arrival, I took telephoto shots from my window of the female militia marching across from the hotel. I took photos of armed installations around Havana and anti-American slogans on billboards. I'd been told Raoul Castro, Fidel's brother, would be speaking at a news conference that night. There were about three hundred people in the audience. After shooting thirty pictures, a militia guy signaled me over and demanded to examine the pictures in my camera. I said I'm a journalist, here's my press card, and refused to hand over the camera. Then I said a stupid thing. I said, "If you take my film, you might as well throw me in jail. I have no other reason for being here." So they took my camera, then took my fat obnoxious ass and threw me in jail. I was charged with espionage.

At Morro Castle, a military prison, I shared one cell with sixty other prisoners and one toilet. The castle was across Havana harbor with sharks circling in the waters outside the massive walls. A chute emerged from the walls of the castle—in the days of yellow fever, the chute was the fastest exit to slide corpses out to the sharks. Charged with spying, I was scared out of my mind, hungry, and had no one to call. I had to shit in front of sixty Cubans, none of them remotely as charming as Ricky Ricardo. The food was some kind of oatmeal gruel. After four days and nights, one prisoner left. I had begged him to go to the American embassy. He did. The next day an official in a suit came from the American embassy and said I'd be released in the next hour and escorted to a plane back to Florida. They returned the empty camera.

I saw that America was hated in Cuba. It was only weeks later when diplomatic relations broke down between Cuba and America. But imagine if the American embassy had only known what I would become. They could have had me executed as a defiant, loudmouthed spy without even lifting a finger.

The Long Island paper *Newsday* did a story on my release. That's how I met Johnny Carson. Before the *Tonight Show*, Carson did a show in New York called *Who Do You Trust?* I was on in 1960 to discuss what jail was like in Cuba. Then another contestant and I were asked questions. I won $225 because I knew who Werner Von Braun was, the head of our rocket program. I'd read about Von Braun two weeks earlier in the *Enquirer*. Years later I wrote Carson and tried to get the clip. He wrote back that NBC destroyed the kinescopes. After *Screw*, I was nonetheless never invited on the *Tonight Show*, or the *Today Show* for that matter. Tom Snyder had me on seven times, Donahue three times.

STATEN ISLAND FERRY

Bellevue makes you leave the shelter from 9:00 A.M. until 6:30 P.M. I still received a monthly social security check. So I learned where every Starbucks was. The first cup of coffee is $1.89, but refills were only $0.54. I bought a thermos and stayed all day. For free, I'd read the *New York Times*, the *Wall Street Journal*, the *New York Post*, recharge my cell phone, use their bathroom. Nobody bothered me and there were beautiful women to look at who are all computer nerds. Starbucks *is* a homeless shelter. Except that only two are open all night, the one on Astor Place and one in Times Square. I had a little Sony radio with TV sound, so I listened to WINS and Peter Jennings. I built my life around this for six months. I learned the whereabouts of every thrift shop. The Homeless Coalition on Nassau Street steered me to the Salvation Army on Wednesdays, where prices are cut in half for senior citizens. My favorite was the Marble Thrift Shop on Twenty-eighth and Third, where I'd buy beautiful two-hundred-dollar Italian jackets for six bucks. Great Brooks Brothers shirts for three dollars. I gave them to my wife to hold, who was back living with her parents. Her family was kind to me. Her father had been a Hindu priest and the oldest daughter was also married to a guy living in a homeless shelter. An old, broken Jew married to the young daughter of a Hindu priest. I'm thankful that before I went under, her parents saw my $3 million house in Florida and knew I was once a contender.

CHAPTER 9

Jackie in Pakistan

I accompanied First Lady Jacqueline Kennedy's Goodwill Tour to Pakistan in March, 1962. Pakistan International Airlines hired me as a commercial photographer. I joined the press entourage as a rep of the airline. I was there ten days, flew first class and was given an expense account. But they didn't let us near her. At one opportunity during the trip, she arrived in the city of Lahore, bordering India. For a moment she stood three feet away from my unsightly carcass and I could snap close-ups. The moment I shook her hand in the press line, I was merely lost in the reverie of being in the presence of Jackie Kennedy like everyone else. No woman seemed so revered, protected, innocent, saintly, pure. I was sweaty and hot, but she remained immaculate. She never had diarrhea, she only drank water flown in from the United States. I wanted to patriotically quaff her bush at Khyber Pass, but these feelings remained deep down and far removed from my professional demeanor.

The Pakistani government supplied hookers to all the press. They were beautiful, but very conservative and didn't like to have their Islamic pussies eaten. I probably jerked off over Jackie during the trip; she had nice thin ankles. Pictures I took appeared in the travel section of the *Chicago Tribune* and some color shots ran in *Travel Digest*. The White House sent a letter thanking me for sending a photo to the First Lady. Unlike Cuba, I took no surreptitious pictures, nothing controversial or remotely sexual, just pictures like everybody else.

Years later, in 1973, *Screw* #206 ran a cover screaming JACKIE O NAKED! Inside was a photo spread titled "Jackie Kennedy's Million-Dollar Bush." It was the single hottest-selling issue of *Screw*, 530,000 copies snatched up on New York newsstands at seventy-five cents a pop. I bought the photos from an Italian magazine called *Playmen* for ten grand. The paparazzi photos were indeed glorious full-frontal captures of Jackie in the buff on the island of Skorpios, shot with an extra-long lens. The pictures were also made into a *Screw* calendar. Six months later, *Hustler* ran the same photos.

In a book by then–*New York Post* Broadway columnist Leonard Lyons, and his son, film critic Jeffrey Lyons, there was an exchange overheard between Jackie and Aristotle Onassis discussing what the Kennedys should do about *Screw*'s calendar photos. She wanted to sue me, but Aristotle is quoted saying, "You don't get in a pissing contest with a skunk. Don't do a thing." The whole thing just perpetuated my reputation as a total sleaze. Having instigated a supreme violation of this magnificent private woman's privates, I was considered more contemptible than bed lice. Had she not been tortured enough? Anything vulgar, vile or disgusting, I would be the one to do it. I didn't have limits and went too far.

Like Jane Fonda and Gloria Steinem—women who would rather commit hari kari than let me near them—Jackie Kennedy Onassis would remain a sexual obsession with me for decades. *Screw*'s brilliant satirist, Dean Latimer, wrote a 1977 fantasy called "If Jackie

O Worked at *Screw*." She had recently gone into publishing and Latimer pondered what it would have been like if she'd chosen *Screw*, rather than editing expensive coffee table books at Doubleday. If only it were true. Jackie followed me to editorial meetings, took dictation, and when she farted, I levitated in rapturous ecstasy, the aroma wafting into my nostrils.

Annette Haven

Annette, the most beautiful creature in porn, was no dummy. The first ego-inflated ice queen of porn films, she ruled her own body. A whole cauldron of feelings boiled beneath the surface, which she kept to herself. But she was only twenty-two, and remained tense, wary, and tight-lipped. Meaning she never gave me a blowjob, no matter how much I begged and groveled for years.

The Las Vegas–bred beauty was attending to college in Oregon, heavily involved in a "triad" relationship with another woman and a man, and had only starred in a few porn films. In *China Girl*, her current release, her character was so saturated in her choice of pleasures, I was sure they'd be having screenings at *Ms.* magazine. The interview was more with myself:

AL: How would a film you made be different from a Gerry Damiano film?

ANNETTE: I don't even know who Gerry Damiano is.

AL: Gerry did *Devil in Miss Jones* and *Deep Throat*. He's a lovely little Italian man. He does shoes on the side in Queens. Soles.

ANNETTE: I had a lot of liking for *The Devil in Miss Jones*. I would want mine to be softer. Much softer. I would like to use effects, like gels on the lights and gauze on the camera.

AL: Wouldn't you ultimately, as a woman, have it so gauzed up that nobody could perceive that people were fucking?

ANNETTE: Oh, God, no!

AL: What I'm really saying is that women in their minds have so sterilized the sexual experience that it's no longer reality. The whole idea of a woman's film, a woman's book, a woman's short story, is softly focused, soft-core pornography. Women almost by definition cannot get into hard-core because it's too explicit. So you take a middle line: you feel you could do it, but it would be almost like Bob Guccione photography, sort of soft and lovely and sensitive?

ANNETTE: (*no response*)

AL: There are shrinks, analysts—who would maintain that somebody in a porn film is ipso facto, by definition, a hooker. Because although they're acting, so much sex is part of the performance that one has to look into their own morality and whether they really are strictly up for sale. One of the reasons Marilyn Chambers entered porn films was she felt too often she had to fuck the photographer to get a role. In porn films there's less hypocrisy. As you look around at the sexuality in your hometown, and as you travel around, do you feel that this country is getting sexually freer?

ANNETTE: I think it's getting sexually freer.

AL: Do you feel in your own heart that what you're doing is helpful to people? Do you think people can learn from going to sex films?

ANNETTE: Maybe it can help them to loosen up themselves. I don't know. I should hope that it would be good for them.

—*Screw*, May 1975

I got my hack license in college and drove a taxi through the midsixties. My shift went from four A.M. to one in the afternoon. I had a girl-friend, Pat, at 500 West End Avenue. I never made money because I would stop at her place at ten A.M. and eat pussy for two hours. I was the worst cab driver. It was more important to give her an orgasm than to keep the meter running. Because of those two hours, many a night cost me more than I earned. Eating Pat's pussy was a feeble attempt to have some control, literally pin her down. She dated other men, keeping me in a constant state of anguish. I became obsessed with her pussy, imagining other men getting a taste. Yet it was unlikely anyone else went down on her. Eating pussy was still con-sidered a perversion and was technically a felony in most states. An unnatural act stemming from the Puritan ethic that could put you on a chain gang in Georgia. Henry Miller wrote about it, and he was my guiding spirit as a fellow tonguesman.

Everyone said eating pussy was a perversion. There was a book called *Ideal Marriage*, by Belde, a theologian. He said oral sex was a true per-version. But he postulated the theory that not only should you only have intercourse, but simultaneous orgasm. So I'm really a product of this world of secrets, and that's why I became a good pornographer. I've been an avid pussy eater since I was sixteen and I'm now seventy—That's fifty-four years of chowing down. That's how I experience the world—with my tongue. Like pastrami, I can never get enough. During my thirty-four years of publishing *Screw*, the vaginal resources flowed. For the rest of my years I've suffered deprivation. I suffer from substance abuse, and that substance is pussy. I have to have pussy every day or I go into cold sweats. I should have joined a twelve-step program. I wish there was a pussy patch, like a cigarette patch for withdrawals.

Another horrible job, though I was good at it, was selling life insurance for Mutual of New York. At the end of my first year, I clawed my way to thirteen in sales out of thousands of agents. But I was burned out. I'd gotten married to my first wife, Lonnie, who left me. But more on that later. I met a guy named Maynard "Red" Ostrow, who now runs the *Circus Circus* shows in Vegas. He hired me as a carnie barker in the Belgian Village at the New York World's Fair in the summer of 1965. My parents then lived in Flushing, Queens, four blocks away from the Fair. I ran the "dime pitch" for a fast $250 a week. If you tossed a dime into a red circle, you won a doll. If your dime hit the middle of the circle surrounded by red, you won a TV set. I'd bark into a mike, "Ten cents right here, take it home for a dime!" Six people won TV sets that summer. We called the crowds "pips," carnie vernacular for building up a crowd. If someone tried to hustle me in a different part of the Belgian Village, I'd say, "I'm with it"—which meant hands off, I'm a carnie. I considered it show business. I even picked up a few groupies as a barker—there were even lower lives than me at the World's Fair. I wasn't scoring Meg Ryan, but to me, it was living, breathing pussy.

Unbeknownst to me, Jim Buckley, with whom I would soon found *Screw*, also worked at the Fair as a fudge maker. I met Professor Richard Brown at the Belgian Village, who taught at NYU with the young Martin Scorcese. He tried to hustle me out of free dolls, he was a real *schnorer*. I think he later felt terrible that Martin made it as a world-renowned director while he remained a mere NYU film professor—where he remains today, hot to trot with college girls. I would sit in at his famous film class at NYU. As soon as *Screw* went under, he, too, dumped me as a friend.

After the Fair closed, I went back to the taxi and took a job selling Encyclopedia Britannica. Except I never sold one. Rootless, with no prospects in sight, I sold blood to Times Square blood banks, like a derelict.

My absolutely pathetic Lonely Hearts personal, as it appeared in several singles publications in 1966:

> I am thirty, am 5'8 $\frac{1}{2}$ inches, blues eyes & brown hair. I have been photo journalist with assignments in Pakistan & Cuba, etc. I am also divorced. I hope that this fact does not dampen your interest. One would hardly know that I am "used" merchandise. I prefer to think that I'm now like a comfortable pair of shoes, "broken in." I enjoy everything with an emphasis on reading, movies, theater, outdoors, & good times of a non-selfish nature. I travel in my work and will shortly be spending 2 to 7 days at a nudist colony at Mays Landing, N.J. Well, I do anything once.
>
> So drop me a line with your response to this brief one of mine & include your address and phone number, etc.
>
> > Yours for future fun,
> > Al Goldstein

Any woman answering this would have had to be a Mongoloid idiot. No one replied.

JACK NICHOLSON

NICHOLSON: I'm not a great sexual person, not a great Lothario by any stretch of the imagination. . . . People that I don't like are not sexually attractive to me at all. In my early twenties I had a few hate-fucks and they were groovy. But not now.

AL: What was your reaction to *Deep Throat?*

NICHOLSON: If you're having a male sexual experience, after you have your orgasm your next impulse is *not* to bend down and look over and watch someone's scrotum pounding against someone's shaved beaver or whatever.

AL: Let me ask you another sex question.

NICHOLSON: What a magazine! *Screw!* Incidentally, this is the best interview I've given in years.

AL: Have you ever jerked off to *Screw?*

NICHOLSON: Yes, I have.

—*Screw,* November 1972

CHAPTER 10

Birth of Screw

Sex is the deepest and most volcanic of human impulses.

—Havelock Ellis

Screw's scathing and scatological editorials railed against a meddlesome government that justified war while imprisoning such erotic magazine publishers as Eros' *Ralph Ginzburg; and after the New York police had closed down the stage production of* Che, *arresting ten cast members along with the theater's floor sweeper because the show included an act of fellatio which was considered morally perilous to theatergoers,* Screw *demanded to know why the police that week had not also closed down the city's streets, on which 145 people had been killed. The frequent police raids against the sex shops, adult bookstores, and porn theaters in New York were reported in* Screw *with cynical alarm, for it saw behind each policeman's angry night-stick a sexually frigid Irish-Catholic mother, a drinking father, and a latent homosexual priest in the confessional deploring fleshly pleasures between men and women.*

—from Gay Talese's 1980 book, *Thy Neighbor's Wife*

Screw *is a huge joke.*

—Henry Miller

If I had to choose to write for either the New York Times *or* Screw, *I would certainly write for* Screw, *just on moral grounds.*

—Gore Vidal

The paper contains the filthiest material I've ever seen in any publication.
—Captain John McKeever, Trenton, New Jersey, Police Force

Desperate for an angle, in my off time from the cab, I concocted my own little start-up "German" news agency in 1965. I got a few free typewriters and TVs. A photo agent named Carl Przybylla gave me some good assignments at a thousand bucks a pop. One was to follow and photograph the Shah of Iran. I spent a month covering some priest in Brooklyn who ran a scam, having his nun girlfriends hustle money on the streets. Then I photographed Malcom X for two weeks at his mosque in Harlem, on assignment for a German magazine, *Bunte Deutch Illustrated.* Harlem was not gentrified then and I was nervous being the only white person present. But Malcom X was nice to me, because it was for a German, not American, publication. He trusted me. He believed the myth of the Chosen People, declared me one of them, and I was flattered. They served vegetarian meals that I enjoyed. I told him about my trip to Pakistan and my time at Morro Castle. I liked Malcom X and felt terrible when he was murdered.

I still couldn't make a living as a freelancer and New York papers were sinking. The *World-Telegram and Sun,* the *Journal-American* and the *Herald-Tribune* all bit the dust in 1966. Little did Gotham's citizens suspect that a radically different type of paper—now just a twinkle in my eye—would soon take its place on the newsstand.

The two jobs I had immediately before starting the World's Greatest Newspaper are what led to *Screw*. I took an unethical assignment in 1967—working as an industrial spy. I'm not proud of this. I did espionage for a subsidiary of Bendix Corporation, P&D Manufacturing in Astoria, Queens. They made ignitions and after-sales auto parts. Bendix was afraid their workers would defect from the local union and join the more powerful United Auto Workers union. A vice president of Bendix, Bob Shear, sent me to Seneca Falls, where feminism started, to take photos of equipment. I would travel through the company sifting through garbage, before they had paper shredders, and listen to pros and cons. I delivered parts, worked in the stock rooms and eavesdropped. It was demeaning, repetitious, and I hated it. My mind would go blank and I almost crushed my hand in the machinery.

I infiltrated the union as a mole and fed all the information to Bendix. Because of me the UAW lost the election. Here I was a scumbag, spying on the UAW when I'm liberal and pro-union. On the other hand, when the UAW lost the workers, who voted 203 to 198 against joining, Bendix closed their Astoria office anyway and moved their whole operation to Mexico City. I finally walked off the job, forfeiting a ten-thousand-dollar bonus.

Disgusted with myself, I approached the *New York Free Press*, a hippie publication. I decided to do an exposé on Bendix and what a lowlife I was. The *Free Press*, at Seventy-second and Broadway, was part of the newly emerging underground, second to the *East Village Other*. It wasn't free, but was published by a guy named Jack Banning who walked around the office barefoot to emphasize how little money they made. It was my fate to meet Jim Buckley there. Jim was an editor/typesetter/proofreader making seventy-five dollars a week. He knew the technical aspects of printing a newspaper. I'd never

learned anything technical about newspapers. My Bendix exposé
came out as a cover story, and while I waited for a media uproar,
nothing happened. Nobody gave a shit about the story.

But I entered the world of publishing. In January 1968 I found an
editorial position through the *Village Voice*. It was a desk job paying
$125 a week writing for the scandal tabloids. Like network TV, they
projected the insidious double standard of trying to titillate while
remaining anti-sex. Nevertheless, I learned the men's mag field here.
Hush Hush News and the *National Mirror* (no connection to Hearst's
Daily Mirror, where my father had worked) competed against the
Enquirer and *Confidential*. They were part of Countrywide Publications, owned by Myron Fass at 150 Fifth Avenue. Fass was a notorious gun-toting newsstand warrior, the "Demon God of Pulp." His
father had worked for the WPA in the sewers in New York; Myron
worked in the sewers of publishing. My editor was Roy Lester, who
hired me.

Every hour I would create a fake news story out of thin air, using
names of old teachers and friends. I reinvented *Romeo and Juliet* and
had them crash into a lake—the girl died and the guy was so
unhappy he killed himself. I wrote Lover Shoves Icepick Up Lover's
Nose, Man Gets Horse Organ in Sexual Transplant, Dancer's
Admirer Sliced Up, Thrown in Sewer, and Cuts off Hand of Jewelry Thief. It was all fabricated sexo-sado-psuedo-mash. My editor,
Roy Lester, accused me of not taking the job seriously enough, but
how could you take it seriously?

These papers were on every American newsstand, their circula-
tions and profits soaring. The *National Mirror* could print fake
details of someone's head cut off or eye poked out. But when covering sex, we had to write, "unmentionable acts." We were restricted
to words like coitus and fornication. You could have specificity of

violence and gore, but in 1968, tabloids couldn't describe human tenderness or hedonism.

There were bottom-feeders even lower than us. Blood and bare-tit stories were the staple of *Midnight* (SEX EDUCATION PERVERTS CHILDREN!), *Inside News* (DREAMED SHE WAS BEING RAPED—SLEEPWALKER HACKED HUBBY TO DEATH WITH AX), *Keyhole* (SORDID JAIL SEX EXPOSED), *Flash* (SEX WITH A HUMAN SKELETON), *National Tattler*, *National Insider*, ad nauseam. This was my entry into publishing and my realization of the state of pornography.

I hired Jim Buckley to do some writing at Countrywide. We talked about how the sexual act was warped and sick in these puritanical papers. Why weren't skin flicks and fuckbooks reviewed? Why were pussy pictures reserved only for the rich who could afford them? Where was the equality and democracy of smut?

Jim said, "Let's do our own paper."

I said, "Let's do a *sex* paper." A newspaper that could be everything that the *National Mirror* was not. To detail sex, but never violence. The *National Mirror* denigrates sex. Why don't we have a sex-positive paper? I'm thirty-two years old, not really getting laid, I'm obsessed with eating pussy, I know all the scams.

Jim, however, was a sexual neophyte. He wasn't that interested in sex. Raised in Catholic orphanages, he was small and lean with lots of black hair. Buckley was considered quite handsome, with an undeniably innocent Catholic schoolboy look. He never cheated on his wife. Born in Lowell, Massachusetts in 1944, he attended fourteen different schools in seven states. He spent years in Catholic orphanages where, as he said, "Life was like a bowl of shit. I've been an anal retentive ever since." After graduating Lunenburg High in Massachusetts, he joined the navy. He was honorably discharged like me. At age twenty he began hitchhiking across the United States,

Mexico, Europe, and North Africa; he became a cook in Greenwich Village, a Kelly Girl typist, and ironically, was a fudge maker somewhere at the World's Fair while I was doing the dime pitch. The *New York Free Press* would fold after Jim left.

We thought up the idea of *Screw* and laid out plans in the summer of '68. That was also the summer I married Mary Phillips, in Taxco, Mexico. She was a Pan Am stewardess, in the days when *stewardi* had to be beautiful, and we could fly discount. I listed Mary as publisher in the first issue of *Screw*. I wasn't sure the divorce was final with my first wife, Lonnie, and didn't want her getting any possible money from it. Mary was a feminist with a great sense of humor. She considered me a psychopath and was proud of it. She flew for Pan Am by day and attended NYU at night for her PhD in anthropology.

Buckley and I invested $350 for the first issue—$175 each. The first printing bill was $217. The printer promptly burned the plates and mats and any evidence that he had printed such a thing. We put a $75 ad in some other underground paper announcing *Screw*. The staff was just me, Jim Buckley, and Mary Philips.

The first issue of *Screw* hit the newsstands on November 4, 1968, the day Nixon was elected. A twelve page, black and white tabloid, it cost twenty-five cents. Newspapers were handled by distributors, none of whom would touch it. So we tried to hustle it onto newsstands by hand. Most news vendors instantly rejected it. For eight weeks, cigar-chomping fat guys with aprons told me I was vile and should be ashamed. They yelled and threw copies back in my face. One called me a disgusting Jew bastard.

I remember the first newsstand that accepted *Screw*. It was at Fifty-third and Third, an all-night stand still there today. It took months to get it on the newsstand at Seventy-second and Broadway. Ultimately, we managed to get it on about twenty-two newsstands— the ones where the news dealers were blind. The first issue was a whopping run of forty-five hundred, which sold out. Myron Fass fired me the moment *Screw* came out. He said it was because my grammar was so bad. I'd lasted ten months at Countrywide, and it was true I still hadn't mastered the alphabet. Before our tenth issue, we were selling over thirty thousand copies per issue, and we surpassed fifty thousand by issue eleven. By the time we were first arrested, *Screw* sales on Manhattan newsstands outsold *Time, Life, Newsweek,* and *Playboy.* Of course, we were only available on Manhattan newsstands.

Beat cops warned our street vendors they'd be arrested along with the publishers for selling *Screw.* All guts and no brains, we challenged the police commissioner to come get us—or shut up. This pronouncement was in issue #3. We didn't yet have a regular office by the third issue, so we announced in the paper where we could be found. But the NYPD was biding their time, collecting issues as evidence.

My very first arrest came from Mineola, Long Island, from Nassau County DA Bill Cahn. Two pedophiles, a cop and his wife, had solicited young girls in a personal ad in issue #6. I didn't know pedophilia from a hole in the wall and I hadn't paid attention to the personals. Had I seen this, I would not have run it. The *New York Post* ran its first picture of me in handcuffs. The great First Amendment lawyer Herald Price Fahringer stepped forth to represent me. Several years later, DA Bill Cahn was charged with tax fraud and spent three years in prison. The Goldstein Curse upon my enemies had begun its magic.

But even by 1969, there was a mysterious draw emerging between my enemies and myself. I had a friendly lunch one day with the young Manhattan assisstant DA, Kenneth Conboy, who busted the off-Broadway drama *Che*, the first stage show to present live cocksucking. *Screw* rallied behind *Che*. In 1986, Conboy became Mayor Koch's investigation commissioner for the City of New York.

Screw gave the world's oldest profession its first advertising medium and enabled the man on the street to get laid within an hour. Gore Vidal called us the only newspaper in America that properly serviced its readers. *Screw* also ran the first weekly gay column of any newsstand publication, by Lige and Jack, before the Stonewall Riot. We were now the sword of the sexual revolution, the *Consumer Reports* of sex. A typical 1970 bust concerned dildo ads. The State of New York argued in Superior Court that dildos could be used for criminally immoral purposes.

There were sixteen early obscenity arrests in a row, every other week. One arrest in '69 involved a depiction of Jesus on the cross. There was a big debate in court with expert witnesses testifying as to whether Jesus's cock was erect or not in the illustration, just as there was with Mayor Lindsay's cock. After Jesus, all the trials just blend together.

But by early '69, *Screw* was so successful on the newsstands, it made Myron Fass irrelevant, driving his whole dreck factory, and others like it, to the very bottom of the newsstand. The sexual revolution was exploding. We embraced a huge market no one knew existed. What was missing from *Playboy* centerfolds, sexploitation films, automobile and cigarette ads with sex—was simple honesty. We soon had imitators on the stands.

We also made enemies fast. On May 30, 1969, we withstood the first NYPD police raid on our office. Buckley and I were fingerprinted, charged with obscenity and held behind bars. Amazingly, we weren't arrested by the NYPD until issue #15. This occurred eight hours after *Screw* hit the stands showing a Mayor Lindsay composite with his cock hanging out. It was a fairly huge cock, and provoked controversy over whether it was real, erect, or in repose.

My third arrest, I'm in the Tombs jail with Buckley, charged again with promoting obscenity—S.235.05 on the books. There are six blind newsdealers arrested for selling *Screw* in the cell with us. Each one holds a cane. I tell Buckley, whatever you do, don't say who we are. They'll bash us on the head with their canes. They were so angry they might have killed us, so we kept quiet. Junkies are peeing against the walls, nodding out and puking over other junkies lying on the floor. One of the blind newsdealers is tapping his cane to find the only urinal, and I'm suddenly overcome with guilt. How could a blind dealer know what he was selling? This was under Mayor John Lindsay's administration. A typical liberal scumbag of the time, I began to hate Lindsay and he holds the distinction of having his head put in the ShitList toilet bowl of my weekly editorial more times than anyone.

It soon became routine: Goldstein and Buckley handcuffed, brought to the Thirteenth Precinct, led away to 100 Centre Street. The cop car veers wildly through traffic, bumping us around. The Thirteenth Precinct cops become nicer, most having now heard of *Screw*; there was even a discernable police readership by now.

"What's the charge?" comes desk captain.

"Obscenity."

"What? How can anyone be arrested for obscenity with all them sex papers out there now?"

"These are the publishers of one of them."

"Oh yeah, which one?"

"*Screw*."

"No kiddin.' Glad to meetcha." Detective Gray and another cop came in to shake hands with great élan. We knew him from a previous bust, when he purchased fifty papers for his "route in Southern Jersey." He was the cop's house hippie, slightly overweight with a red beard. Buckley and I liked him. Then we'd be fingerprinted, photographed, and incarcerated.

I compared the cockroaches at Rikers and the Tombs. The cockroaches were stronger and faster at the Tombs. But the worst part of jail was having, on several arrests, to share a cell with "Old Archie," the distributor of *Kiss*. *Kiss*, *Pleasure* and the *New York Review of Sex and Politics* would sometimes get busted with us, so we endured the poor company of our tabloid imitators. *Screw*'s arrests were now reported in the *Times*, *Post*, and *Daily News*, as well as on local Metromedia TV and sometimes network news. The imitators rode our coattails. Morality in Media, led by Father Morton Hill on the east side railed against us, a resurgence of the Inquisition, breeding sexual fear and ignorance.

People of the State of New York v. *Al Goldstein*. It was exciting; I felt alive.

I was making money. And I paid a price. To the general public, I was dirty, hated, and decent citizens just wanted me in jail. But the attention was a validation of my narcissistic shortcomings that made the fight worthwhile. If the City had left me alone and paid no attention, I probably would have gotten bored and quit the magazine.

Herald Fahringer was winning my trials. They were getting bigger, becoming a cause celébrè. My proudest was a 1971 conviction for showing pubic hair. Pubic hair! It was considered dirty and illegal. After this pubic public hurdle, *Penthouse*, and then *Playboy* began to show hints of the dark triangle.

At one trial, the prosecution put forth two expert witnesses who testified that *Screw* was legally obscene: Father Raymond Schroth, journalism professor at Fordham University, and Ernest van den Haag, sociology/law professor at NYU. Bravely coming forth to testify on our behalf was Paul Zimmerman, senior editor at *Newsweek*, Rev. William Glensek, pastor of Spencer Memorial Church, Dr. George Stade, chariman of the department of english at Columbia University, Herbert S. Altman, film producer and director, Dr. Sol Gordon, a clinical psychologist degreed from the University of London, and two of our first staffers—ad manager Marcia Blackman, our first hire, and associate editor, Peter Ogren.

As pointed out by Albert B. Gerber in his intro to *The Screw Reader* anthology in 1971, our expert winning defense demonstrated that if something is funny enough, it isn't "dirty." The great newspaper man, Heywood Broun, famously quipped that "if the width of the wit is wider than the depth of the dirt, then it is not obscene." Our shocking material was mostly put-on. These trials helped us clarify our purpose and improve the paper.

Ernest van den Haag testified against me in my first trial, but then we became friends. He always asked me to get him hookers. If I've run into anything in my years publishing *Screw*, it's the difference between the real world and the fake one.

Screw was not an evolution of men's mags, but a counterreaction to them, especially the "acceptable" sadomasochistic tabloids. No one was mutilated or beaten in *Screw*. *Screw* was part of the underground hippie counterculture emanating from the East Village, a few blocks below our office. Sally Eaton, from the cast of *Hair*, wrote in *Screw*, "I think fucking is the friendliest thing two people can do. . . . America is such a deodorized country that we have to surround something as simple as fucking with romance."

Marilyn Chambers

Imagine what a collector's item a 1972 Ivory Snow box must be. When it was revealed the wholesome vision of sweetness holding a baby on the cover was the star of *Behind the Green Door*, the film became a sensation. Marilyn pointed out that porn was not a business you have to fuck to get into, like Hollywood. You get in it and *then* you fuck. Her then-husband, Doug, joined the interview:

DOUG: I like to eat her when she has her period. That bothers her more than it does me.

MARILYN: Well, you know you like to feel clean. You have to wash your cunt ten times a day so it doesn't stink.

DOUG: One of my favorite erotic acts is to eat her asshole out after she hasn't had a bath in three days.

MARILYN: I'm kind of hung up on the asshole trip.

AL: Linda Lovelace still beats you by about five inches. Is it because you had less cock to work with or that she has more throat?

MARILYN: I think she has more throat. But I don't think good cocksucking depends on how deep you get it.

—*Screw*, November 1973

Hundreds of *Screw* staffers came and went in a blur over the years. *Screw*'s first three art directors, Steve Heller, J. C. Suarez, and Bob Eisner, were hired away by the *New York Times*. Heller was so young that, during one of our busts, he was thrown in juvenile lockup. Some staffers I remember vividly. *Screw*'s first three managing editors were women. Our first hire was Roslyn Bramms. It was early 1969 (*Screw* #15–23). Roz stayed with us for eight issues, then quit with a temper outburst, charging we were "tools of the chauvinist revolution." Next came my beautiful wife, Mary Phillips, who somehow managed to put out the magazine each week without ever once viewing the contents. Then came Managing Editor Heidi Handman, who later became managing editor at *Penthouse*. And finally a man, Peter Brennan, who next became managing editor of Hefner's *Oui*.

Marcia Blackman was our ad manager for eight years. She was every guy's fantasy of what a *Screw* woman should be like. She sold her pubic hair to *Screw* readers through a personal ad, for a couple hundred extra bucks a week. We went to Florida once and I asked to eat her pussy. I thought we should just get it out of the way. But she said no. My feelings were hurt, and remain so to this day. She started off pretty then morphed into a fat bull dyke.

Marcia came up with this prank concept of listing a massage parlor called the Golden Tongue, for women. The ad promised that the most agile and powerful tongues would be assembled to satisfy women in a plush setting, with men whose cocks were so strong, you could hang 'ten umbrellas on them. We said the men would be dressed in blue, and that the Golden Tongue would resemble a police station. The address and number we published was the Midtown North Precinct on Fifty-first Street. The ad ran for five weeks and trouble started when the cops' *wives* began complaining. Until then, I think, the cops were enjoying some off-duty action—when my secretary called to make an appointment for a Golden Tongue massage, they told her to come on down. I heard a lot of New York's Finest were asking to be transferred to Midtown. But finally, I was arrested on the dumbest charge of my career: "harassing a police station."

After *Screw*, Marcia opened up a Body Shop in California. She always liked guns. During a robbery attempt at the store, she opened fire and blew the perpetrator away.

The first issues were basically written by me alone. I was first to actually review porn films and test drive sex aids. I remember taking this inflatable doll to Seneca Falls and trying to fuck it. Rubber compounds were like tire treads for such gimmicky equipment then. It was rough and hurt my dick. I went to all the early porno theaters. The one closest to our office, Variety Photoplay at Third Avenue and Twelveth, was crawling with guys giving blowjobs in the bathrooms. We called it Suck Theater. The first film I recall seeing there was called *The Screening Room* by Alex deRenzy. Next I remember seeing something called *Electro Sex*. Most porn was coming direct to the East Coast from San Francisco, after the Supreme Court had ruled on *Censorship in Scandinavia*, which was a "documentary." Once the Court allowed a documentary with two minutes of hard-core, the floodgates opened up. Nobody could stop it.

Screw was first to interview sex actors, which in 1969 would have been akin to doing interviews with terrorists, or bed lice, today. Considering the playing field today, maybe it would have been better if we never started the trend. Ten-minute 8 mm loops, the bread and olive oil of mafia porn, were illicitly produced criminal affairs, with black market distribution like heroin. Pornographic feature films were making their baby-steps transition from smoky stag parlors to Times Square grind-house marquees. No publication had ever considered or bothered to interview the bodies that appeared in them.

But the *Screw* interview soon became a rite of passage for the first generation of made porn stars—it was their first and sometimes their only feature interview.

Terry Southern
Just as his current book, *Blue Movie*, projected the whole porn movie future, Southern predicted the whole video and digital revolution to come in his 1970 interview:

SOUTHERN: Now we're getting into a golden age of filmmaking with video tape. There'll be no censorship or sponsor problems. It'll be the era of the homemade dirty movie. Imagine the enormous impact that will have. They have prototypes now for four or five hundred bucks. Instant playback. I just saw a demonstration—fantastic!

SCREW: Will there be restrictions on it?

SOUTHERN: They can't restrict it, because it can't go through the mails. We're right on the threshold of total freedom in that area because of the Polaroid aspect of these video tape movies— that they can be shot privately and you don't have to take them out to get them processed, but immediately play them back, erase them, shoot them again—and this aside from the stuff that will be made in the studio under professional conditions with beautiful people and so on and then sold. If they *have* to be sold in a clandestine way, say like pot now, that's all right. I mean, there won't be any stopping it—any more than they can stop people smoking pot by saying it's against the law.

Screw: Do you think satire is still a viable weapon after everything the country's been through—Nixon, the hardhats, the war?

SOUTHERN: Yes, but it will take stronger satire, like the movie *Joe. Joe* is a satiric treatment of hardhats, but it goes beyond a conventional notion of satire because it gets into . . . well, it takes up where *Easy Rider* left off. It really gets into a depressing statement ultimately. *Satire* may not be the right word anymore. I mean, with its connotations of Thurber-type lightheartedness. But maybe we have to get into a heavier type of satire, the kind that Mark Twain and the guy who wrote *Gulliver's Travels*—Jonathan Swift did. More bitter, but controlled.

Screw: What was it like working with Dennis Hopper on *Easy Rider?*

SOUTHERN: Den Hopper? Also called "Grass," like in, you know, *Grasshopper?* "Great Grasshopper" we called him. Well, it's a lot of fun working with Den—except sometimes he asks you to hold his head, you know, while he shoots a lot of weird dope and drug into it—right into the top of his weird old head.
        —*Screw*, October 1970, interview by Michael Perkins

Great Ray, our eccentric resident cunnilinguist, put weekly pussy-eating ads in the back of the paper. *Screw* published his life story in installments. About his great obsession, he recalled, "I was eating four girls on the school marching band majorette corps in Ridley High School. . . . In my second year of college, I had four steady eating cunts. After college, it was sweet eating for three years. But then sucking declined for reasons I can't well remember."

Honeysuckle Divine wrote a regular column, "Diary of a Dirty Broad." Legend had it she was a Jekyll-and-Hyde case—a schizo-phrenic nun who escaped an upstate convent by moonlight like a werewolf and transformed into the "Dirtiest Girl on Earth" on Times Square burlesque marquees. She was able to shoot Jergen's lotion and ping-pong balls into the audience and play kazoo from her circus-trained vagina. She would put a broom in her cunt and sweep the floor. Although she looked like Brigitte Bardot, she was a one-woman slum. She could sicken a gynecologist. She was so dirty, even I wouldn't touch her. But, oddly, she was also a sweet, seemingly innocent creature who was the only one on staff who called me Mr. Goldstein.

Honeysuckle reported her misadventures in Times Square and around the country. Her diary noted the deteriorating burlesque market. This dispatch from 1971 reflects the hardships of a poor stripper on her own, without a suitcase pimp:

Dear Diary:

After I left Baltimore a month or so ago, I went to Chicago and looked up an agent one of the girls had told me about. I felt since she was a woman agent at least I wouldn't be expected to put out. But she shared her office with a man agent and he zeroed in on me right away. He booked me in a theatre in the West End of Chicago. Lord—it was the worst place I've ever worked. Not only did the agent come to the dressing room with subtle hints about having sex with him, but the boss, the manager, the ticket agent, the popcorn machine attendant, the projec-tion room operators (day and night shift), and about five guys who were doing repairs and painting the building were all flowing into the dressing room in a steady stream. They were all on the make and not the least bit subtle about it. The stage was filthy and I couldn't do any floor work without getting caked with dirt and dust....

Jim Buckley and I had a hooker named Maureen Kelly come in every Tuesday at two o'clock to blow us for a hundred bucks. By the third week, it felt like a dental appointment. Oh, shit, I gotta wash my balls. If it's scheduled, it's just business, it loses spontaneity.

Screw's first office was on Thirteenth Street at Union Square. A year later we moved to the eleventh floor at 11 West Seventeenth Street. The American Communist Party headquartered on the tenth floor below us, with old lefties roaming the halls. The *Monster Times* shared the building, from where *Screw* editor J. J. Kane would be hired, and a scandal sheet called *Peeping Tom*. An upscale massage parlor on the ninth floor, Experience One, began to advertise its phone number and address, and soon dozens of massage parlors followed in our pages. Milton Glaser came in to redesign *Screw* in 1971, to separate us on the stands from dozens of imitators.

My mother's attitude was "*Screw* is good, he makes fun of sex." My father's attitude: "Who cares. He has people working for him."

My mother remained proud of me. She liked that her son Alvin had such a big mouth, even when in handcuffs, the opposite of my father. I'd fallen far from the tree, far from my father's self-effacing world of cowardice. She could beam to befuddled old ladies who used to work at the Rainbow Shop, "That's my son, Alvin—the Great Pornographer." During one of my trials, my mother picketed the district attorney; my father stayed far away, didn't want to make a scene.

Screw's headline, Is J. Edgar Hoover a Fag? broached this hushed question for the first time ever, while Hoover was still alive and kicking. A grand jury called my mother in to explain how her son determined the FBI's founder was homosexual. She was listed on *Screw*'s masthead as "business manager," as a joke. She was a Jewish mother from Brooklyn, what did she know?

I was in the vortex of chaos. I was a madman. I ran centerfold illustrations of Nixon's two daughters eating each other, and Attorney General John Mitchell fucking Tricia. I became the feature interview of the October 1974 *Playboy*. That put me on the national map. Public taunting of scumbags J. Edgar Hoover and Nixon would soon reach critical mass. *State of New York* v. *Al Goldstein* would soon escalate to *United States of America* v. *Al Goldstein*. When my federal indictment came down, I would have sixty-five years in federal prison staring me in the face for three years.

Meanwhile, *The Screw Reader*, a coffee-table compendium of *Screw* articles, came out in hardcover from Lyle Stuart in 1971. The articles seem quaint, dated, from a faraway time and place called 1969. Typical was Jim Buckley's "Interview with a Cocksucker." But back then, *Screw* screamed of blasphemy and sexual revolution. We overturned every rock and crevice revealing dark secrets heretofore untold. I was being found guilty of obscenity every other week, paying ten-thousand-dollar fines and moving on. New York newsdealers were baffled, local politicians befuddled, churches outraged, morality watchdogs and decency groups called to arms.

I became a walking caricature of anti-Semitism. "The world's foremost pornographer," according to the *New York Times*. The Clown Prince of Pornography, to men's magazines. The Devil Incarnate, to women's magazines. Gandhi with his dick out, to sexual

freedom fighters. Dirty Alvin, to old Brooklyn cronies. A bona fide
New York eccentric, to city boosters.

Al Goldstein, the Great Pornographer.

LENNON

I had so much respect for John Lennon and the Beatles. In the midseventies, Yoko put me in one of her art movies, *Knees*. I had dinner
with John and Yoko twice at the Four Seasons. Gena was with me;
John was with actor Peter Boyle and another friend or two. I felt like
a chosen person to be in his presence; I had touched the face of God.
He liked the fact there was no repression in New York, he seemed
happy, he seemed to like the irreverence of *Screw*. Yoko wasn't too
good with her English. One of John's guys picked up the tab both
times, money was irrelevant to him. John and Yoko did the *Screw*
interview from Montreal during their 1969 Bed-In for Peace, which
he had to hold in Canada; the American government wouldn't let
him do it here. Lennon was the only sacred cow in *Screw*'s long history, the only figure whose life and death transcended parody. When
Screw reprinted his interview in December 1980, the introduction
was more somber than anything we'd ever done editorially:

> The sickening circumstances of John's tragic departure have left us
> dumbstruck. His importance to many people far exceeded that of any
> president or world leader, and he was one of the most beloved men in
> the world. He struggled to eliminate the aura of godliness that people
> thrust on him, as the following reprint demonstrates. Alas, in the
> worst way of all, we have seen that he was not a god, but a mortal man.
>
> In June of 1969, issue #18, John and Yoko granted an interview to
> Screw magazine, conducted by Jim Buckley, Goldstein, and assorted
> staffers. The interview, during John's Bed-In for Peace days, also
> occurred in the first year of Screw's existence. Needless to say, it gave

the paper a great boost in credibility and prestige. The transcript, in which John relates some of his sexual feelings, stands as a highlight of our own twelve-year history.

An excerpt below:

Screw: What was your first sexual experience and how old were you?

John: Oh, probably around six, you know, I don't remember anything before that, really, I mean I suppose your first sex experience is fiddlin' with yourself, but the first of my big episodes was a little girl up in entry and we had her knickers down and some guy came along, you know, and she ran off with her knickers around her legs and we all ran away. She was about four years old. All the other guys got caught but me (heh, heh!), so that's why I remember it so well. We were just lookin' and before that I can't remember anything.

Screw: You want to pose naked for our centerfold? We'll be glad to take the picture.

John: You and whose army? I even took the photograph for *Two Virgins.* We were alone when we took that photograph. We're very shy people, you know. What do you think we are, some kind of sex perverts or something? You're talkin' to Abbott and Costello.

Screw: Do you still want to get into the United States?

John: Sure. I want to see Nixon, to give him an acorn. . . . We think the whole scene's too serious, that's why *Screw* is good. . . .

The whole movement is all a load of intellectual shit. And all them "hippie-aware" people are just a gang of snobs.

Screw: I was once managing mditor of a paper called *The New York Free Press* and the main problem with it was it took itself so serious. If I wanted to say that this cop was kind to children I'd probably get censored.

John: Right! That's where it's at. Like the Underground in England is so serious. The *International Times* is so serious they won't even review our records. Because we made it. We "sold out" and it's a real laugh. Now they're talking about changing it and talkin' about Gandalf and fuckin' Alice in Wonderland. The hobbits.

Screw: Are you guys ever planning to get together again to do something?

John: I've tried to get them all on the road, but Ringo doesn't want to, so . . . I'm not that mad about it, but I'm interested in going out. So I'm just doin' a few gigs with Yoko.

Screw: Have you gotten out of the bed all these past few days?

John: Just to shit and pee.

Screw: You got that *Screw* reader? Get closer to the mike.

John: Yeah, we got out of bed one day and we just SHAT!

SCREW: This is going to be hard to take. A lot of little girls are going to be very disappointed to find out that a Beatle shits.

JOHN: I used to wonder about the Queen.

SCREW: Why did you come to Montreal?

JOHN: Because they wouldn't let me in the States.

SCREW: But you could've gotten in?

JOHN: They only would have let me in if I did an anti-narcotics thing with a senator. McGovern, I think.

STATEN ISLAND FERRY

It's rare to find a real *mensch*, a standup guy, in the porn biz. Or anywhere, for that matter. Let me tell you who stuck by me: Steve Hirsch of Vivid sent me five thousand dollars. Paul Fishbein of *Adult Video News* sent me five thousand dollars. Writer Ratso Sloman's been there, Don Imus; Howard Stern reached in his pocket and gave me five hundred dollars. The brilliant Herald Fahringer, the lawyer who defended me throughout my First Amendment trials, "loaned" me five grand. The not-so-brilliant Ron Jeremy gave me money, which is amazing. He's cheap, but also my best friend. My new criminal lawyer, Charles DeStefano, threw me a couple grand.

CHAPTER 11

DiB

A lot of wiseguys saw me as the father of their industry, the guy who fought and beat the system. If I was shot, they could fill up Yankee Stadium with suspects. But I knew it wouldn't be the mob. They were pleased to have a public face on an illicit business rising out of the gutter. If I ever figured in a mob hit, it would be from some low-level scumbag who hadn't been set straight about who I was, some punk or son of a gangster. Little did I know, as I will later mention, there would someday be a contract on my life from John Gotti. It was squelched by my friend DiB.

Robert DiBernardo, aka DiB, was the powerful Gambino capo in charge of "union negotiations" for the teamsters, while simultaneously being the Family's "porn kingpin." He was *Screw*'s protector for almost twenty years. He was a debonair, good-looking gent, with excellent sartorial taste. DiB's name was feared and respected throughout the underworld, probably for good reason, but he was also widely liked.

Six months before I started *Screw*, while still at the *National Mirror*, I answered an ad in the *Village Voice* seeking porn writers.

The operation, Star Distributors, was at 150 Lafayette Street. They paid twenty-five dollars on five-hundred-word wraparounds for their pseudo-porn periodicals sold on racks at Times Square bookstores. The words were supposed to offer redeeming social value. Nobody in the office could write them, they couldn't spell.

There I met DiB and his partners Teddy Rothstein and Steve Alba. It was a boring office, a lot of books, ledgers, file cabinets; nobody got laid there. U-hauls at the sidewalk were loaded with Mafia porn, going out twenty-four hours a day all over the country. DiB was thin, but still had high blood pressure.

I soon came to DiB with the first issue of *Screw* in November '68. He thought it was "too dirty." Pornography, extortion, union-fixing, rub-outs—that was just business. The Gambinos were otherwise conservatives. They believed in the Vietnam war. When I attacked J. Edgar Hoover or the church, DiB, a patriotic Italian-American businessman, was outraged. When *Screw* covered the Pope's visit to New York, alleging his entire tour consisted of visiting men's bathrooms, he felt I went too far. But they were impressed with my public battles, setting legal precedents, the first proud pornographer. The world was changing. As smut became more mainstream in the wake of *Screw*, DiB's Star Distributors became the largest porn film distributor in the country. And the word on the street was nobody fucks with Goldstein.

DiB and I made fun of Rick D'Matteo at Astro News, because Rick was a Damon Runyon character, a dese-dem-and-dose guy. Astro News was *Screw*'s distributor in New York. But DiB was my national distributor, and he had us do an out-of-town edition. The out-of-town *Screw* was the same as the in-town one, sans the hardcore photos. John Zaccaro, the husband of Geraldine Ferraro, who ran for vice president, was DiB's office building landlord. When

Zaccaro's Mafia connections were made public, it hurt the Mondale ticket.

DiB was not present the last time I went to his office, in June 1986. I dropped off a TV as a gift. He never picked it up. He had "disappeared," according to the press, but we knew that meant he was gone. It was revealed a decade later, in *Underboss*, by Sammy "The Bull" Gravano and Peter Maas, that John Gotti ordered DiB's hit over some minor ego slight. I loved DiB. He was only forty-nine, fourth in the Gambino hierarchy. He had been convicted on federal pornography charges in Miami and was still awaiting a five-year prison sentence. So at least he beat that.

I was recently astonished, while watching a History Channel documentary, to learn that DiB was one of the five shooters of Gambino boss Paul Castellano at Sparks Steakhouse. I never knew he had it in him.

CHAPTER 12

A Blowjob from Linda

This week I am reviewing the very best porn film ever made, so superior to others that it defies comparison. . . . The film was supposed to be called *Sword Swallower*, but the distributors realized that it would be impossible to advertise that title in the sterile newspapers so they opted for the equally bewitching title of *Deep Throat*. It opens next week at the New World on Forty-nineth Street. At the time of this writing, the distributors were not sure whether their film would be booked for June fifth or twelveth, so call the theater. . . . The star of the film has fine legs, firm tits, a not unattractive face and the greatest mouth action in the annals of cocksucking. . . . The girl with the deep throat is almost a *Ripley's Believe-It-Or-Not* as she takes the whole joint down her gullet. No, it's not a small-potato penis but a roustabout rod of ten inches that plummets into the deepest recesses of our lady's oral cavity; down, down, and down it plunges until nothing remains. It seems a miracle. . . . I was never so moved by any theatrical performance since stuttering through my own bar mitzvah.

—*Screw* #171, May 1972

Both Mayor Lindsay and I were responsible for making *Deep Throat* the most profitable movie ever made. It cost about twenty-five grand and legend has it that it grossed $600 million to this day. And porn was a cash business then. Sammy Davis and Johnny Carson showed up with entourages in limousines; it became the first must-see porn film for millions who never before ventured to a porn theater. And New York became the only city in the United States where *Deep Throat* was considered obscene, in 1972.

Deep Throat debuted at an L.A. porn theater and closed in four days. The week before it played New York at the World Theater, where I made my usual rounds, I happened upon a screening. After my review, lines formed around the block. Mayor Lindsay confiscated the print which, without precedence, suddenly gave national headlines to a cheap porno film.

Linda Lovelace's first interview was with *Screw*. We met at a small, cold, seventeen-dollar hotel room, and it was the most difficult interview I ever conducted because Linda was utterly inarticulate. Chuck Traynor, her handler, did most of the talking. After the interview, I said, "Listen, I'd like you to suck my cock."

I figured Linda was a hooker anyway. She said fine and Chuck said okay. Here I was with the world's greatest cocksucker, and yet it was a lonely experience. I had never fucked a woman in the mouth like that. It seemed hostile. I felt alienated. We were both sweating. Though I've often felt I was hung like a rodent, I have a slightly above-average cock, seven inches, and the fact that it disappeared down her throat interfered with my concentration. I kept thinking, "Am I *that* small? Is she *that* good? Should I come now?"

She then sat on my face in a 69 position, and as I was eating her, I wasn't bringing her any pleasure. Her pussy was hairless, which I didn't care for, and I noticed ugly scar tissue running down her torso.

Suddenly I realized why she wasn't shown fully naked in *Deep Throat*—Damiano had to shoot around that scar tissue. She later said she considered me a pig, but it was easier to give a blowjob than an interview. It dawned on me that this was arranged as a nonmonetary gift from the distributors for my review. *Deep Throat* was financed by the Peraino crew, a division of the Colombo Family. Butch Peraino's Miami office became so crammed with cash-stuffed garbage bags, nobody could walk. With Linda, I felt like a hooker faking orgasm with a john, and left feeling sad.

My partner, Jim Buckley, photographed this summit meeting. Jim would never drop trou in public, and kept his repressed cock zipped up. We ran the photos of Linda sucking my cock in *Screw* with my commentary, which became my paradigm of personal journalism. But the photos in *Screw* didn't show my face, so my wife Gena wouldn't see what I was doing.

After the Lovelace story ran in *Screw*, I ran anything I could find on Linda. She became *Screw*'s Marilyn Monroe. If I were a faggot, she would have been my Judy Garland. But it soon became apparent that Linda had no talent whatsoever, and couldn't maintain a career in show business. Her attempt to exploit her momentary fame with a singing-dancing Vegas act bombed outright. She couldn't act, dance, sing, or be merry. There was only one thing she was great at. Linda Lovelace's one witty line: when asked if she would ever do an endorsement, she said she'd like to do one for a mouthwash.

The book, *Inside Linda Lovelace*, came out exactly a year after I met her in that hotel room. She had a literary cocktail party in New York to launch the book. I'd never seen the press more awestruck. They were fighting for autographed photos. Everything about Linda was news, and I had come across her earlier loop *Dog Fucker*. *Screw* ran a photo of Linda *in flagrante* with her co-star, adding yet another dimension to the Lovelace *oeuvre*.

During the party, Chuck Traynor called me over and said there were grand juries trying to nail her on the dog photos, that they had these big movie contracts brewing and I should lay off. He was furious. She publicly denied having done the loop, and I said, well, let's have the dog testify. Later, during a question-and-answer period, I waved the photos and said, "In these hands are photos of you, Linda, being fucked by a dog." She ordered, "Have Al Goldstein thrown out of this press conference." And three goons threw me out. I was now considered her enemy. Only in America could a cocksucker go so far.

Eight years later, in desperation, when Linda aligned herself with anti-porn feminists, she made fantastic claims of being held hostage by Chuck Traynor. She claimed to be the Patty Hearst of porn in a best-selling book, *Ordeal*, published by porn turncoat Lyle Stewart. This book was quite different from her previous two tell-alls, *Inside Linda Lovelace* and *The Intimate Diary of Linda Lovelace*. The dust jacket blurb claimed "she was beaten with savage regularity, hypnotized, and raped . . . forced into unspeakable perversions, sold to high bidders, passed from one celebrity to another." She claimed that the whole "deep-throat phenomenon" was one big scam—that she was drugged, beaten, forcibly pimped off to sleazy strangers and celebrities, and otherwise coerced into becoming a secretly unwilling yet virtuoso dick-eater by her ex-husband/pimp/Svengali, Chuck Traynor. Rather than admit that she and Traynor were involved in the classic pimp-prostitute relationship, where a weak woman seeks the strength of a surrogate father figure, Linda would have us think that she was pummeled into performing her legendary acts of fellatio. She became a symbol for antiporn feminists, appearing as their mascot against the porn industry. Gloria

Steinem took up her cause as an indictment against porn. She wrote the introduction to Linda's follow-up book, *Out of Bondage.*

The whole situation irked me because, though I obviously had a vested interest in the porn business, it was crucial to buck false perceptions held by society. As Traynor himself said, "There are millions of straight people out there who don't know anything about the world you and I live in, and they really believe that people are snatched off the street—like in the [George C. Scott] film *Hardcore*—and forced into pornography with guns held to their heads. Naturally, if you're going to write about that, people are going to buy it, because it's already *their* fantasy."

This perception denies the idea that women operate by their own free will. In every interview I did with porn actors who worked with Linda, I asked whether she seemed coerced. Typical was Eric Edwards, who said he was himself brought into the business by Lovelace, who solicited him to appear in his first loop. She hired him afterwards for more of her "one-day wonders," as porn movies were known. (In Eric Edwards's own bedroom, he collected mannequins from department stores, dressed them like a film crew and assembled them with lights and camera around his bed.)

Bankrupt and unemployed by 1976, Harry Reems was convicted in Memphis of "conspiring to transport obscene materials across state lines" by acting in *Deep Throat,* for which he was paid one hundred dollars. Warren Beatty and Jack Nicholson supported his defense, but Hollywood did nothing for him career-wise. He was tainted by smut. He was not a good actor. But Harry was as facile with offscreen social intercourse as onscreen sexual intercourse.

REEMS: As far as the aesthetics of the art of acting or film, I think anything important that had to be said about fuck films was said in the first film made, when a cock went into a cunt and you could see it. . . . Pornography is *not* my way of life nor my reason for existence. It's a thing I do for income.

AL: With Linda Lovelace, when did you realize you were being eaten by greatness?

REEMS: Instantly. We were doing a test for a feature. Damiano wanted us to do an anal scene and I asked her if she wanted any lubrication and she said, "No, just let me give you a little bit of head." She goes down and the next thing I know I'm being devoured by this set of jowls, my cock disappearing. Damiano has this look of disbelief. We're all going, "What's going on here with this amazing chick?" Two days later Damiano came up with the script for *Deep Throat*—and that first loop is *in Deep Throat*. Damiano took some loops we had done with Linda and blew them up from 16 to 35 mm and used them in the film.

—from *Screw*, May 1974

Traynor, who ran an all-nude biker bar in Florida during the hippie days, had the distinction of managing and marrying Marilyn Chambers after Linda, the next porn starlet to become a household name. He rebutted Linda's claims in a 1980 *Screw* interview. Linda, like so many other porn starlets, sprung from trailer trash to, in her case, national prominence—without a trace of talent to sustain her projectory. She bombed in her headline act at the Aladdin Hotel in Vegas and in Philadelphia. By the time she drifted into Traynor's low-life world, she'd had a kid who was taken away by the father (not Traynor). Traynor said she left him when the character that he "created" became famous, a commodity in which he had a custodial interest. Hers was a sad life.

AL: She claims she was your captive—your sexual slave—and that you turned her into a zombie. Did you make her do all the things she said in her book?

TRAYNOR: No, actually she was more of a pest. Basically, I was in the sex business a long time before she ever arrived. I owned a topless/bottomless bar in Miami. . . . There was a lot of partying, and she was screwing other guys, but not necessarily for money. In the circles I travel, it's not uncommon for ladies to be passed around. . . . In her book, she indicates that from the first time she got near me, I somehow captured her. Well, that's a bunch of shit. First of all, there were ten or twelve girls who were a lot better looking than she who I was fooling around with. She was sort of the outcast because she had that god-awful scar down the front of her. I think the first time she fucked for money was in exchange for carpeting in the upstairs part of the house.

AL: Did you love her?

TRAYNOR: There was definitely a period when I loved her. I mean, I married her.

AL: You say you loved her. When did you start beating her up, and how did that happen?

TRAYNOR: Well, that's kind of stretching it. As you know, I was raised in the country, and I don't consider slapping your old lady when she does something wrong as beating her up. To me, that's almost a sign of closeness, of feeling. Of course, she stretched that brutality unbelievably in the book. The marks on her legs, I think, were from her car accident. I didn't beat on her legs with chains or any of that bullshit.

AL: Did you ever knock out any of her teeth, blacken her eyes, disfigure her in any way?

TRAYNOR: No. I mean, as for her teeth, I had them all fixed. They were capped by a dentist because they were screwed up from her car accident. She wanted to have them capped when she started getting well known in the movies. So, I would be stupid to knock her teeth out. And, of course, I didn't because they're still in.

AL: At what point did you teach her to deep throat?

TRAYNOR: As far as teaching her to deep throat, that was just us partying around. I never did it with an ulterior motive of creating a sexual superstar. She never actually went out and turned any tricks. She was too stupid for that. In fact, I used her in an 8 mm loop doing the deep throat, and that's where Gerard Damiano saw her do it. . . . I've taught a lot of chicks to do it—before and since. She never really had any special ability. . . . As a manager, I felt that you've got to sort of lay out a plan and stick to it. And, since I was the brains and she was going to be "the Throat," I kind of had to direct her. . . .

In 1986, the Meese Commission consisted of an eleven-member panel of retired vice cops, right-wing academics, "porn victims," a smut-busting D.A. and the soon-to-be-exposed child-molesting priest, Father Bruce Ritter. Like HUAC in the 1950s, the "Attorney General's Report on Pornography" was a prefabricated, and quickly discredited, conclusion against "the graphic representation of people having sex." They were able to intimidate Southland Corporation into banning *Playboy* and *Penthouse* from thousands of 7-Eleven's. When Linda Lovelace testified against porn for the Meese Commission, I showed up waving copies of *Dog Fucker*, her 1969 loop. No doubt this endeared me even more to the angry, fat antiporn feminist, Andrea Dworkin and her radical-in-arms, Catherine MacKinnon, who stood behind Linda. Lovelace had understandably denied doing such a loop, but was caught with her pants down. Linda would eventually renounce the feminists, saying they "exploited" her just as much as the pornographers. She went back to posing naked for *Leg Show*, the year before she died from a car accident at age fifty-three in 2002. Traynor was sixty-four when he died of a heart attack the same year. The dog died earlier, but was denied entry to the Motion Picture Country Hospital when it reached old age.

CHAPTER 13

Wives and Other Strangers

Every woman I have ever dated, been married to, or hired to work for me has broken my heart and/or attempted to relieve me of my last red cent either legally or illegally. With the exception of my current wife—so far.

Attacking corporate America over the years had validity; but attacking those close to me is another story. As I walked the streets in my homeless year, unable to feed my gluttonous hunger for the material world, with nothing but time to reflect, I came to the realization I was wrong. And I will never be forgiven. Printing illustrations of the Pillsbury Doughgirl with a yeast infection is different from running obscene pictures of my ex-wife Gena along with her phone number in *Screw*, and accusing her of introducing AIDS to America after sleeping with a witch doctor in Haiti. Running a parody of the Pope is different than running baby pictures of my son Jordan for subscription ads (Wahhhh! I want my *Screw!*). I went too far. I've burned bridges. I have regrets.

LONNIE

My first wife, Lonnie, was a short, fat Jewish yenta at Pace University. She was a pig. She had big tits, which I've never liked. Her pussy tasted like vinegar. It was a marriage based on spite because her family hated me and forbid us from dating.

I was captain of the debating team at Pace University. Because I'd been in the army, at twenty-seven I was older and more worldly than most students. Lonnie was on the team. More importantly, Lonnie had a wonderful quality that was rare in women: she admired me.

Lonnie's mother, father, and two brothers despised me. They were a family of vile Jewish lawyers, and I was not a lawyer nor did I have a high-status professional career; they felt I was beneath them. Her father, Irving, and her brother worked at 16 Court Street. Little did they know how much I would be supporting lawyers in just a few years. They put a warrant out and tried to have me arrested, because she had just turned eighteen. We had to get married fast. Their attempts to destroy our relationship were an added incentive that made me persist. Finally, in January 1963, the day after Lonnie turned eighteen, we eloped. We got married by rabbi under a tent at Leonard's of Great Neck, the ultimate Jewish embarrassment.

We hated each other and our families never met, but we remained married for about two years. I knew it was over when she graduated from Pace. As a graduation gift, her parents gave her a trip to Europe—a trip for one—and Lonnie went. But the clincher came one evening when I returned home from work at Mutual of New York. Gay Talese has described what I saw in *Thy Neighbor's Wife*:

> He found his apartment ransacked, the furniture gone, and his clothing tossed around the room and cut into pieces. His expensive cigars had been broken in half, his stereo was missing, and the bathroom floor was covered with broken glass and smelled of his aftershave lotion. His wife was nowhere in sight, and she had left behind none of her own personal possessions.

MARY

The greatest woman of my life was Mary Phillips. She was a Pan Am stewardess with a PhD who was independent, self-confident and smart as a whip. When I met Mary she was twenty-seven years old, a beautiful blonde *shiksa*. Her father was a professor at the Citadel in Charleston, North Carolina, the country's top military school. She was not into money, she was a hippie. She once lived with a Negro, which was really pushing it back then.

Because of Mary's Pan Am travel schedule, it took weeks of calling her on the phone before we met in person and went on a date. Mary admired my persistence. Of course what she perceived as persistence was actually my howling desperation. Begging women, worrying into them like a dog—that was part of my M.O. My sex life got so bad, I kept a photo of my right hand in my wallet. Sex was good with Mary. Her pussy tasted fantastic.

Mary didn't want to get married, but she gave me the nuptial equivalent of a charity fuck—because I was so persistent. We tied the knot in Taxco, Mexico, on August 5, 1968; I was thirty-two and on my second marriage. When I started *Screw* the following November, we listed Mary as publisher—I didn't want Lonnie to get any money if *Screw* made it, and there was some question as to whether I was legally divorced yet.

My mother flew down to Mexico for the wedding with my old diet doctor, Dr. Harry Stone, the guy she was *shtupping*. My father was too timid to make the trip, and rarely traveled after WWII. Ever the Jew, I picked Taxco because we could fly down at a terrific discount. My mother took the opportunity to fight a bull while she was there. There was a deal where tourists could get in the ring with a small bull, probably the size of a Pekinese. So there was my mother on the occasion of my wedding in a toreador costume fighting

Chihuahua-sized bulls, with Dr. Stone in the bleachers cheering her on. Unlike bullfighting in Spain, Mexicans don't typically kill the bull; it's a contest of "bravery" between bull and toreador. But I knew Dr. Stone was there in case my mother got gored to death.

Mary's family didn't attend. Even before *Screw*, they weren't thrilled with their daughter marrying a Jew, and not just any old Jew, but Alvin Goldstein, to boot. I used to chase her with gefilte fish—no wonder she eventually ran away. We lived on Jane Street in the Village, and she was such a feminist, she would pay half the rent.

In 1970, Mary wrote an article about women's liberation for *Screw* #56 that directly led to her firing from Pan Am. Her termination was communicated in a registered letter she received while on vacation; there was no hearing and no chance for appeal. Today it would be grounds for a lawsuit; back then there was no recourse. Unless your husband happened to own a certain pornographic newspaper. And so, I relentlessly hounded Pan Am CEO Najeeb Halaby for seventeen years in the pages of *Screw*, in over two dozen "ShitLists" and "Screw You" columns. I compared the airline to the Luftwaffe, accused them of being Nazis, Commies, Jew-haters, reported their yearly losses, reveling particularly at their $61 million loss during one quarter of 1980, when they laid off 20 percent of their workers. And Halaby wasn't even there, he'd been forced out in 1972. His daughter married King Hussein, becoming Queen Noor of Jordan. It took twenty-one years before the Goldstein Curse finally shut down Pan Am in 1991.

So Mary was fired and suddenly I went from having a wife who was constantly flying around the world, to having a wife who was around all the time. We started to get on each other's nerves. Mary had written not only for *Screw*, but for Grove Press publisher Barney Rossett's *Evergreen Review*. I thought she was good and encouraged her to write more. But I missed not being able to fly discount. I would fly Hitler Airlines if it offered triple mileage.

We attended our first orgy together during a party at the house of Betty Dodson, the erotic artist and sexologist. Betty Dodson is the Mother of Masturbation, the groundbreaking pioneer of women's sexual liberation. A sex-positive feminist, she helped womankind break through the ancient shame of masturbation, teaching work-shops and writing books like *Viva la Vulva: Women's Sex Organs Revealed*. She came from Wichita, Kansas, where she began as a commercial artist for department store ads. Wichita was where I would endure my three-year federal obscenity trial. Betty moved to New York in the 1950s to attend art school.

Swinging may have existed in some shadow dimension before, but by 1969 wife-swapping was in the air. Mary, being an inquisitive soul, was up for it; and as publisher of *Screw*, it was my duty to push my own envelope. By the time Betty and I met she was divorced and deeply involved in sexual experimentation. She was going through a weird stage in which she was eating a lot of raw garlic and shaving her head. Totally off the wall.

When we entered Betty's big apartment on lower Madison Avenue, there were about twenty couples; most of them naked or getting naked on couches and mattresses. Some were licking balls or sucking cocks. Betty greeted us, presented drinks and some pot. I was already some-thing of a celebrity in 1969, making headlines for my *Screw* arrests. It felt like something new, like visiting a hotel in Casablanca.

Mary and I couldn't just tear off our clothes and dive in; there was some small talk, some joking around. But after thirty minutes or so Mary was down to her panties and I was out of my Jockeys; we were sitting on the floor leaning against the couch. Mary turned around and started kissing a guy who was reclining on the couch above her, a boyfriend of Betty's named Graham. As a once-repressed Brooklyn Jew, just slightly younger than the Greatest Generation, this was a startling situation. For sweet Mary from Charleston, North Carolina, it was also unprecedented.

Then she started sucking his cock. Graham's was the first cock she had that night and it was also the first cock other than my own I'd ever seen her suck. Amazingly, I didn't find it very threatening. In part that was because I knew Graham distantly and didn't find him intimidating. If he'd had John Holmes's dick, I might have *plotzed*.

Before we'd gotten to Betty's, I had been anxious about this inevitability. I still came from a mindset where men were allowed to stray, but one's wife was a no-go. Would I be possessive? Would I find it disturbing to see my beautiful blonde wife with another man's cock in her mouth and cunt? This was the first swing I'd ever been to. But as the evening progressed, I was fascinated by how *dis*interested I was. There was a certain disconnect . . . and yet it was mildly titillating watching my wife do to another what I'd only seen her do to me.

I recall Mary sucked his cock rather slowly and dreamily, occasionally stopping and masturbating him, then teasing him with her tongue. The most startling image I remember is the moment Graham came. He was lying on the couch as Mary sucked him; but she had shifted her position, and as Graham groaned and ejaculated into my wife's mouth, she was staring directly, unblinkingly . . . at me. When Graham finished, she swallowed, licked her lips, and smiled. Then she leaned over and kissed me on the cheek. I faintly smelled the scent of the sea on her breath. Did I hallucinate all this, or was my marriage turning into a cheap porn novel?

There was a certain loopy equity to the whole scene. It seemed fair. It was the heyday of women's lib, and though my wife sucked a guy's cock, and soon afterward fucked him, over the course of the evening the high priestess of masturbation, Betty Dodson herself, was blowing and fucking me. So it all seemed wonderfully fair. The whole point about swinging is no one is really cheating. There's no power imbalance. Somebody is always getting something.

Later on when I went to Plato's Retreat, things were different. I sometimes got pussy because I was Al Goldstein, publisher of *Screw*. I was good friends with Larry Levenson, exempt from the rule that you had to be in the club as a couple. Thus at Plato's I felt I was getting away with something. At Betty's that night it was all so understated and mellow, there was no sense of power play or getting away with anything. And no sense of cheating.

That orgy was the only time Mary and I swung together. Been there, done that. I came in with "coin of the realm"—a beautiful woman. I had something to offer and so did everyone else there. But Mary was a lot prettier than Betty Dodson, this being Betty's shaved-head-and-garlic-eating period. So maybe I gave more coin than I got.

Mary and I broke up the next year, in 1970. I fucked it up by cheating. She came home early and found me with another girl. And it wasn't Betty Dodson. She left me and I felt horrible. I loved her. She found me intolerable, impossible, a control freak. With my new arrogance in publishing *Screw*, getting all this action, the bottom line was I really became a piece of shit. When we got divorced two-and-a-half years later, she insisted on paying me all the money she owed me.

We stayed friends over the years, doing better than we had as a married couple. Yet to this day I regret I didn't work harder at the relationship during our marriage. Mary Phillips was clearly deserving of far more careful consideration than I gave her.

Mary never wanted a kid. She found a boyfriend named Irwin, who was stoned all the time, lived in a dream world, always said he was about to have a show on Broadway. A delusional, disturbed human being, but that turned Mary on. That's probably what attracted her to me in the first place. I liked Irwin anyway, and invited both to my home upstate. Here's a guy who couldn't get a job, and his wife's ex-husband is the publisher of *Screw*. Most likely it made him feel inadequate. I suspect he may have been the one to call the FBI and tell them I had illegal guns in my house.

Mary was the best wife I had. I love her because she had the intelligence to walk out on me. She was the one class act in my life. I miss her terribly.

GENA

I met my third wife, Gena Fishbein, mother of my son, on a blind date. A hairstylist I knew said he had a schoolteacher client who lived on Fifty-second Street in Manhattan. Gena was in group therapy. After we'd gone out on several dates she would complain to her group that all I ever wanted to do was go down on her. Everyone in the group told her life could be worse.

I showed off my new Corvette on our first date, driving around her block unable to find a parking spot while phoning her on my newest gadget—a high-tech mobile phone, which was new and unheard of at the time. I ate Gena's pussy on our first date, which had a school-marmish, academic kick to it, at least in my imagination. She was smart and quite attractive, a daily *New York Times* reader like me. I was confident, aggressive, and once again, persistent.

Gena grew up in Miami and now had her own apartment in Manhattan. Her father died two weeks before I met her. Her mother asked me if the company publishing *Screw* was called Milky Way Productions, which it was. It turned out Gena's father had been a subscriber to *Screw*. I regret that I never knew Joe Fishbein. We missed meeting each other by just a few weeks. Gena felt he would have liked me. He was loud, bombastic, opinionated; constantly correcting her, telling her what she was doing wrong. He was a big man who smoked cigars. More significantly, he was a leftist, a commie. With the anarchic political criticism I put into every issue of *Screw*, I was an extension of what he had been.

Considering the madness of my career, I liked going out with a nice, pleasant grade-school teacher. However, wouldn't you question the better judgment of a woman who would marry Al Goldstein? Maybe I should have. We got married in 1973, two years after my divorce from Mary, at a singles club called Barney Google's. By the second year of marriage all women slip into their true behavior pattern—which in Gena's case was passive aggression. Our relationship became purely annoying. On the surface, Gena was a charming hostess at our east-side townhouse during celebrity-filled cocktail parties—which could have nearly passed for soirées hosted by the French embassy. She acknowledged me with pride anytime guests praised her husband as a heroic free-speech apostle. But she herself never said anything positive about me.

Jordan was born in 1974, the same month I was featured as the *Playboy* interview. All in all, a banner year. I was thiry-eight. I'd take my toddler to playgrounds and there would always be good-looking mothers to hit on. I'd buy high-tech presents for myself making believe they were for Jordan. He was smart, he read a lot. Jordan was a total pleasure.

Gena was rightfully terrified I might come home and give her V.D. She said it would take her a long time to get over hating me if I gave her anything. This was a constant area of tension. When she found out about the Linda Lovelace photographs in *Screw*, she displayed a Jewish-princess cuntiness that she learned from her mother. She sulked, went into another room and slammed the door. I told Gena she gave a much better blowjob than Linda Lovelace, but that only made it worse. Why couldn't we be more like the Buckleys—Jim kept *his* pants zipped! God knows what her mother thought. Before we got married, my analyst wanted to meet with her to explain why I wasn't the best candidate for marriage. A prenup deal was made that I wouldn't write in *Screw* about my sex life with Gena. That would rightfully remain private. She wanted me to wear our wedding ring, to announce to the world that I belonged to her. I wouldn't, on principle. "But honey," I pleaded, "I'm spearheading the sexual revolution."

Life with the Goldsteins. If there was something even potentially damning in *Screw*, I wouldn't even take that week's paper home. But then she'd say, "What are you hiding *this* week?" Our relationship was a classic double standard. Considering the life I led, I was amazed to find how some of the old values stuck with me. And those values embraced cheating—for the man. The stress was an enormous weight to saddle upon a conventional marriage, to test the limits of her original vow, *Do you take this man?* When she married me, she assumed she could change me, as all women do. But I was the fucking publisher of *Screw*, for Christ's sake! Was I not entitled, even *required*, to be the George Plimpton of sex; to try everything sexually, to sample the goods of my profession, to write off hookers as tax expenses?

Gena simply insisted that none of my extramarital sex interfere with *her* time. As soon as it got dark, I became married again. But she was afraid I'd get into a meaningful relationship and leave her. She asked how would I like it if she did the same? I said if *she* cheated, the marriage would be over. She got upset, said that was unfair. I admitted it was not only unfair, but medieval—but that was my chauvinistic position at the time. I figured she'd eventually get so pissed, she'd start to fuck around anyway. Probably not for another few years, and maybe then I'd care less. The first scratch on your new car hurts. It doesn't matter after that. After there were a few more dents in Gena, maybe I'd be willing to lend her out. For now, I loved her and was too insecure.

Then Gena began turning into her mother. She was getting a fat ass, her legs were thickening and I found her less attractive. Boredom set in. Familiarity bred contempt. The worst sex in the world is married sex, because it gets boring quickly and has no spark or passion. Serendipitous, unscheduled sex is the best sex.

As *Screw* peaked throughout the seventies and eighties, I had money in the bank, a townhouse, a chauffeur . . . and yet sat isolated in the back of my limousine thinking, *If I'm so rich and famous, why am I so unhappy?*

We had so many fights, they could have been assigned numbers. Fight number 27 was about the blowjob I got in *Screw*'s film, *It Happened in Hollywood.* Fight number 61 was about the orgy I attended on a yacht on the East River; fight number 73 was the time I was manacled upside down by dominatrix Monique Van Cleef in the Hague. "But honey, I didn't even get a hard-on," I insisted.

However, it wasn't as one-sided as it seemed. She also extracted a price, beyond the credit cards and millions I made. Some psychiatrists theorized that in a sadomasochistic relationship, the masochist really has more power than the sadist. Because I was dependent on her accepting my strictures—she was actually in control.

In reaction to my endless succession of sex partners, Gena finally took one herself to checkmate me. But I liked the guy. His name was Chuck and she was with him for about four years, starting around the time our fourteen-year marriage was ending. The thing that delighted me was, Gena tortured him the same way she tortured me. She became nasty, caustic, and sarcastic.

Jordan lived with Chuck and Gena after our separation, and Chuck was very good with Jordan. He was an attractive hippie-type; an astrologer. As a straight schoolteacher, I figured Gena would come to her senses and hook up with a boring doctor or accountant. But there she was with her astrologer. From pornographer to astrologer. And she now believed in astrology.

Jordan was eleven when we divorced. Gena was represented by the legendary, ruthless super-lawyer and closet homo, Roy Cohn—the only other figure in history, along with Mafia don John Gotti, that I was actually too frightened of to attack in *Screw*. She chose Cohn to cut my balls off. I prefer not to tangle with tough fags, and he was the toughest. In the settlement, Gena got our house on Fire Island and I kept the townhouse in Manhattan. She got a three-bedroom apartment on Fifty-sixth Street; I kept the chauffeur. She got $275,000 cash. I had money in Switzerland at the time, so I had cash to give her. All things considered over time, she got nearly $4 million. The first $2.5 million bought me joint custody of Jordan. I knew no judge would give me joint custody, so I would have seen him only two weeks a year. It was extortion, but I did it willingly. What more commitment can you make as a father? We lived five blocks apart and Jordan stayed with his mother half the time. When Jordan was eighteen and his trust fund matured, Gena demanded I give him even more.

Most people graduate college and law school owing hundreds of thousands of dollars. Jordan had three hundred thousand dollars in the bank. I spent seven hundred thousand dollars on Georgetown and Harvard, not including his tutoring at Horace Mann School in the Bronx. I went to Georgetown, where Jordan actually finished first in his class of 741, and met the president, Father Donovan. We shared Cuban cigars.

At Harvard, I was the picture of propriety, posing in photos with college officials and Jordan. I always acted appropriate for the moment. I'm not Larry Flynt. My will stated Jordan could never enter my business, my world.

I took Jordan with me when I debated Jerry Falwell at Dartmouth, and took him with me on the *Tom Snyder Show*. I took him to Japan and Bangkok. I paid *Incredible Hulk* star Lou Ferrigno $750 an hour to work out with Jordan when he was a kid. He worked for me summers and I put him down as creator of the *Gadget* newsletter. I got him a job on Court TV through Lyle Stuart. I gave him a million dollars' worth of gold watches to hold for me, as *Screw* started to sink.

But the moment he graduated Harvard Law School, I was not invited to the ceremony. As an alumnus of lowly Pace U, I lived for the day my son went to Harvard. He was suddenly embarrassed to have a pornographer for a father—even though a million tricks turned by hookers in the back pages of *Screw* are what financed his Ivy League education. Here I was, a renegade degenerate, yet I secretly harbored the same wishes as any middle-class American parent. I *kvelled* at his success. If I had been a surgeon, an entrepreneur, if I had been a CEO that bankrupted Enron, he would have been proud back. But his father was a pornographer.

The last time my son Jordan ever phoned me, he announced that not only was I not invited to the Harvard graduation, but he couldn't wait for the day to read my obituary in the *New York Times*. I remain devastated to this day by that remark. He and Gena held a $2 million life insurance policy on me, and Jordan wouldn't return my watches, even when I was homeless. I blamed Gena for turning him against me.

As *Screw* degenerated into a morass of personal hatreds and lawsuits, Gena had me arrested on aggravated harassment charges in

2002. It was not a banner year. I'd just gotten released from a near-death experience at Rikers Island for "harassing" my former secretary, Jennifer Lozinski.

Insanity became the only rational response to my life. What did I do to deserve the wrath of my ex-wife?

I merely printed a mockup of Gena fellating our "dead, gay son Jordan." I wrote that Jordan had died a bizarre death in the company of transsexual hookers. I published composites of my enemies, with Gena fucking District Attorneys Charlie Hynes of Brooklyn and Robert Morgenthau of Manhattan. I published a picture of Morgenthau, in his eighties, with come dribbling out of his mouth. I ran the full-page spread, HOW AMERICA GOT AIDS, depicting Gena blowing a black witch doctor, accusing her of introducing the disease to America after a Club Med trip to Haiti. A fake photo of her rolling around naked with a hog, calling her "a dirty pig-fucker," whose "cunt ain't kosher."

Finally, I ran a full-page photo of Gena in *Screw*, headlined A WORLD-CLASS CUNT. It was requested that readers phone her at the Allen Stevenson School and "ask her to stop being a cunt." A hundred called and the Manhattan DA's office issued an order of protection. I was arrested for aggravated harassment.

Represented by my superb new attorney, Charles DeStefano, I pled guilty. I apologized in court to Judge Renee White, who I slandered in print for having "rabies coursing through her corrupt, decrepit body." She loathed me, but remained unbowingly professional and level-headed in the face of my insanity. Judge White sentenced me in the Gena case to three years probation while I lay in diabetic shock during a nine-hour coma. I was ordered to attend fifty hours of anger management classes. I couldn't travel to my homes in Florida or

Holland; I was walled in as a resident of Manhattan, even though by that time I was sleeping on the floor of *Screw*'s office. Yet I still had porno fans coming up to me saying, "God, I wish I had your life."

Dr. Lou Arrone, my obesity surgeon, helped nurse me back to health, while my psychiatrist of twenty years, Dr. Theodore Rubin, agreed I might be better off committing suicide. It was probably the first time an esteemed member of the medical profession ever gave such a prognosis, considering I wasn't even terminally ill. Being Jewish, I decided to gas myself in an oven. I was even too depressed to go out the way I'd prophesied: death by pastrami.

PATTI

After several divorces, I often wore a tee shirt that said Death Before Marriage. It became my mantra. It even appeared each week in a diagonal stripe across the top of *Screw*'s cover. Yet, as soon as some pussy came a-knockin,' I crumbled once again. Men will do anything.

On my cable show, *Midnight Blue*, I'd complained about losing weight at great personal expense and effort, yet received no compliments. I should have been like a bakery; women should be taking numbers. I appealed for women to contact me for sex. Patti saw the show and wrote a letter offering herself.

She came to my townhouse on Sixty-first Street. She was elegant, blonde, slender, and very Irish. She cleaned apartments for a living. Henceforth, she became known in my personal mythology as "Patti, the Irish Cleaning Lady."

Her father had managed a New York hotel. I never knew anyone who grew up in a hotel, like the children's cartoon, Eloise of the Plaza. Except instead of growing up to be a guest of hotels, she grew up to be the maid.

I liked Patti's manner of quiet obedience. I kept thinking of *Pygmalion*; I'd be her Jewish Henry Higgins; she'd rise from an urchin-like washerwoman existence to become the erudite, cultured wife of an Upper East Side pornographer. While we were dating, the sex was outstanding. She would blow me at the drop of a hat—at the airport Ambassador Club, for example, reducing my travel stress. A nip at her pussy was like a nip of Jameson's whiskey.

Both my parents died in 1989, but they met her first. Quietness was a characteristic my mother appreciated in other women, and she liked Patti a lot. So I married Patti as a memorial to my mother. But Patti kept working even after she married a rich Upper East Side pornographer. My limo took her to cleaning jobs, though the limo cost $40 an hour while she was making $8.

Once we married, my Eliza Doolittle didn't spend any time with me. It had all been a setup, I was a mark. She married into money. When we lived together in Florida, I eventually realized she had a girlfriend . . . a woman who came to our house constantly, and ultimately moved in. Patti spent every evening with Darlene, who would scamper up to her bedroom every night to slurp her clam. I married a bull dyke. And Darlene became pregnant by a guy who owned a chain of department stores. It was all a plot to milk him for paternity-suit money.

I was in terrible shape during my Patti period: I ballooned back up to 350 pounds; I was depressed, deeply unhappy. Both my parents had died within six months of each other. I stayed married to Patti for two mind-numbing, self-loathing years. So I never really knew her. She remained a cipher.

Even though we had a prenuptial agreement, when we finally split up in 1992 she was awarded $1 million in our divorce settlement, so she could continue living in the manner to which she had become accustomed. She now stays in hotels.

LINNEA

I wrote a *Hustler* piece about my relationship with scream queen Linnea Quigley. I had a box of love letters and treasured pictures of me eating her pussy that she shot. Bruce David, the most loathed scumbag in men's magazines, won't give it back. I probably took him and his wife out to dinner thirty times when he worked at *Screw*.

Linnea made over fifty low-budget movies, the best being *Return of the Living Dead*, but none of them porn. She was the finest sex partner and cocksucker I ever had. Best-tasting pussy I ever ate. I loved eating her ass. That delicate little body, delicate tits. She had great orgasms.

I was with Ron Jeremy at the Friars Club in L.A., who brought over "Hollywood Madam" Heidi Fleiss and Linnea. Heidi didn't like me, she was too professional. But Linnea did. She seemed wounded, but so beautiful. She was born in the Midwest, a nut case. We went to my apartment and she blew me on the couch. She said two hundred dollars would help her, so I happily gave it to her. Then we got in the habit where I always gave her two hundred dollars. Once we were engaged, being a Jew, I made a deal. I said, "Look, we're going to get married, you're my fiancée. I'd like a special price. After the first two hundred dollars, my second ejaculation's only one hundred dollars." She accepted. It was our wedding vow.

I understood that no matter how many times I made her come or how good the sex was mutually, she expected money. It's always money for girls, for whom *money is love*. That's the deal. I'd insist she come four or five times. She'd say it hurts, her pussy was sensitive. "Shut the fuck up," I told her, "and be eaten." Eat them first, then by the time they suck your dick, they're so happy. They owe you.

I miss Linnea deeply. But she dumped me soon as the money ran out.

VENICE

I used to see a working girl named Venice. I got a blowjob from her every year on my birthday. She worked for Heidi Fleiss, drop-dead beautiful, twenty-eight years old. She was a fifteen-hundred-dollar call girl, but because I'm a Jew, I got the Jew rate, two hundred dollars. I'd been eating and fucking her since she was eighteen. She was Ron Jeremy's best girlfriend. She and Ronnie picked me up at the homeless shelter and, would you believe it, she gave me a thousand bucks. Can you imagine a hooker giving a john money back?

One time, Venice was blowing me in my New York townhouse. She said, "Load up your shotgun." I always kept a 12-gauge, I was afraid of being assassinated. She wanted it against her head with my hand on the trigger. So I put it against her head and cocked it. She wanted to see if I'd lose all control and blow her head off when I came. I knew the cops wouldn't believe it. I'd be like Phil Spector, charged with murder. But this got her so excited—don't forget that as a hooker, she was bored by everything. All I kept thinking while she's sucking my dick is, *Don't squeeze the trigger, don't squeeze the trigger.*

Hookers are actresses, I can't give them an orgasm, sex doesn't mean anything. You're just renting them like a car, they have so much sex they're blinded by it.

Women constantly told me, "My girlfriend eats me better than you do." Venice loved when girls ate her pussy, so I set her up with Sara Gardner, who published some catalog on Kosher products. I'm not sure if it was Glatt Kosher or Parve. But Venice felt so good being eaten by another girl, she was then able to enjoy it when I stuck my dick in her mouth. Ronnie stood by asking, "Did she swallow?"

Venice is a class act. I will never forget her kindness when I was in need.

MYSTERY WIFE

My fifth marriage, to my mystery wife, is perhaps the strangest and most potentially tragic of all. She doesn't want her name used.

Everyone told her not to date me, I'm a *player*. That turned her on. Everything that makes me Al Goldstein, being a rebel, my tenacity, not taking shit—that's what she likes. So she married a *player* at the end of his game who suddenly became homeless. And she stuck right by me—from a distance. She's the first wife I ever wore a wedding ring for. Her faith in me is misplaced. She's very sick with Crohn's and had to move back with her parents, rather than join me at Bellevue homeless shelter.

Her family's conservative, she has three sisters, her mother's a nurse and her father was once a Hindu priest. Can you imagine, an old Jew winds up with the daughter of a Hindu priest? I lived with them for two months when I first became homeless. I'm festering among all these girls, cluttering the house with my thrift shop purchases. But all I had was support from these beautiful people.

I love her tasty little pussy. I gave her her first orgasm. She's cute, pretty, and crazy. We're trying to be loyal to each other. My testosterone level is low, and I've already done every sex scene in the world. But she woke me up at 2:20 in the morning and said, "Eat me," and I was the happiest fucking guy in the world. She loves knowing I've been with all these women and now I'm with her. *Al Goldstein is eating me!* It turns her on.

Like many young women today, thanks to President Clinton, she doesn't consider fellatio to be sex. Which for me is the best sex. According to a panel of sex experts on Katie Couric's NBC show, 55 percent of girls fifteen to eighteen will not have intercourse, but they'll suck a guy's dick. In their mind, it's not sex, because they haven't been penetrated. Who would have ever imagined this sea change? My young wife has blown guys and never considered it sex. I found that so horny, thinking of all these young girls with cocks in their mouths, not having sex, I ran to the bathroom and whacked off.

We were married with the blessing of the state—although that state was Nevada. It was in Las Vegas with Ron Jeremy as best man. She was twenty-seven, I was sixty-seven. We don't have a prenup. I said, "Honey, you can have everything. I'm washed up, finished, old dirty socks." She kept telling me, "You're Al Goldstein, you're Al Goldstein, you're Al Goldstein." But I looked good, I'd had some stapling done, a gastro pouch. Dr. Arrone did it free. I'd known him fifteen years and when I was fat I took him to Le Cirque, my favorite restaurant.

I love her youth. I have to tell her who the Beatles are. She doesn't know James Joyce, Alfred Kinsey, she never heard of Jimmy Hoffa. But do I really need a young girl who's up-to-date on Jimmy Hoffa?

I was arrested for shoplifting when I was homeless. I had two big bags with me. Homeless people keep everything with them, if you leave it at the shelter, it'll get stolen. I also wasn't on my medicine, so I kept fainting. I went to Starbucks on Sixty-seventh Street to have my fifty-four cent refill and read the *Times*. I was supposed to meet a guy at 5:00 who was taking me to a Tony Bennett concert at Lincoln Center. At 4:30 I left for Barnes & Noble next door to buy two books on Crohn's and colitis, to study up. She's in and out of the hospital for blood transfusions. I asked the salespeople where the books were—if I was going to steal them I would have stayed low profile. I was getting dizzy, so I put my two bags down before paying. I put the two books in the bag to look for the cash register. Then security swooped down. I had three hundred dollars cash on me, which my lawyer, Charles DeStefano gave me. I was going to pay for them. But the bottom line was, I never left the store's premises. Why would I steal books on Crohn's and colitis, you can't even jerk off to it. They made me spend another night at Rikers, and I missed the Tony Bennett concert. The case was dismissed in court.

RONNIE

Ron "Hedgehog" Jeremy, one of my closest, hairiest girlfriends, did a movie with me called *Al Goldstein and Ron Jeremy Get Screwed*. My fifteen-room house in Pompano Beach, Florida, was featured in it. Ronnie paid me five hundred dollars to eat the pussies of two twenty-year-old girls; he offered another thousand if I'd come on camera. I was sixty-seven, this required 400 milligrams of Viagra. Being a Jew, I took the Viagra and popped a load. I was nominated for best supporting porno actor. I couldn't leave New York by court order, so if I won at the Adult Film Awards in L.A., I had the Association for Retired People ready to accept it.

Ronnie has done some two thousand porn films, more than anyone, and we shared many evenings sexing up starlets, mano-a-manatee. He would bring the porn bimbo of the day over to my L.A. apartment. His urgent question was always, "Did she swallow, did she swallow?" Ron is a voyeur. He'd stay in the living room and peek.

I was watching the Animal Channel and told Ron he's not a hedgehog, he's a hippo. Hippos eat a hundred pounds of food a day. So did Ron. There was never a reason to take him to a good restaurant because he has no discernment, never tastes anything—he just engulfs like a shark in a frenzy. I took him to Chinese buffets where he could refill his plate five times. He was always late and I'd yell, "You're not Marilyn Monroe. I'm not one of your flunkies, call me so I don't have to wait, my time's valuable. I don't even drink."

We set up a rule. If he arrived more than thirty minutes late, he had to pick up the tab. He was late to Spago one time and had to buy me dinner for $180. Since then, he hasn't been late in twenty years.

GLORIA AND JANE

After seeing *Klute*, I wanted Jane Fonda with a hunger. If she were spread-eagled before me, not even a pastrami sandwich between us would have stopped me. I desperately wanted to stick that bitch. I would have given up *Screw*, joined NOW, sought to protect all the sardines of the world, any cause she wanted. Her body, her intelligence, her intensity was superb. I cared about her in a deep way.

I won the right to take Gloria Steinem out to dinner once at an auction. She reneged.

The Problem of Women

There are a lot of women who just want to be my friends. Most of them are young and pretty and eminently fuckable, but they just want to be friends, nothing more. There seems to be a vast fund of these women, since I keep running across them in day-to-day life.

It is a new platonic plague. Now, some of you *Screw* readers out there will only wish you had a problem like this. You'd appreciate it if a woman would deign to spit on you, much less talk to you, much less offer to be your friend. And if you behave yourself with your keepers and don't rattle the door to your cage too much, maybe someday you, too, will meet up with this new breed of friendly, feckless, but fuckless female.

But whereas you might take whatever you can get from women, I don't have to put up with it. I am here to announce that I am tired of these naïve women. They strike me as fundamentally misinformed about life's basic realities. It's as if when you talk to them long enough, you'd discover they hold other quaint beliefs, too—like the earth is flat.

Can men and women be friends? Well, yes. A whole movie was constructed around this premise, *When Harry Met Sally*. But even in that film, the two leads had to try out their sexual apparatus with each other before they could punch through and be friends.

It's not an easy question, which is the way these women want to treat it. Oh, I don't want to fuck you Al, I just want to be friends. As if they were announcing they'd like to go shopping with me at a Bloomingdale's white sale.

But it ain't that easy, darling. Why would I want to be your friend? Most of these women bring nothing at all to the table. They have no life experiences worth talking about. They haven't traveled. They've written no books. They couldn't tell a joke if it was written on a cue card. They have no talents, no prospects, no history. On the radar screen of life, they don't even qualify as a blip.

But they want to be my friends.

They just want to be near me, hang out with me. They want to bask in the reflected glory of what someone called "the greatness of my grossness." I am the sun, and they want to orbit me.

No thanks. I have a much more rigorous test for friendship than these women imagine. I require people to be lively, witty, well-connected. I number among my friends and acquaintances some of the leading lights of Hollywood, New York, and the world.

What do these women think? All it takes to qualify for friendship with me is that a person be breathing? Sorry to burst your bubbles, but the world doesn't work that way.

I find myself having to break it to these women that the only reason people want them around is as sperm rags, as receptacles for genetic material, as warm holes, all of which are perfectly respectable things to be. We all serve our function in life, and a fuck object is like any other. These women should wear their sluttishness with pride. Instead, they all want to be something else.

Part of this is because society is so fucked up about sex. It denigrates fucking to the point where it no longer becomes an honorable purpose in life. So these women, who really have no other purpose, desperately seek to hide behind some kind of charade. *I just want to be your friend* . . . .

Tough! I want to scream at them. Who cares? Flop and drop! On your back or on your knees! This is your role in life, and you better get used to it!

These women whine about their college professors. "They just want to fuck me," one after another will say.

Again, I want to scream, what else do you expect your professors to want? To discuss ideas with you? Sorry to break it to you, but your intellectual conversation falls a little short.

Again, there shouldn't be any blame in this. College-age females are not supposed to be brilliant conversationalists. They are not supposed to have had scintillating life experiences. Sadly, though, this society has seen fit to strip them of pride in the one thing they do have—tight, taut, fuckable bodies.

Women who "just want to be friends" are living in some media-inspired Neverland. They are in heavy denial about that magic patch between their legs. And they are losing out on the best thing in their lives, during the best years of their lives. It's almost enough to make you want to toss them a long, arduous, all-night pity-fuck. Almost.

—*Screw* editorial, June 1994

TINY TIM

AL: Have you ever masturbated?

MR. TIM: Unfortunately, yes.

AL: Was it something that filled you with pleasure or shame?

MR. TIM: Shame entirely, because I believe it's an act that's reserved only for marriage; I've asked the Lord for strength never to do it again, and I vowed that if I did do it again I would never, never stop trying to stop until I quit. I think that the organ down there was meant only to have Blessed Events, for the joy of God's grace, and I believe it's a very delicate instrument and only in the use of its proper place can it really function right.

AL: Before you go on, there's one question that I've been thinking about for this whole interview. How big is your cock?

MR. TIM: Oh! Well, I must say . . . smaller than an acorn. But look how small King David was, and look what he did to Goliath. It's not really the size of anything; it's always the quality that counts.

—*Screw*, October 1981

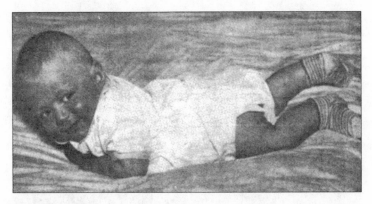

Mamas Don't Let Your Babies Grow Up to be Pornographers: Baby Alvin, 1936

Brooklyn-Jewish Gothic: I would later wear this bar mitzvah suit for my first hooker.

THE AL GOLDSTEIN ALBUM

Took 'Shots' of Raul Castro

Flushing Photographer Freed from Cuba Jail

MORE EVIDENCE THAT AL WAS A SOME-
BODY BEFORE HE BECAME A PORNOG-
RAPHER IN 1968:
(Above) Al snapped these shots of First Lady
Jackie Kennedy with her children John and
Caroline. (Top Right) Two-time Pulitzer Prize
winning Poet Carl Sandburg. (Center Right)
President Truman and his daughter Margaret
in 1957. (Center) Newspaper clipping of Al's
release after being arrested in Cuba on
charges of spying. (Bottom right) Mob-buster
and Presidential hopeful Robert Kennedy.

Photos by Goldstein

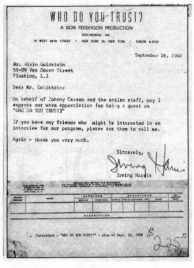

(Who Do You Trust?)

Adam-and-Eveing It: Driving the *Daily Mirror* radio car for Walter Winchell, I ran into Marilyn one night, Jayne Mansfield the next.

On the scent of Fair Jacqueline in Pakistan, 1962

Pride of the Yankers: Serving my country in a Mexican bordello

"Weird Beard": The beatnik of Pace University

Mary Phillips: My second wife—the greatest
woman I ever knew.

Bush People: Goldstein & Buckley, in days before landing strips

Christ, You Know It Ain't Easy: John & Yoko's *Screw* interview, '69

Shayna Tokhis: Serena at *Screw*, 1978

Screw's first NYPD bust came hours after running Mayor Lindsay's cock in 1969

Buckley & Goldstein were jailed for running this photo (sans bar), considered criminally obscene in 1969

Beginning of an Error: Screw staff, '69

Winner Take Al: Seka owed me five of these after losing a bet

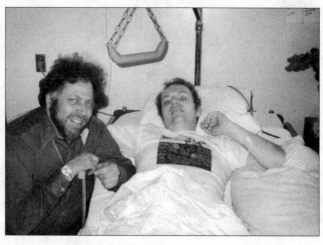

Moral support for Larry Flynt after he was shot

My "real" life with Gina and Jordan

Masturbatin' Rhythm: Disco nights with Gloria Leonard

Jordan performed magic tricks for Hef and bunnies

I bought a few chatchkas in my time

Casa de Al: Boatloads of tourists gave
the finger back

Beach Blanket Hippos: Frolicking with
Ron Jeremy

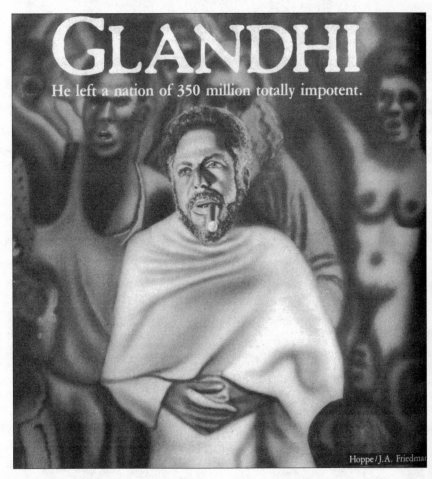

Screw movie ads ran each week

Illustration by Drew Friedman

Illustration by John Mariano

Illustration by "Uncle Tom" Hachtman

Illustration by "Diddler on the Roof"
Curt Hoppe

Illustration by Julius Zimmermann

Illustration by Joe Coleman

Illustration by Michael McMahon

Illustration by Yossarian

Illustration by Rene Moncada

Illustration by Curt Hoppe

Japanese *Screw*

CHAPTER 14

Holmes

John Holmes, aka Johnny Wadd, the star of a thousand 8 mm loops and feature porn films, was equipped with what even satchel-cunted women called "fourteen inches of dangling death," and used it to schtup more female orifices than any man alive. I suffered from penis envy. I felt that if I, Al Goldstein, had a fourteen-inch dick, I would caress it, I would walk it, I would study it. I would tie myself to a base with a spotlight and present it like a museum piece. I would probably turn myself over to the Museum of Modern Art and be a display.

AL: You are the ultimate sex symbol to so many people.

HOLMES: Isn't that disgusting?

AL: Yeah, but your name sells movies. Who turns you on? Where does your fantasy begin and end?

HOLMES: A one-on-one. Quiet atmosphere. I'm a romanticist.

AL: Who are some of the people who appeal to you?

HOLMES: Actress types. I would fuck Elizabeth Taylor, just to say I've done it. Desire-wise, I don't know. Who's the girl who played in *Butch Cassidy and the Sundance Kid*?

AL: Katherine Ross.

HOLMES: Her I would fuck.

AL: Free, too?

HOLMES: Several times.

AL: Who would you pay to fuck?

HOLMES: Nobody.

AL: Do you jerk off a lot?

HOLMES: No more than anybody else does.

AL: In your case, if you jerk off, it's almost like you say, "Jesus, if I didn't jerk off now I could have made fifty bucks." Do you look at it like you're a wasted natural resource? You're like Yellowstone National Park.

HOLMES: I can get it in my book and I can call a freebie, or I can call a trick. But then I'm accommodating them. There's a hassle about cleaning up, and the drive, or having them come

over, have to be a host. I mean, you beat off, you don't even
have to brush your own teeth.

AL: Have you ever met Linda Lovelace?

HOLMES: No.

AL: Do you think she could handle you?

HOLMES: I don't know. She said she can.

AL: I don't think she can.

HOLMES: I've never been deep throated.

AL: Neither has a crane.
                          —"King of the Cocks," *Screw*, June 1975

To see Holmes loops and films was to see hundreds of beautiful
women driven to sloe-eyed ecstasy with his cock buried in them. His
fourteen inches of dangling death was an instrument of shuddering
awe to porn starlets, who succumbed weakly under its powers. And
so went my obsessive fantasy that a fourteen-inch cock could con-
quer any and all women, and if only I had such a weapon.

But Holmes, in his first interview with *Screw*, concocted a fairy
tale that we all fell for, hook, line, and sinker. I was like a boy in the
locker room with Jackie Robinson again, regaled by his exploits.
With casual matter-of-factness, Holmes related a storybook childhood being reared by a "wealthy aunt" who took him to live in Paris
and London. As the Berlin Wall was being erected, he fucked

Brunnhilde wives of potato farmers. He had a Swiss nursemaid who gave him head when he was six-years-old, and taught him to suck her pussy. His aunt had a cook, butler, and maid. He fucked every girl in his high school class but three, and fucked the entire senior class ahead of him. He claimed he had rich, married housewives and spinsters who still flew him to Europe for gigolo gigs. When he was eight, he fucked a girl who was seven. He said he had twenty-seven fan clubs around the world that vie for locks of his pubic hair, and that he would clip hair off the neighbor's poodle to send. He said there was a John Holmes Film Festival in Paris, where his wealthy aunt still lived. She attended all twelve films shown, then took him aside and told him, "You bastard! You never told me you were built like that!"

Holmes said he got laid in airplanes, helicopters, trains, elevators, kitchens, bathrooms, rooftops, storm cellars, bomb shelters in Europe, under tables in crowded restaurants. He claimed he'd received a thousand marriage proposals, eighty propositions per month by mail from girls, and two hundred from gays. Prostitutes paid *him* to get off. Mothers made pilgrimages with their daughters for him to take their virginity, then stayed on to get stuffed with cock as well. Husbands paid to watch him fuck their wives, including several governors and congressmen. Though a "romanticist," by 1975 he estimated he fucked six thousand girls. He only got "a great deal of satisfaction with about three hundred of them." And then in his spare time, on days off from fucking chicks, John Holmes did "free-clinic charity work" and painted. Though no doubt some of Holmes's number crunching was in the ballpark, such was my awe of this man's pecker that I believed him. And it was virtually all bullshit. He was a better actor than his films foretold.

J. P. Donleavy

Donleavy met our editors, Peter Brennan and Jay Molishever, at the New York Athletic Club. He looked like he just stepped off the back of a book jacket: wooly tweed overcoat, tweed suit, tweed beard, tweed hat in hand. An air of self-satisfaction about him that came from being born in Brooklyn, raised in the Bronx, and making it into the New York Athletic Club on his English accent. An ex-pat American, Donleavy had lived in England and Ireland since the late forties. *The Ginger Man* was first published by Olympia Press in Paris in the fifties as a porno book; it was now literature. Olympia was first to publish *Lolita*, *Candy*, and *Naked Lunch*. After being ripped off royally by Olympia publisher Maurice Girodias, many years later, his own wife now owned the entire Olympia catalog, hundreds of books originally published as pornography.

"Pornography is a really important thing," said Donleavy. "It's kind of a mark of the freedom and ease in society. It could be very beneficial to a country like Ireland if pornography was widely disseminated throughout the country. . . . The further you go from Dublin the more censorship is still imposed by local officials. But to a large degree, Ireland is losing its puritanical streak. The younger people have broken away. They don't want to be laughed at. . . . But the traditional Irish thing is a fist in the goff. The drunken husband comes home, beats the wife up, and throws her out into the back garden where she shivers all night."

In 1976, *Playboy* and *Penthouse* were still banned in Ireland. An Irish magazine called *Man Alive* showed the upper part of ladies, but no full-frontal nudity. Though it had been a best seller in America, Ireland imposed a second twelve-year ban on *The Ginger Man*. But Donleavy still considered Ireland a far better place for a writer or artist to live and work than America. "I have a friend over here who sends

me copies of *Screw* in a wrapper so it looks like private mail, of course."
The packages, to get through customs, used some Catholic organization for the return address.

—*Screw*, February 1976

CHAPTER 15

J'Accuse! Hypocrisy!

The only vice that cannot be forgiven is hypocrisy. The repentance of a hypocrite is itself hypocrisy.

—William Hazlitt

Hypocrisy is the homage vice pays to virtue.

—La Rochefoucauld

Civilization will not attain to its perfection until the last stone from the last church falls on the last priest.

—Emile Zola

In 1984 the New York Public Library presented an exhibition called *Censorship: 500 Years of Conflict*. It featured Renaissance works, Negro authors, once censored, now accepted. *Screw* and *Midnight Blue* were barred from the event. "It's not something we feel you should cover," said the shrill female public relations hack in charge, under Library chairman Vartan Gregorian—if indeed that is his name. As long as censored words remained safely diffused behind a wall of centuries, everyone was safe. *Screw* reprinted the Library's full-page *Times* ad, revising it to "501 Years of Censorship." A year later, *Screw* editor Josh Alan Friedman brought a stripper with him to the Library's "Locking Out Burlesque" symposium, part of their Suppression and the Stage in Twentieth Century America program. Dressed inappropriately, she was denied entry and Friedman had to send her off in a cab.

Chemical Bank, Morgan Guaranty Trust, and the Republic Bank of New York all threw out my accounts when they found out I was publisher of *Screw*. I ShitListed all three. Soon after, two top Chemical Bank executives were sentenced to jail for using the bank as a money-laundering operation for a drug cartel. Anyway, I was pleased to take my business to the First Women's Bank when it opened, an outgrowth of the heady days of feminism. The gals promptly bounced the largest check of my business career, with no notice, no courtesy call. I immediately ShitListed them in *Screw*, and in no time at all, *Crain's New York Business* reported that "men" had been called in to take over nearly all leadership posts. I ended the account, this time by my own volition. But I kept a Women's Bank Gold Card because I liked people's reactions when Al Goldstein, demon chauvinist incarnate, whipped it out to pay at restaurants.

In 1986 I was escorted out of the Jacob Javits Convention Center, the new I. M. Pei–designed palace. I paid three hundred for two tickets to an AIDS benefit. I found myself standing next to Calvin Klein during a photo op. But Klein demurred to be in the same photo with me. So a photographer, Gordon Munro, bitchily ordered me out of picture. Security was summoned. Munro ingratiated himself to the powers that be—Klein over Goldstein, thus demonstrating the pecking order of things. Munro, a mere sycophant, flogged away a beggar from a king's court. Calvin Klein's ads were nothing but *Screw* dressed up in money and glamour. Sex swathed in hypocrisy. At a benefit for AIDS victims who were refused housing, medical care, or freedom of movement, Klein, who never publicly came out of the closet, had a knee-jerk prejudice against being seen with a pornographer.

During a 1983 visit to England, I was stopped at Heathrow Airport. Ten customs agents descended on my bags, unearthing fifteen copies of that week's *Screw*. They spent ninety minutes turning pages, ripping out images apparently offensive to Margaret Thatcher. The leader of the customs mob, when I confronted him, exhibited the comic poofter mannerisms of the overbred, hemophiliac British upper class. "I'm just following orders," he said, repeating the immortal words of Adolph Eichmann.

If I ever wanted to help a local politician get elected, all I had to do was endorse his opponent. No politician wanted any association with a vile pornographer, I was poison. In the pathetic case of mayoral candidate Mel Klenetsky, entering the field against Koch in 1981, Klenetsky attempted a smear campaign against Koch by plastering the subways with flyers headlined: SCREW PUBLISHER ENDORSES KOCH!

I then changed my endorsement to Mel Klenetsky, he's our man—campaigning tirelessly for him eight hours a day, until he lost heavily in the primary, never to be heard from again.

No other figure from the sixties sold out harder than Jann Wenner, publisher of *Rolling Stone*. Less than a year old when *Screw* began, it had the most exciting music coverage in the world and spearheaded the coming revolution. It never quite came, of course. Twelve years later, *Rolling Stone* degenerated into a corporate cesspool. Deeming it necessary to keep his bloated ass afloat in the publishing wars,

Wenner—who I named Water Retention Poster Child of 1986—
abandoned the ideals of the 1960s in the age of Reagan. Even Abbie
Hoffman called Wenner "the Benedict Arnold of the sixties." Once
Reagan was elected and Lennon assassinated, Wenner joined the gath-
ering forces of dark and evil and leapt on the Republican bandwagon.

An insidious *Rolling Stone* ad in *Advertising Age* went "Perception: McGovern. Reality: Reagan." Wenner and his staff of
yupped-out trend vultures boasted the "reality of *R. S.* is a readership that voted overwhelmingly for Reagan." Another double-
truck ad in *Time* appeared in 1980 to attract commercial
investment. It showed a bullish market while graphing their readership with cattle icons, offering "how to own a piece of the rock."
But there was no longer any joy in the rock they chose to cover,
only the stink of conspiracy with record companies and bottom-
line corporate interests.

This became clear to a legion of betrayed readers as early as the
midseventies, when cover stories began to take their leads from television, putting Donnie & Marie or John Denver on the cover. Though
their tribute issues to Lennon, and later George Harrison, were excellent, they wallowed in celebrity worship of Madonna and Bruce
Springsteen. They heralded the age when agents, like David Geffin,
began getting top billing over musicians. This toilet of a magazine
completely lost its soul; its then-new Fifth Avenue offices resembled
an oil company more than a music paper. Balding wimps, as bankrupt
in spirit as the junk culture they idolized, walked through the halls
like death-row inmates. They still harbored the illusion they were
some final cultural word, the "bible of rock." *Rolling Stone* record
reviews came to epitomize the worst writing known to journalism—
that of humorless "rock critics" studying their own belly button lint.

• • •

The biggest all-time sellout of the entire 1960s: Jann Wenner.

The blatant lies and hypocrisy of all religions assume that male testosterone could be muzzled and men could be monogamous. In 1983 I was arrested on the steps of St. Patrick's Cathedral dressed as Jesus, bearing a huge cross designed by vagina sculptor Rene Moncada. The vertical line was in the shape of a vagina. The Catholic Church and more than a few pedophile priests, like Father Bruce Ritter of Times Square, were *Screw's* perennial nemeses. I railed against them almost as much as Hammacher Schlemmer, Forty-seventh Street Camera, and the dry cleaners that continually ruined my shirts. The following editorial, from April '87, is typical of dozens:

The great thinkers of history—from Rousseau to Freud to Al Goldstein—have always railed against that viperish thicket of superstition and idiocy, the Catholic Church. It is astounding to me that such an anti-quated institution still exists in these supposedly rational times. I'm appalled that the battles won so convincingly in the Enlightenment, some three centuries back, still have to be so tiresomely re-fought today. The Catholic Church is a scabrous bloodsucker on the body politic, thriving on ignorance, poverty, and dread of death. The Pope is the chief mafioso of this gang, and he deserves nothing better than to live over and over again the miserable lives to which he condemns others.

You may have read that one of the gaseous eruptions emanating from the Catholic Church in New York City was its objection to being targeted by gays angry at the Church's medieval pronouncements on homosexuality. Actually, the Church did not object itself to the demonstration, but used its front organization, the Irish-Catholic goon squad called the NYPD. The police said the demonstrations would likely lead to violence, using the same tired illogic of anti–free speech forces of eons past.

The courts exposed the Police Department's reasoning for the charade it is and said the demonstration must be allowed, essentially
pointing up the fact that the Catholic Church has no preferred status
in a free society.

In 1983, *Screw* artist Rene Moncada, a *Midnight Blue* camera
team, and yours truly, dressed in my usual churchgoing garb, set off for
a minor protest at St. Patrick's. We were reviling the Church's anti-
quated views on sex, just as the gays were to do some four years later.
We were arrested by the NYPD. Some of us took our incarceration
like the principled free-speech agitators we were; others, like the
sniveling artist Moncada, tried to weasel their way out of jail. But the
court case wound up with a total vindication for me, *Midnight Blue*
and the right to parody the Catholic Church. . . .

I have had more than my share of ex-editors and ex-employees turn
against me. For example, Gil Reavill, a corn-fed Midwesterner who
came to Fun City in 1981 seeking literary fortune. He was greeted
by a wall of busboy jobs. Managing editor Richard Jaccoma selected
him from among dozens of job interviews to fill *Screw*'s associate
editor opening. Soon out of the gate, the academic young Reavill
was co-writing assignments on my behalf for *Playboy* and *Penthouse*
as extra freelance income. He reviewed Manhattan's many new Ori-
ental Spas (which came with gratis "massag-ees" and "handjob-ees"),
and we dined at the Old Homestead. He even accompanied me to
the Playboy Mansion, nailing one of their black-chick centerfolds.

Reavill developed an uncanny ability to inhabit the Goldstein
persona as my ghostwriter, and wrote *Screw*'s bogus interview with
Albert Speer, Hitler's surviving Third Reich architect. It seemed
authentic and many readers believed it. Years later, Reavill went
turncoat for a big book advance. In my universal quest for truth, I
cannot altogether dismiss his assessment. From *Smut: A Sex Industry*

Insider (and Concerned Father) Says Enough Is Enough (Sentinel, 2005):

All [Goldstein's] humanity seemed to have been stripped away, reducing him to a single attribute—appetite. He was all mouth. He ate, sucked, consumed, inhaled. . . . He was diet-maddened the whole time I knew him, and ballooned up and down in girth like a blowfish. Watching him eat was a poor exchange for his always picking up the check. He resembled a massive, squalling, undiapered infant, always screaming to be fed something—new food, new toys, new sensations. . . . I eventually came to understand that there were two Goldsteins: Goldstein the symbol, and Goldstein the man. Goldstein the symbol was the one lionized by the media. . . . In the pretzel logic of my imagination, the fat slob who sat chomping a cigar in editorial meetings was an important crusader for the First Amendment . . . but gradually I recognized that Goldstein was an ultimate opportunist, selfishly using free-speech guarantees to satisfy his appetites."

DESIREE COUSTEAU

AL: Have you ever worked the O'Farrell Theater in San Francisco?

DESIREE: Yes, once.

AL: Did any guys eat your pussy?

DESIREE: They wanted to, but I didn't. I'm very conscious about keeping myself clean and healthy. I go to a doctor a lot, and I take vitamins and things. I just couldn't get turned on to letting any guy off the street just grab my pussy or fist-fuck me—which I know a lot of girls do.

AL: Are there things you won't do in films?

DESIREE: Anals. But, I did an enema scene in *Pretty Peaches*—I'd been taking them for health reasons for a long time.

AL: What else won't you do in fuck films?

DESIREE: I don't know if I should say this . . .

AL: Say it!

DESIREE: I don't do blacks.

AL: You won't fuck blacks? Is that because of your Southern background?

DESIREE: Sort of, yeah. I did it for Swedish Erotica. I worked with Johnny Keyes. That kind of cured me of ever wanting to work with blacks again.

AL: What was Keyes like? Is he arrogant?

DESIREE: Very, but it wasn't that. I don't know what it was. I just started crying.

AL: Are you into big cocks at all?

DESIREE: Yeah . . .

AL: Did you ever fuck Johnny Holmes?

DESIREE: Yeah, I have. He is an amazingly nice guy. He really is. He's very sensitive.

AL: I bet his big cock spoiled you. Now, since you don't fuck little cocks, that means you never fuck Jewish guys, right?

DESIREE: No!! I had a boyfriend once who had a very small cock, and we did a lot of anal sex. That's the only time I've liked anal sex.

AL: What do you think about when you come?

DESIREE: God . . .

AL: God? You think about God?

DESIREE: That's a new one, huh? Sometimes when I'm making love I fantasize that it's an animal or a black guy—something that I would not normally want to do. I get very turned on when I'm embarrassed. It's kind of exciting, being humiliated in sex. Normally, I think of myself as a goddess on a pedestal, so I like to be brought down.

AL: You were raised in the Bible Belt [Savannah, Georgia]— are your parents religious?

DESIREE: Strict Baptists.

AL: No offense, but at first glance you *look* rather straight. I can't help but notice the cross around your neck. You're from the South. What are your morals? How do you feel about what you're doing?

DESIREE: I quit for a year because I felt so guilty. I had a nervous breakdown. I finally went to a psychiatrist and had been seeing my medical doctor, and they both said, "There's nothing wrong with sex; don't feel bad if you want to do it. Sex is clean. It's not like murder." I feel a lot better about the whole thing now.

AL: You made the mistake of accepting society's values?

DESIREE: Absolutely.

—*Screw*, June 1980

CHAPTER 16

Spent

While Long John Holmes is outside sunning himself, his latest chick is in the shower dreaming of what they did last night. . . . John takes her to the bedroom to help her get it on again. This will really turn on John Holmes's fans as he plunges his incredible manhood deep inside this tender young girl, driving her to climatic exhaustion!
— Swedish Erotica film #64, *Lost Weekend*

There was a time, not too long ago, when pornography was dirty and exciting and illegal. It seemed like an invasive peek at behavior deemed so private and personal, it was unbelievable that anyone—particularly female—would ever expose themselves to be gawked upon and photographed while fornicating. Before perinea went public, with landing-strip pubes and anal bleaching, when each woman's bush was a private jungle. Little did we know that women had secretly been waiting for centuries to show it all—and then some.

Before today's endless pool of bleached blonde automatons shaved their snatches and received assembly-line boob jobs, there was Swedish

Erotica. Produced under covert conditions throughout the 1970s, the ten-minute, 8 mm peepshow loops featured dirty, unrehearsed hard-core sex, with gorgeous females. Stag films were never like this. Gone were the masks and the black socks.

In the thousand-page Swedish Erotica catalog, the ordering manual used in the porn underworld, one man stood supreme, his cock towering over every other page. He held his manhood in a two-handed grip, like a ballplayer. The films from 1973 have him billed as "Fred," "Rudy," "Dave," "Stan," and "Big Dick." But the distributors quickly found they had a star on their hands. Soon, the name John Holmes was encased within an electric-red splash of lightning, stamped across the box of each 8 mm loop. He got top billing over every female, even Annette Haven, Desiree Cousteau, and Seka. If Holmes was in the loop, they didn't even mention the names of the broads. Little did my dream-fuck, Gloria Steinem, know at the time, but the feminists finally got what they wanted: a male sex object.

Mafia-composed capsulizations appeared on each page:

> *Film #20*, Pier Passion: *Long John is on the prowl again.* . . . *He quickly locates a beautiful horny yung* [sic] *girl on the beach and wastes no time getting her into a motel where he fills her waiting mouth with his enormous tool. Then he rams it up inside her, and when that isn't enough, he goes in the "back door." That's too much for John, and he covers her with liquid passion.*

How any woman was able to handle Holmes up her rear end remains a mystery, but the evidence is plentiful. Big-cock standup jokes came easy, and provided no amusement for Holmes. He was just a two-bit hustler trying to grind out a living, and any hero worship he generated says volumes more about us—the arrested-development masturbatory public—than poor John. But who else had ever orchestrated a thriving show-biz career based solely on the size of their cock? Walter Cronkite? Some of Holmes's female co-stars reported a "spongy" quality to his penis, which may account for how he was sometimes able to stuff so much cock in. No one knew if he achieved an official erection—he used the two-handed batter's grip to hold it up. Like the lost silent two-reelers of Fatty Arbuckle, many of Holmes's early loops on cheap 8 mm stock have dissolved, lost to schlong scholars forever.

But Holmes's career came to an abrupt halt. Based on a palm print found at the Laurel Canyon murders in 1981, John Holmes was arrested and charged with the four killings nearly six months after they took place. He listed his trade as "actor and screenwriter." The press had a field day with sex-and-death porn-star headlines, reminiscent of my days at Countrywide. Holmes's arraignment sent shock waves through the tightly knit porn industry in California.

Back in New York, the unwelcome news about Holmes filtered into my office. This was not just porn's leading man, but one of my personal heroes. Although a jury, not convinced beyond a reasonable doubt, would eventually acquit Holmes, I would soon learn everything about him was a lie.

I recall the first time, in 1972, *Screw* remarked upon a certain newcomer on the scene, then anonymous, as "that schmuck from L.A. with the enormous cock." A star was borne between Holmes's legs. Now, with the connection between Holmes and the Laurel Canyon murders, I couldn't help marveling at the direction Holmes's life had taken. Johnny Wadd, one of his main personae in films, was a sullen, macho, gun-wielding Sam Spade—porn's stupid caricature of a hard-boiled dick—exactly the type who would be involved with criminal figures like Eddie Nash, and something cops referred to as the "four-on-the-floor murders." Calls came in daily from porno and publishing luminaries with gossip about the case.

Through it all, I tried to graph the porn world's connection to the Laurel Canyon murders, trying to define the limits of porn's culpability. Were the moralists right? Was this the domino theory of immorality—masturbation leads to pot leads to coke leads to heroin leads to murder and mayhem? Was there really a short distance between shooting "one-day wonders," and sheer criminality?

Holmes and I had appeared together at countless sham celebrations of porn's success, the type of nonevents at which men with unclean fingernails glad-hand actresses whose pussies are more recognizable than their faces. Holmes and I shared an insider's disdain for the porn establishment. He felt it had ripped him off. And I was sickened by the bad-faith hypocrisy that infected it—that organization of bald-headed businessmen whose wives tell people that their husbands are in import/export, who call fuck films "erotica," who feel comfortable only when they can apply the word *genre* to porn. Had those pretentious, hypocritical businessmen distorted the ethics of poor Long John to the point that he thought it was all right to commit murder?

I considered myself a friend of Holmes. *Screw* always reflected my obsession with the size of his cock, comparing it to a woman's forearm, a cannon, a Sunday paper when the rest of us were just dailies. If that prick were just attached to my body, this would be a very different world. I remember an exchange with my celebrated psychiatrist, Theodore Rubin:

> AL: [*on the couch*] I meet all sorts of people through my job, and
> they all have large pricks. I envy them. I'm intimidated by a guy

like Holmes, because his schlong makes mine look like a pack of Tums.

RUBIN: What would your life be like if you had a larger penis?

AL: I just feel that I would get laid a lot more often. Women would be begging for it. That moment of excitement when I dropped my pants. I wouldn't even have to show them my bankbook. Or seven hundred issues of *Screw*. I would drop my pants, even in a hallway, and they would all drop to their knees and genuflect. I mean, instant power. It would be the same way the Pope feels with his cross. If I were a street beggar, it wouldn't matter. A big dick would be my great equalizer.

RUBIN: Would you trade places with John Holmes?

At the time I seriously considered the proposition. Holmes's prick was awesome. I had certainly seen too much of it in movies, and somehow, thought if you knew the prick, you knew the man.

Film #44, The Architect: *A pair of lovely young girls feel that the apartment they share could stand a bit of basic redesigning. They call Long John Holmes, who is an architect. They go to his place where he keeps a studio so they can go over some plans, but John has other plans. He takes them right to his bedroom for the view, and then shows them his best design . . . thirteen inches of high rise action.*

But now I wasn't sure I knew him. He once again became an anonymous schmuck with an enormous pecker. A shadow figure, an enigma to me, a cipher.

For five months after he was arrested on the murders, Holmes was unavailable. Following the murders, Los Angeles police had immediately picked him up on an unrelated charge and shunted him around to various downtown hotels under heavy guard, grilling him about Laurel Canyon. When they released him on his own recognizance, he disappeared.

I searched for new ways to pin down his personality. There was, for example, a disturbing story from Gloria Leonard. Discussing Holmes in the weeks following the murders, Gloria told me of the last time she had seen him. They had once worked together in France but had gone a couple of years without seeing each other when Holmes called her to set up a reunion at her new Los Angeles home. He arrived at 9:30 A.M.

"He looked like he hadn't been to bed yet," said Gloria. "He looked—well, he's so painfully thin, you know, he's all cock." In the course of two hours that morning, Holmes freebased more than three grams of coke. A week later, he and Gloria were to meet at her home again—at noon, since, as she told him, she had an appointment that morning. When she returned to meet him, her house had been burglarized to the tune of twenty-five-thousand dollars—jewelry, electronic equipment, guns. Holmes never showed for their appointment.

"I heard he had a serious cocaine problem, but it wasn't until after that particular encounter that I realized how serious it was," Gloria said. "I heard he lost a lot of his possessions. His cars, his house, his jewelry, everything else. He had obviously not worked in films for about a year or more, because he was just so immersed in the drug culture."

AL: As you know, he was involved in and beat a drug-related murder rap. Were drugs on the set a lot?

SEKA: If they were I didn't see them. If he was doing drugs, he kept them to himself. He was a bit strange the last time I worked with him—he would go hide in closets and detain work on the set. We would sometimes wait an hour because we couldn't find him. He would be hiding in a closet in the dark somewhere because he didn't want to be bothered. So he therefore lost us a lot of money and caused a lot of aggravation. And I was a bit disappointed. But John has always been my favorite and always will be.

AL: Did the drugs affect him to the point that he couldn't get it up?

SEKA: I saw where he had problems with other women. John never had any problems with me, but I mentally eliminated everyone else on the set. I paid 100 percent attention to John and we got along very well.

—*Screw,* January 1983

It was while Holmes was on the lam that *Exhausted,* his last film before the trial, was pushed into release. Suzanne Atamian, aka Julia St. Vincent, a twenty-two-year-old former girlfriend of Holmes's, produced the film and engineered a publicity campaign to coincide with the notoriety provided by the murders. It's a strange fuck film, a pastiche of interviews, clips, and testimonials, a "documentary" on John Holmes the man. Watching it amid the hype of the murders— the screening was invaded by cops who thought Holmes might be there incognito—I felt unable to separate shadow from substance. In the film, sex goddess Seka said that Holmes was the man who erupted with "the come of God." That was the Holmes I knew and idolized. The film was fascinating but about as phony as the tip that had caused police to bust the screening.

> *Film #68*, Seaplane Sex: *Beautiful scenery rolls below the wing of his private seaplane as John Holmes, a busy executive, approaches a meeting with a lovely Oriental girl. When Big John lands, he rushes to the fantastic chick who has been waiting. They really get it on, including some sensationally exciting sex that leaves her exhausted and limp. He drags himself up, and runs out on the dock to his waiting plane for his next "meeting."*

I found a few facts. Holmes's cock measured twelve-and-three-quarters inches when erect, not the fourteen inches of the publicists. When I knew him in '75, during his two-part *Screw* interview, there were no paranoiac tics, no rolling up in an embryonic ball, no coke habit to dwarf all other elements of his life. That was the period of Johnny Wadd's greatest success, with hundreds of different Holmes loops and films playing peep show booths and theaters across the country.

But it had become clear over the years that Holmes was a pathological liar. Take for example, the question of his early years:

AL: At what age did you become aware that you were "abnormally" large?

HOLMES: When I was eight. When I lived in Florida with my aunt, she was always running to Europe to get married or get divorced. . . . I had a Swiss nursemaid. And whenever my aunt was out of town, she would give me head. She taught me to

give head. It was just great. I loved it. We had this huge house
all to ourselves. We had a gardener and a cook and a butler,
altogether, and then we had a maid who cleaned the place. . . .

—*Screw*, June 1975

I found out myself that the entire aunt story was fabricated. Being
charitable, I can imagine the notorious Johnny Wadd contriving the
ruse to shield his family from the awful truth. But it is odd how con-
veniently the ruse aligned with Holmes's self-aggrandizement, his
need for a more romantic, less mundane personal history. Parts of the
interview embraced typical American-male fantasies.

AL: Did you have any sexual experiences involving . . . the girls
you went to school with?

HOLMES: Oh, yeah. I fucked a lot in high school. I think I got
everybody but three girls in my class, and then the class before,
quite a few of 'em; and then the senior class ahead of me, I got
most of them.

—*Screw*

I spoke with a woman from Holmes's high school, the head of the
alumni association, an ex-cheerleader, Miss Popularity. She gradu-
ated the same year Holmes would have. She didn't remember him,
she said when I called her, but she was going to a meeting later in the
day to organize the twentieth class reunion. She would ask the
people there. When I got back to her, she reported that Holmes was
in none of the yearbooks. One girl had vaguely remembered his
"walking to school all the time." This was in a graduating class of
fewer than one hundred people.

It was then that I decided to check things out myself—at a place I usually make it a point to fly over, preferably asleep while cruising at high altitude.

Film #67, Away Too Long: *"John Holmes plays an airline pilot who has been away from his girl for a very long time. . . . They go off to the bedroom for some heavy stuff! While he's been gone she's taught herself the trick that 'Linda' made famous, and she's become an expert."*

Ohio is, for me, an utterly foreign and almost surreal sector of America. The countryside around Columbus was impoverished, blank, vaguely menacing. It was into that border-state environment that John was born, as John Curtis Estes, on August 8, 1944. Two years later, the birth certificate was corrected to list the child's name as John Curtis Holmes. The original listed Carl L. Estes, railroad laborer, as father. The correction listed no father at all, though the man from whom John took his surname was evidently a carpenter named Edward Holmes. He married John's devout Southern Baptist mother. John seems to have been born and raised in rural, depressed Pickaway County without anyone's particularly remarking upon his existence. The only man I could find who remembered the Holmes clan told of the large family "across the tracks . . . We used to call that type of folks something that rhymes with 'might clash,'" he said.

Some remarkable information about Holmes's Ohio upbringing was to come later, from his lawyer. They had obtained his Sunday school attendance record. It showed perfect attendance for twelve years. I got goose bumps when I heard that, as a quote from the *Screw* interview surfaced in my consciousness: "It's totally insane," Holmes had said. "The perfect child that always goes to church and goes out and cuts fifty people's throats."

It was also said later that Holmes's stepfather was an alcoholic who beat him. Holmes spent three years in the Army Signal Corps, like myself, and was stationed in Germany. Standing urinal to urinal once, some guy supposedly peeked over the divider and suggested he should enter pornography. The Ohio experience only depressed me. The idea that my hero might be a murderer depressed me.

There was a rumor circulating that proved what a chameleon the Holmes persona was. The rumor was that Holmes was actually Ken Osmond, the actor who played Eddie Haskell on *Leave It to Beaver*. Haskell was the sneering, sleazy friend of big brother Wally, who always feigned innocence before the skeptical Ward and June Cleaver.

Holmes did resemble Eddie Haskell to some degree, and people were indulging in an irresistible poetic justice believing that Eddie Haskell had ended up a porn star with a giant cock. Osmond even sued the distributor of Holmes's films in an attempt to halt the rumor, and the whole bizarre situation concluded with a twisted irony: Osmond was a Los Angeles cop.

My desultory investigations were interrupted when, on November 30, 1981, Holmes was arrested in a Florida hotel on a fugitive warrant from California. He was taken in on a charge unrelated to the Laurel Canyon murders but on December 9, as soon as he was extradited to Los Angeles, he was charged in the deaths. Three days later, I flew out to see him.

Film #147, Balcony Pick-Up: *"John Holmes, while walking his dog, is invited in the home of two lusty girls. All three get down to exploding sexual pleasure. . . . John using his steel-hard cock to penetrate the different love nests of each girl . . . ending this erotic trio John's volcano erupting while the girls lick up the lava.*

What I found was a terrified man looking out at me from behind the thick prison Plexiglas with strangely bulging eyes. Cocaine withdrawal eyes. It seemed astounding that this was the man I had idolized. He wore a nondescript uniform and complained wearily through the phone intercom of the lousy prison food and the lack of bail. I resisted the impulse to ask him whether the famous Holmes cock was being used in jail. Later, there were more rumors that while in prison, Holmes was bribed with beer and contraband by sadistic guards to sodomize prisoners they wished to punish.

Even at that meeting, as long as he held together the mangled shreds of his personality, we were comfortable with each other. I was moved and astonished when John asked me how my son was, by name, after what was a six-year gap in our relationship. I worked the conversation gingerly around the question of the murders. It was a mistake.

I thought the best way to find more information was to talk to my Los Angeles porn contacts. But I found that the porn community had turned its back on its favorite fourteen-inch son. The murders, coming after a year or two of Holmes's erratic behavior as an addict, made Holmes a pariah in his own backyard.

Bill Margold, a producer and self-styled Renaissance man of porn, was the only one with something positive to say. His agency had its offices in the crumbling Cineart Building on Sunset Boulevard, across from the Chinese theater. He told a story of giving Holmes $1,500 up front for a one-day shoot in a swimming pool. When the temperature of the pool proved to be too cold for Wadd's hard-on, he backed out of the shoot. "He actually gave me back the $1500," Margold recalled. "All of it and at once. After that, no one can tell me that Homes isn't a straight guy." With a final touch of irony, Margold noted that the Cineart Building, with its fading Chandleresque glamour, was owned by Eddie Nash.

Authorities had hammered away at the Holmes-Nash connection. Nash opened a sandwich stand called Beef's Chuck in 1960 on Hollywood Boulevard and somehow built it into a million-dollar empire of night clubs, strip joints, and restaurants. "He's pure power," said Ron Coen, the prosecutor in the Laurel Canyon case. He owned the defunct rock showcase, the Starwood, the soon-to-close Seven Seas, Ali Baba on the Strip and a lot of gay clubs. A local gangster, he had Americanized his name from Adel Nasrallah. Nash was busted three times for drugs in the months surrounding the murders. Once, when police came up with $1 million in coke from his private safe, his lawyers argued that it was for personal use. After the murders, his name would crop up in the L.A. papers with increasing frequency— in an arson ring of which he was the only one acquitted among four coconspirators, the others convicted of racketeering and mail fraud. His driver/butler died of an overdose at Nash's Studio City home.

But it was the Laurel Canyon murders that would prove most troublesome to Nash. Greg Diles, his massive, blubbery bodyguard—at three hundred pounds a mountain of black lava—would be arrested for the murders and then be released for lack of evidence. But the prosecution characterized the four deaths, committed at Wonderland Avenue in Hollywood Hills, as "the gruesome revenge of Eddie Nash."

One scenario put forth by the police on the Nash-Holmes connection had Nash fronting coke to the group of hardened, professional burglars who lived on Wonderland Avenue—of which Holmes was a member—and taking stolen property in return as collateral. But there was another connection police pursued, even more ominous. Two nights before the Laurel Canyon massacre, Nash's house in nearby Studio City was burglarized and Nash was robbed. Later, in court testimony, robber David Lind would admit that he and his gang had pulled off the break-in with tactical and logistical help from Holmes.

Holmes mapped out the floor plan of Nash's residence, rehearsed the robbery, insisted it was a good mark. Nash was something of a porno groupie—who else do you take to parties to impress people like John Belushi?—and an intense relationship had grown between him and Holmes. Holmes went to Nash's house the evening of the robbery and unlocked a sliding door. Then he went to the Wonderland Avenue house of the robbers and awaited the results.

Four robbers pulled off the heist, one waiting behind the wheel of the getaway car. The other three entered through the door Holmes had left open, flashing fake police badges to confuse Diles (it didn't take much). One of them delighted in terrorizing the inhabitants of Nash's home. The heist netted a cache of dope, twenty-thousand dollars in cash and some jewelry. Holmes got $12\frac{1}{2}$ percent of that. It also led police to suspect that the later murders were the result of vengeance and that Holmes, with his close connections, had either led the Nash gang into the Wonderland house or participated himself.

The level of violence in the deaths appalled me and gave me a peculiar sense of dislocation. I could not connect Holmes to it; it was too distant from the soft-spoken man I idolized as the greatest cocksman in the world.

Film #80, Horseshoes: *Long John Holmes, as a successful executive, takes in some horseshoe pitching on his lunch hour. One of his tosses goes too far, and almost hits a beautiful black chick. . . . John apologizes, but the girl is very angry indeed. . . . When they get inside her pad all the hate has vanished, and been replaced by lust. They get it on as only John and an uninhibited black chick can.*

I decided to attend the Holmes trial. To get my bearings, I mentally listed three trials that would help me get through this one. My own

federal trial, in Kansas, was for obscenity and tied into the sensa-
tionalism of the Holmes case. The whores and bottom-feeders of the
media couldn't pass by a chance to turn up their disapproving, snot-
nosed faces at porn, even while using it to trump up the lascivious-
ness of their stories. Like the *National Mirror* all over again. The
Holmes trial also coincided with the start of the John Hinckley trial,
tagged by the press as another saga of love and madness in the
shooting of Reagan, to "impress" Jodie Foster. The Patty Hearst case,
replete with elements of coercion and forced wrongdoing, completed
the trio of precedent-setting trials that prepared me for this one.

Throughout the preliminary hearings, Holmes sat with his attorneys, looking alternately haggard and flip, uncomfortable in a Sears
& Roebuck leisure suit. The same high white-trash fashion he might
have worn in his early loops. While the reporters from the *Los Angeles
Times*, the *Herald Examiner*, and the *Daily News* attentively took
notes, I felt dazed by the proceedings, as if the courtroom atmosphere had lobotomized me. All I could think about was cocks.

*Film #136: John Holmes and his partner deliver furniture to a voluptuous
beauty and it is found she cannot pay them, therefore they decide to take it
out in trade. . . . But it is John who make* [sic] *the big scene as his enormous
penis assaults the anus of the girl, all to the pleasure of the threesome.*

Penis size, when it comes right down to it, is basically a concept of
the rational mind. It is quantitative, safely within the realm of reason.
It seems perfectly reasonable to take a tape measure to your dick.
There isn't any Bureau of Standards and Measurement for this
procedure—porn studs cheat, starting their measure from the asshole.
But where do you start? Seen from the emotional female side,
though, the whole concept seems ludicrous. That side wants soul,

passion, exuberance—those messy things that push sex into the realm of mystery.

I tried to imagine the weariness with which Holmes looked at society. For anyone with a foot-long cock, everyone else was a size queen. Seeing Holmes, tic-ridden in the courtroom, wearing that pathetic mail-order double knit, made me imagine that if I had that *shvantz*, I couldn't be Al Goldstein. I couldn't whine and complain about my feelings of inferiority and not getting laid, and there would be no *Screw*.

The months on the lam might have provided relief for Holmes. "I grew a great big ugly beard and hung out," he said. Freed from the onus of his cock, Holmes was finally unburdened of his public identity. He lost himself in the wastes of Montana, visiting his sister, changing the plates of his car (legally, oddly enough) and painting it a different color. When cops were tipped to his presence in Miami, they found him working as a handyman at a local hotel.

Film #184: The Handyman: *Mending the tree house is only one of this guy's jobs, as to his pleasure, when a ravishing brunette and luscious blonde relaxing in the grass beckon to him. All three romp together and his cock finds its way into the brunette's beautiful ass.*

He had left Los Angeles, he said, because shots had been fired at him. "There are good guys, bad guys, and the in-between, and they are all out for me, one way or another," his wife had quoted him as saying in an interview she gave to the *Los Angeles Times*. The wife was another revelation to me. She seemed to have dropped from the sky into the *Times* and was, even then, filing for divorce. I was astonished to find out they had been married for seventeen years, though no one in the X-rated biz had known about it.

I recalled Holmes railing against marriage in the *Screw* interview: "Marriage is wrong. And it always gets messy with marriage. You can't break it off. One out of a thousand marriages breaks off beautifully." I wondered how the former Sharon Gebenini, married to Holmes for all of eight years when he said those words, felt about them. According to her *Times* interview, Sharon was getting out because Holmes had run up thirty-thousand dollars in "household debts" by charging goods to credit cards and then selling them for cash. She also spoke of his fear of Nash, saying that Holmes had called him "evil incarnate."

The trial itself left Holmes between two terrible decisions. If he testified, he feared he would be killed as a stool pigeon. If he didn't testify, he would be tried for murder—and mass murder and murder committed during a robbery were both capital crimes in California. He would testify and die or lie and fry. There was testimony from a homicide detective that Holmes admitted taking the murderers to the Wonderland Avenue house but strongly denied that he had done any of the killing himself. By his own account, Holmes had been the finger, he told the detective, because Nash wanted revenge and threatened him and his family. Nash had gotten hold of Holmes's address book, copied the names of his relatives and told him they would be killed if Holmes informed on Nash to police.

Prosecutor Coen, a stocky, square-shouldered man who wore the sleeves of his shirts too long, reminded me of a white Jim Brown. His strategy seemed straightforward: scare the fuck out of Holmes and force him to finger the real killers. Until he does, keep the pressure up, to the point of trying to prove that Holmes actually killed someone that morning on Wonderland Avenue. One of the surviving robbers of Nash's home, first identified as a Sacramento bounty hunter by trade, was asked on the stand for his occupation. "I rob," he said fiercely. He told the court about the robbery at Nash's home that set up the murders. Nash's huge, blubbery bodyguard, Diles, lay whimpering on the floor after a robber's gun accidentally discharged and left Diles with a powder burn on his thigh. You got the idea that Diles was someone who would kill for Nash, even if Nash were dead. The primal image of the robbery, though, was of Nash on his knees, praying for his life to be spared for the sake of his children.

The fifth victim barely survived with her skull bludgeoned, and was the estranged wife of one of the burglary-ring victims, having arrived to try and patch things up. She drifted in and out of consciousness for twelve hours after the massacre, until a neighbor finally heard her low moans. She was to be the star witness if she survived, and when she did, she said she remembered seeing only "shadowy figures." Shadows don't kill, they told her. Another dead victim, Barbara Lee Richardson, who was not a member of the hardened burglary ring, was in the wrong place at the wrong time. She was one of the robber's girlfriends, crashing in the living room.

After the revenge killings, a thirty-minute video was made by police just hours after the bludgeoned bodies of the robbers were discovered. It was the first time in the history of American jurisprudence that a videotape of a murder scene was allowed as evidence at a criminal trial. Every advance made by video and DVD technology was presaged by porn, even in the judicial system. In the darkened courtroom, I watched the monitor while the tape was played. The lousy technical quality of the tape, the graininess and the gaudiness of the color, brought out the film reviewer in me. Save for the subject matter, the cinematography was like one of Holmes's loops.

Film #137: John Holmes and his rugged black friend visit this gorgeous, lusty girlfriend. . . . John shows the girl new sexual dimensions, that make

her insane with lust, taking John's friend with her to heights of unbeliev-
able passion. All three come together in a sexual act that is beyond belief.

The images in court, however, were those of a death camp—inhuman.
I watched Holmes as the camera panned in on the brutalized body of
Barbara Lee Richardson, lodged between a couch and a table on the
floor of the living room. *Had Holmes watched this woman being murdered?*

Robbery/homicide detective Tom Lange was allowed to testify
about Holmes being tailed to Nash's home. According to Lange,
Holmes had a closer relationship with Nash than with the burglary
ring. He visited Nash repeatedly *after* the murders, once less than
two hours after telling another detective that he had let the killers
into the Wonderland Avenue house out of fear of Nash. I couldn't
help wondering the obvious: if the killers were going to brutally rub
out four people (an attempted five), why not add Holmes, the only
witness—unless he was allied with the killers himself? What if
Holmes killed one of the victims himself, as police theorized?

Had the jury been influenced by Holmes's *oeuvre* in porn? I found
it odd that although none of the jurors had, in the selection process,
evinced any prior knowledge of Holmes, Johnny Wadd, or any other
Holmes personae, several knew my name—that according to a clerk,
who said the jury was impressed that I was in the courtroom.

All my life, I had prayed for a bigger dick; just a few more inches
and I would have everything: success, women, happiness. John Holmes
had those inches, and look where they had gotten him. He was no
more than a haggard, hounded man sitting in the courtroom, waiting
for his own life sentence to be passed.

On June 26, 1982, the jury acquitted John Holmes of the Laurel
Canyon murders. Despite his acquittal, Holmes was kept in jail, first

on a stolen-property conviction, then on contempt-of-court charges for refusing to answer the grand jury's questions about the Wonderland Avenue killings. He spent 111 days in jail for contempt, way beyond the norm. Word on the street had him finished in porn. Even I wondered whether or not audiences, or more specifically masturbators, would want their fantasies acted out by a man involved, even tangentially, with such a gruesome crime. The firm of Hansen and Egers was appointed by the court to defend Holmes in Superior Court. Hansen was the articulate, dapper, gray-haired senior partner. "John really loves the [porn] business," he told me, after an hour-and-a-half session we had with Holmes. Hansen listed me as a witness for the Laurel Canyon case, giving me access to Holmes that no other journalist had. Holmes, in the months he spent in jail, missed the world of porn, the circles he had traveled in. Hansen couldn't help him, but I could at least gossip and give him a sense of his world. Hansen gave Holmes cigarette money from his own pocket, and Holmes openly considered Hansen a hero.

But his lawyers could not protect Holmes from jail. "He's going to stay there until he tells us what he knows about the Laurel Canyon murders," vowed prosecutor Coen. Holmes spoke of Coen's "vendetta," his "hatred" for Holmes. "It's political," Holmes said. "Coen knows I didn't do it." Under California law, a person may be jailed for contempt for coercive but not for punitive reasons—to force him to testify, but not to punish him for failing to do so. Holmes went on a hunger strike. "A fast between meals," sniffed Coen, saying that Holmes ate—even gained weight—during his strike. All I could think of was the famous Holmes cock wasting away from malnutrition.

Film #51, Polynesian Princess: *Long John has a new challenge—a beautiful young girl from the islands. He arrives at her apartment where she has laid out everything for a feast, including herself. . . . After a little wine and a tasty morsel or two, her hands stray below the belt to feel and see for herself if the legendary manhood of John Holmes is for real. It is—all of it— and it's what she came to get.*

While Holmes was in jail, the wheels of justice were slowly grinding down on Eddie Nash, but this time the charge was drugs, not murder. Nine days after the Laurel Canyon murders and only a few days after Holmes had implicated Nash in his statement to the police, the cops launched a successful drug raid on Nash's house. Then, a few weeks later, they raided it again. And again. In all, they found more than $1 million worth of drugs, and Nash found himself in jail, unable to meet his $5 million bail.

It was frontier justice at its best. The authorities had both their murder suspects in jail, despite the fact that one had been acquitted and the other not even charged with the murders.

Holmes might have been silent, but Nash was not. First he told Coen that Holmes had taken part in the murders, then he wrote Holmes a letter that read: "Jhon [*sic*] you know as God is your witness that I am innocent and that I never sent anybody with you to kill anybody anywhere or anyplace. So don't you think it's about time to tell the truth?"

Another letter followed: "Jhon [*sic*] I swear man I will forgive you for what you did to me if you snapp [*sic*] out of it and tell them the truth and come and save me out of my miseries."

Still, Holmes kept quiet, at least until the day of Nash's sentencing. Nash, not surprisingly, was hit with the maximum sentence: eight years in prison and $120,350 in fines. His lawyer was furious, claiming that the average term for similar drug charges is two to three years. "There is no doubt he was not sentenced for crimes that he committed but the crimes he was suspected of," thundered his attorney to reporters.

Holmes then had a change of heart about testifying, and did so under a set of extremely agreeable conditions his lawyers were able to arrange. Holmes would not be prosecuted for perjury, no matter what he said, and major probation constraints against him would be dropped. The proceedings were secret and some insiders thought the testimony Holmes gave to the grand jury was useless. Nevertheless, John Holmes walked out of prison on November 22, 1982. A paranoid, but free, man.

On the second day of the 1983 International Winter Consumer Electronics Show in Las Vegas—where I indulged in a yearly orgy of gadget-buying gluttony—Holmes strode up to me out of nowhere. All the X-rated companies were ghettoized in the Hilton, across a parking lot from the mainstream, where Toshiba and Sony reigned. He was signing autographs for Caballero Control, a distributor of many films featuring his third leg. He gave me a nudge in the belly. "You're gaining weight, Goldstein," he rasped. "You should be on the same diet I'm on, the cocaine diet." He was thin and emaciated, just like in jail.

He was once again in porn, on coke, and in need of another Eddie Nash. We spoke of my victory in the Kansas obscenity case. "That's what makes us alike," Holmes said. "We're both winners. Sometimes the good guys win." His eyes were glittering, unfocused. Holmes spotted the watch I had on, a garish, gold-and-gem-incrusted monstrosity mounted on a Mickey Mouse dial face.

"You give gold a bad name, Goldstein. I wouldn't be caught dead on the streets with you."

I asked about a large diamond he used to wear as a ring, a sort of trademark, visible in many of his films. It was his signature, and a phrase tossed about was that he wore "a diamond as big as his dick." The dick jokes never ceased.

"Gone," he said, "with the rest of it. Up my nose in a couple of toots." Drugs had stolen the man's only identifiable characteristic outside his pants.

"So this whole thing was coke, John?"

He looked away, the unfocused eyes narrowing. His whole life, from Ohio to Hollywood, had been a hustle and a sham, and coke was a facilitator. John Holmes was a foot-long cock hanging from an empty persona. He was disappearing, dissolving before me.

> *Film #34*, Marilyn's Portfolio: *This film marks the introduction of a Beautiful Blonde Superstar who bears striking resemblance to "MM"! (You know who!) Her beautiful face and figure not only look startlingly like the famous sex symbol, but her sexual appetite is as unquenchable as her legendary look-alike's! Here she visits the equally famous Long John Holmes. . . .*

Poor John was soon diagnosed HIV positive and died of AIDS in 1988 at age forty-three. He was cremated. That way, no mortuary joker could erect a phallic tombstone over his grave.

STATEN ISLAND FERRY

I have nothing but time now for TV. I'm addicted, as only an addict can be, to television. I watch CNN, the History Channel, Court TV and *Strictly Sex with Dr. Drew*. My TIVO screen is programmed to fifty different food shows: *Everyday Food, The Naked Chef, 30 Minute Meals, Calorie Commando, Good Eats, Barefoot Contessa, How to Boil Water, License to Grill, Cookin' in Brooklyn*. I can't cook, I just mentally masturbate over food I can no longer afford. I watch the morning shows with Katie Couric, Diane Sawyer, and Kelly Ripa. If only they knew me, I'm convinced they'd let me eat their pussies. If I could get my tongue up Katie Couric's asshole just once, she'd follow me around like a dog. She already had a colonoscopy on air, why not Goldstein's tongue? If I was a giraffe with an eighteen-inch tongue, I could lick her ass and pussy at the same time. When I'm especially depressed, I watch Nixon's resignation over and over on videotape. It cheers me up. Tricia's standing near and I imagine eating her pussy.

CHAPTER 17

Pastrami Whore: How I Became 350 Pounds

Katz's, at Houston and Ludlow Streets on the Lower East Side, has probably been my favorite delicatessen since 1888, when it opened. I've eaten there in previous lives. Unchanged since WWII, a beloved sign still hangs from the ceiling: "Send a salami to your boy in the army." The men's room still has a sawdust floor, like the great restaurants of yesteryear. Hands down, Katz's currently makes the finest pastrami in New York—and by definition, the country.

On a recent lunchtime visit, I was greeted by head chef, Kenneth Kohn.

"Whaddya still here, Al, you want desert now? Cheesecake or something?" And then he turned to my lunch date: "One day I gave Al a whole bunch of different cuts of pastrami to demonstrate the differences. People don't realize what a wonderful man Al is. For every Pat Robertson and schmuck out there, you need an Al Goldstein to balance things out."

Pastrami Master Kohn describes the ruthless use of his carving knife on dead animals: "Pastrami is actually just a spice mixture. You have salmon pastrami, herring pastrami, you can have any kind of pastrami. We, as New Yorkers, use it strictly as a meat. You want the juice from above the navel, the top part of the navel piece. The same with corned beef, you got the top deck or the bottom deck. The bottom cut is always lean. So you start cutting pastrami in the middle, where the two pieces of fat cap together. You separate 'em, trim that fat back, and now you got the best of both worlds. We get a kickback from every cardiologist in New York."

I learned more about pastrami during my homeless year, when I briefly worked for Jack Lebewohl at the Second Avenue Deli. There are three ways pastrami is served: one is extra lean, with little taste. Inbred *shtetle* Jews prefer it too fatty. To me, if it's too fatty, it's gross. Katz's serves it perfect, just the right balance of moisture and fat. Don't give me too fatty, don't give me too lean, give me right in the middle. The Second Avenue Deli is kosher, which fares poorly for pastrami—you can't have uncured pastrami, it ain't spicy. You might as well put mayonnaise on it. But the brisket is great. And for *cholent*, you can't beat Second Avenue Deli.

The Carnegie once had good pastrami. I became friends with Leo Steiner when he owned it; he cured his own pastrami in the basement. Leo Steiner and Abe Lebewohl were true deli owners, Brooklyn boys like me. Being in the food business is the epitome of being Jewish. The more repulsive-looking the proprietor of a restaurant, the more delicious the food. And these guys were not easy on the eyes. Leo died of cancer, probably from the nitrites in his own cured meats, and Abe was murdered.

I couldn't go to the Stork Club, Lindy's, or the Stage, all of which closed or changed by the time I hit the big time. Money and fame opens doors, and I didn't have it then. These days, the Stage is rotten, they don't even smoke their pastrami. The Stage autopilots on its old rep. Once king of the neighborhood in Times Square, the Stage became a tourist joint after Max Asnis retired.

A joint called Pastrami King used to reside on 144th Street, near the courthouse on Queens Boulevard in Queens. They served incredible pastrami. The guy's wife took it over when they moved to the Diamond District on Forty-seventh Street in Manhattan, and it was never as good.

To me, corned beef is just boring.

Stanley Zimmerman, who owns Sammy's Romanian on the Lower East Side, gave me two-thousand dollars recently. Sammy's has the best skirt steak I've ever had, a steak that falls off the plate. I sold Stanley my blue Rolls Royce in 1976 for fifteen grand, less than half of its worth. He kept it parked in front of the restaurant for years. The older generation of Jews who became successful lawyers and doctors would travel back in time to their peasant stock at places like Sammy's. Today, young, yupped-out Jews don't care, they want hot new restaurants.

In L.A., I love the cheese blintzes at Canter's, open all night. The Jewish cookies and pastries at the bakery are good, and the restaurant serves great pickles. I made a move on Jacqueline, the manager there, very pretty brunette. I wanted to eat her pussy for dessert. I didn't realize she was married to a doctor who later became my doctor.

Schraft's on Madison and Sixty-fourth had my favorite malteds in a cold steel container. It poured out two-and-a-half glasses, for $1.10. At Chock Full O' Nuts, I loved the cheese sandwiches. Later, I loved Rumplemyer's in the St. Moritz Hotel, for wonderful sundaes and malteds, but pricey. The onion rolls at Ratner's on Delancey Street were legend, and everybody would stuff a few in their pockets before leaving. I loved the Belmore Cafeteria, Twenty-eighth & Park, where all the cab drivers went. We had *Screw's* twelveth anniversary there. Cafeterias excite me, all that food. I liked Grant's Cafeteria on Forty-second Street, where they put a lousy Nathan's franchise in the 1970s. The aforementioned seven restaurants are all gone.

I never discovered a good delicatessen in Florida.

STATEN ISLAND FERRY

It's been my restaurant cronies, not the porn world, who've kept me alive. Noel Stein, who used to run the Playboy Club for Hefner, owns the great restaurant, Bice, on Fifty-fourth. We go back twenty-five years. While I was homeless he'd serve me lobster free. I didn't want to be *shnorrer*, a pig, about it, so I attended Bice only every other night. He'd slip me fifty or a hundred dollars with a meal. Sirio Maccioni, owner of Le Cirque, the most important restaurant in New York, comped me four out of five meals. Rotating, I'd eat lobster at Bice one night, then pasta at Le Cirque the next. But I had to go early to make the homeless shelter by eight to sign for my bed. (I hope I didn't contribute to Le Cirque's recent closing, after forty-five years.) Drew Nieporent, the owner of Nobu, the exquisite Japanese restaurant on Hudson Street, also gave me free meals.

Before hitting absolute bottom, I landed a menial job at Second Avenue Deli for $10 an hour. It was like a sympathy fuck. Greeting customers and showing them their tables, a salesman for their catering service. In 1978 they catered my huge celebration at Plato's Retreat, after I won my federal obscenity acquittal in Wichita, Kansas. I flew the entire jury in.

But I always preferred food to sex. Often while lunching out on a daily hooker, my mouth really watered for Pastrami King or Katz's. Just nine years before, in 1996, I posted half of the hundred-thousand-dollar reward still offered for the unsolved murder of Second Avenue Deli owner Abe Lebewohl, who was shot outside the restaurant late one night. There were rumblings about the Russian Mafia. I could use that money back. Abe had been one of many alter cocker restaurant cronies. His younger brother, Jack, hired me, quoting a Yiddish saying from his mother: "Better to lose on a smart person than to win with a fool." They lost.

Former mayor Ed Koch was cordial to me when he came in before the Republican convention. He mentioned to Jack that I'd once put his head in a toilet bowl in the pages of *Screw*. Even Hizzoner felt honored being targeted in my weekly editorial. But I was fired for sleeping overnight on the Second Avenue Deli floor.

CHAPTER 18

Fat City

In my worst corpulent Walter Mitty nightmare, I am at my fattest, over 350 pounds, a Macy's Day Parade float. I am on a hotel bed, ordering pounds of takeout pastrami from the Stage, a bucket of chopped liver from the Carnegie, and gallons of Häagen-Dazs double chocolate ice cream. I'm propped up in bed, so bloated I must balance my mass against gravity and wedge myself against the headboard. I'm still ordering take-out when my dial-a-hooker walks in, appalled by the sight she sees.

I'm in bed with the hooker, wiping oily potato salad off my sausage-like fingers on the hooker's blouse, flinging leftovers against the wall like an infant. My body is a sac of protoplasm shot through with nitrites and calories. I drift off to sleep.

And then I awake without the faintest memory of how my hotel room reached such an incredible state of disarray. There are blotchy, bloodlike streaks everywhere, on the sheets, pillows, walls, and floor. My God, there are what look like bones on the floor. The hooker's blouse is soaked in an evil-looking red substance. Carnage. I then vaguely remember a hooker on my bed. Could I have? It wasn't possible! And just left her bones?

I call up Ron Jeremy. "Ronnie, you know that hooker I had last night?

"Yeah?" comes Ronnie, his mouth full of food.

"Well, I think I ate her!"

"So what?" says Ronnie, clueless. "Isn't that what you always do?"

"No, man, I mean I actually fuckin' ate her! All that's left here is blood and bones!"

Such is the albatross of anguish a fat man must carry on his shoulders. Whenever things got this bad, I booked myself into the fabled fat farms of Durham, North Carolina. I first had myself shipped to Durham in 1979, at 325 pounds, to enter a diet program. At the behest of actor James Coco, I began to attend Structure House, a rigorous behavior-modification program that took 140 pounds off my frame and added years to my life.

Durham has been a mecca for flab since the 1940s, when an autocratic doctor named Walter Kempner of Duke University created a diet for patients with kidney disorders, which also happened to reduce weight radically. The Rice Diet was born and, publicized by Buddy Hackett and other celebrities, went on to bring hordes of "ricers" to Kempner's program. Kempner and other diet gurus are responsible for turning Durham into Fat City, USA.

Every week, "flab flights" land at Raleigh-Durham airport, trundling in obese patrons desperate for treatment. Amazingly, I was able to get laid on my sojourns. Herds of jabbering, perspiring women, their weight averaging out to, say, Stan Musial's lifetime batting average, threw themselves on men. Many were ordered here by their husbands, who could no longer stand the sight of them. Fat women are outcasts. They were too busy sucking down sundaes in their adolescence to ever have normal sexual development—no dates, no dances, no feverish fumble with their bra in the backseat of a Chevy. The touchstones of female experience are foreign to them.

The swimming pool at Duke Towers, where many fat people kept apartments, resembled an African watering hole beset by a herd of hippos. But as revolting as this may seem to skinny people, for the fat ones, it is the first timid step to some kind of sanity about their bodies. The dieting and attention given refocuses their attention. As the pounds drop off, so does all pretense of sexual subtlety, and the fatty becomes a sexual being. Local men, especially the black *playas*, knew that fat women were easy pickings.

Sexually, I could not bear to see myself when I was corpulent. The thought of having a mirror over the bed seeing myself fucking would be like examining my puke. I wanted the lights out. Airline treatment was but a small example of a fat person's humiliation and persecution. Fat people got a seat-belt extender placed around them. As if they cared to save a fat person's life. Fat people were treated like eight-year-olds by the stewardesses.

By 1979, when I lost 120 pounds, I went from being pornography's biggest ego and belly to a svelte man-about-town. I could suddenly see my own schlong, hidden for years behind layers of blubber. I had always eaten pussy, but now I could fuck again. Now the stewardesses would look at my eyes. I was perceived as a man, a possible sex partner. That was such a joy. Even food wasn't equal to that. It's a choice between being dead and alive.

I was particularly repulsed by fat guys in porn, at the very audacity that they could snag a part, no less maintain a career. Like that hirsute walrus, Ron Jeremy. My self-loathing was reflected in a 1983 *Screw* review of *Centerspread Girls*, which featured a fat leading man from Texas:

An indication of the film's bankrupt creativity is the appearance of a porno actor who, for me, is the biggest blob on screen. His name is Michael Morrison. And other than looking like the globular owner of Plato's Retreat, Larry Levenson, his attempts at sexual activity are self-burlesquing and moronic. This man should be forced to watch his own footage and then be compelled to attend Weight Watchers for twelve months until he has human dimensions.

At least when I was a fat slob I had the self-respect to keep my body out of the public arena. It not only upsets me to have to look at Morrison but, even more importantly, to feel utter contempt for the people behind this film for being so desperate to utilize his body in sex footage.

After writing this cruel assessment, I became friends with Morrison and interviewed him. Bawdy Blubber-Boy Tells All read *Screw*'s coverline that week, featuring an interview titled "Beauty and the Obese." Michael Morrison was humble and explained his popularity. "How can you identify with a Mike Ranger?" he said. "The guy's six-foot-two, gorgeous, he's got a twelve-inch cock, and it works. If the only people in X-rated films were gorgeous, then ninety percent of the guys in the audience would sit there and go, 'The only way you get laid by Seka or Marilyn Chambers is if you're gorgeous.'"

Morrison did fuck Seka and Marilyn Chambers and got paid for it. He had a small cock, but became a leading ladies' top choice for anal intercourse because of it. I prodded him about Jewish guys being preoccupied with cock size—but he remained a secure, self-effacing Texan, while I remained an insecure, self-loathing Jew. Morrison was totally secure about his small Irish cock, and he knew how to use it.

David Allan Coe

At country singer-songwriter David Allan Coe's home, they had a "quarantine" house rule—he put his girlfriends and wives in quarantine whenever they were on the rag. Coe also shared my desire for smaller tits:

AL: David, I'm going to ask you the kind of questions Tom Snyder always asks me. You're a fucking degenerate. You've been a pimp. You served tweny to thirty years of your life in prison. You killed a homosexual in prison. You live with seven wives. You're the ultimate degenerate personified. Where did you go wrong?

COE: [*laughs*] I don't know. I used to sniff a lot of glue and typewriter fluid when I was a kid. Maybe it fucked up my head. But, seriously . . . I first went to reform school when I was nine years old, and I grew up in institutions. My morals are different.

AL: According to what I've read about you, you killed a homosexual in prison. What motivated that violence?

COE: I'm not sure he was a homosexual . . . but I guess he was, because he wanted to fuck me in the ass. I might not have killed him if he wanted me to fuck him in *his* ass. It happened because he was trying to force me to do something I didn't want to do. The guy was threatening me physically. Fucking wasn't something that I wanted to do with him. Besides, he was a big, grizzly nigger.

AL: In other words, if he was a white WASP and said, "I love you, I want to have a meaningful relationship with you," you would have let him fuck you in the ass?

Coe: No, I don't think so. Like I said, I might have fucked him in his ass. You know, having been sent to institutions at such a young age, I spent most of my life warding off that kind of thing. It was just a matter of kill or be fucked.

Al: By the way, how big is your dick?

Coe: I would probably say, in all fairness to my dick and my seven wives, that it's probably maybe nine-and-a-half, ten inches.

Al: I read that you like women with small tits.

Coe: I don't like big tits, the reason being that I don't identify big tits as being feminine. Feminine to me was the guy in prison with the nice ass.

Al: You've said that you love pussy, but hate women.

Coe: I think it's because all the women that I'd ever met in my life were basically cunts. Now, I'm growing an awful lot in my relationships with women. When I first got out of prison, it was, "Hey, cunt, hand me a glass of water, and if you're not fast enough I'll knock your fuckin' brains out." And now, it's "Hey, babe, how about getting me a glass of water?" It might seem that I act real hard, but to me, it's coming a long way. Most of the women I used to come in contact with were dummies. I was never around businesswomen or any woman that had a fucking brain or idea. Now, I *have* been around those kinds of women. Some of my old ladies are very high in my organization.

They design album covers, make logos, run video equipment, and I'm realizing that they are, you know, people.

AL: Why are you so aggressive in pursuing yourself as a product?

COE: Okay, let's get this straight. It's sort of like the Indian selling shit-turquoise jewelry to the white man . . . I've packaged up the penitentiary in a book, and I've sold it right back to the motherfuckers that put me in prison. I packaged up the penitentiary in albums, and I sold it back to the motherfuckers that put me in prison. I only had twenty dollars when I got out. [As a kid] if I stayed out after eleven o'clock, they sent me back to the fucking joint. I got busted for possession of obscene literature. I had two pictures in my wallet of a naked girl, right, and I went to prison for one to seven years. I did six-and-a-half fucking years for possession of obscene literature, and now it's not even a crime.

AL: You could have been a publisher.

—*Screw*, April 1981

CHAPTER 19

The Mitchell Brothers

Why was porn so bad? It struck me as the ultimate self-fulfilling prophecy. This country stigmatized porn, ghettoized it, made it bear the burden of shame for centuries of antisexual Puritinism. It made adult entertainment a profession of guilt and then wondered why Mafia losers, failed hacks, and no-talent greaseballs got into it. Society gets exactly the type of porn it deserves.

There still hasn't been a significant, big-budget Hollywood porn film as envisioned by Terry Southern in his 1970 novel *Blue Movie*, nearly forty years ago. This is a tall order that remains to be done. Some of us tried to get sex out from under its rock to take its place beside other great urges of the human animal, like intellectualism or emotionalism—to assume its natural role in an integrated psyche. Most publishers in porn kept their identities a dark secret. They shared society's loathsome attitude toward sex, but were eager to make a living off it. They wanted the money and had no care for the social implications.

Cleveland smut mogul Ruben Sturman, for example, went incognito, on the lam while distributing an avalanche of pornography.

Cowards like Carl Ruderman, shadow publisher of *High Society*, had a near monopoly on phone-sex numbers, probably outgrossing AT&T. Ruderman stirred up the ire of environmentalists by building a heliport on his pristine Connecticut property, scattering wildlife every time he 'coptered in from New York. Publishers ashamed of the sex business included the late Chip Goodman (*Swank*, *Stag*), Murray Traub (*Oui*), and partners Bentley Morriff and Ralph Weinstock, who kept their names off the *Adam* family of men's magazines (*Adam Film World Guide*, etc.).

Hefner, Guccione, Goldstein, and Flynt—once the frontline Detroit of sex in America—proudly used their own names. In the case of Larry Flynt, he had to keep his disreputable name *off* any shitty mainstream periodicals he published—like his magazine for fat women that snagged a cover interview from the yapping prude, Kathie Lee Gifford.

Porn film directors born unto bland names used obvious pseudonyms, like Henri Pachard, Henri Paris, Damon Christian, Armand Weston, Alex deRenzy, Bruce Seven, on and on. Carter Stevens, for instance, was born Mal Whorb. But there were two siblings using their own names, present from the beginning, who held the lowly mantle of pornography high. They were the Mitchell Brothers.

I knew Jim and Artie Mitchell well, or so I thought. Whenever I visited San Francisco, Jim and Artie sent a stream of pussy to my hotel room, where I got stoned and indulged. I saw them as pug-faced, black Irish, salt-of-the-earth, passionate pornographers. But in 1991, Jim shot his younger brother Artie to death. Theirs was the second disturbing case, after Holmes, that made me question the culpability of pornography.

The Mitchell Brothers opened the two-hundred-seat O'Farrell Theatre in 1969. Hunter Thompson called it "the Carnegie Hall of public sex in America." The Mitchells' best movie, *Behind the Green Door*, was third in the triumvirate of porn films, after *Deep Throat* and *The Devil in Miss Jones*, to become a cultural phenomenon in the early seventies. Costing sixty-thousand-dollars to produce, it initially grossed $30 million, and continues selling as a staple of porn to this day.

At the debut of *Green Door*, the movie reels were shown out of sequence, but nobody noticed. "The only Art in this business is my brother," said Jim. They had an ongoing battle with San Francisco mayor Dianne Feinstein, echoing my own with Mayor Lindsay. Taking a cue from *Screw*, perhaps, they would post her private phone number on their marquee: "For show times call . . ." As soon as the mayor changed her number, they'd somehow find out and repost the new one.

The Mitchells came out of the sweetness-and-light side of the porn world, the side born during the Summer of Love in San Francisco. It held that sex was honest, healthy, a path to human enlightenment. Their own brand of enlightenment began in college, when Jim would pay girls five bucks to be photographed topless, then sell the pictures to sex stores at a profit. When the brothers were kids, it was said, their transplanted Okie parents would bring home road kill to cook for dinner. They spoke with a slight Oklahoma drawl, growing up among other dust bowl migrants in Antioch, California. Their father was a professional gambler who made his living playing lowball and Texas hold 'em in smoky back rooms of the East Bay. After workers got their paychecks from the U.S. Steel foundry or the local paper plant, pappy Mitchell went to work.

The cop who arrested Jim Mitchell, on February 27, 1991, received a report of gunshots at 23 Mohawk Avenue, across the Golden Gate Bridge in the San Francisco suburb of Corte Madera. He saw a man stiff-legging it down the rain-slicked street, clutching a folded umbrella even though it was raining. There was a .22 rifle stuck down Jim Mitchell's pants, the reason for his odd, Charlie Chaplin tramp walk. Jim had just fired the three shots that killed his brother Artie. Artie was forty-five when he died, and Jim forty-seven, so it was the end of a two-brother tag team that had spent their lives watching each other's back.

People were forgiving of Jim Mitchell, recognizing that he probably punished himself more severely than any court could. He may be the country's only pornographer to have had a public official testify to his character during his bail hearing—State Senator Quentin Kopp was among a dozen people who spoke on Jim's behalf, just before he was released on a half-million-dollar bond. For a short time after the murder, the O'Farrell Theatre posted a sign reading Closed Due to a Death in the Family. Then it was back to business as usual.

"I love Uncle Jim," said Artie's seventeen-year-old daughter Mariah at her father's memorial service. "No matter what, he's my uncle, and I love him."

Why would Tweedledee kill Tweedledum? Did Jim totally lose his marbles?

"That conclusion is consistent with the facts as we know them at this point," said his attorney, Michael Kennedy, at the time. Jim Mitchell's defense lawyers were Dennis Roberts, a civil rights advocate and defender of Black Panthers, Chicago 7 members, and pot activists; and Michael Kennedy, the legal overseer of *High Times* magazine, who'd represented Timothy Leary and the Weather Underground.

As with John Holmes, the whole case was tailormade for blood-to-ink media stories. *Hard Copy* and *Inside Edition* did their obligatory sex-drugs-and-fratricide rave-ups. I ran across four scripts in the making, while covering the trial myself. "The private life of a slain pornographer: is it a movie, or a mini-series?" asked the *Los Angeles Times* in an article on Karen "Kay" Mitchell, Artie's ex. She went to L.A. to "explore the Hollywood options of her life." It ended up a lousy Showtime movie, called *Rated X*, with real-life brothers Emilio Estevez and Charlie Sheen as the Mitchells.

Kay tried to get Artie into rehab and engaged the help of brother Jim a few weeks before the killing. The prosecution stated that Jim parked three blocks away, slashed his brother's tires before he went in and shot him. "This was a premeditated murder, and the suspect was involved in careful execution of the crime," said the dick on the case. But no one could offer a viable motive.

"These guys were just like twins," said Chuck Traynor. "They drove the same cars, rode the same bikes. They ran the business, did everything together." The Mitchell Brothers had a strong sense of family, and spawned a brood of nine kids from two marriages each. The media loved to harp on that theme, questioning how such good family men could be smut merchants. In 1990, Artie almost drowned trying to save his son Storm, whom he thought was lost in a riptide off Ocean Beach, and Jim almost drowned trying to save Artie. Everyone wound up safe—the Surf and Rescue Squad that showed up got a ten-thousand-dollar contribution and lifetime passes to the O'Farrell Theater.

The Mitchells probably made thousands of shit-quality, hand-held camera loops, starting in the late sixties, when an underground railroad of pornography began steaming in from California for East Coast distribution. Theirs was a hippie porn aesthetic, promoting free love. They opened the O'Farrell on July 4, 1969, a counterpart to the sexual revolution *Screw* was spearheading in New York. San Francisco authorities saw it as a return to the pirate depravity of the Barbary Coast, and the place was busted three weeks after opening.

The Mitchell Brothers versus the Censors paralleled my battles in New York. At first they were fighting for their lives and livelihood. They wanted to stay out of jail and keep the O'Farrell marquee lit. But then they started to become First Amendment idealists, and that would become their legacy.

Jim and Artie would spend up to half a million dollars a year on legal fees—an amount that rivaled *Screw*'s own defense budget. Artie would say that half of the twenty-dollar admission to the O'Farrell was taken right off the top to feed the barracudas in suits. One of the most far-reaching court battles the Mitchells ever fought—and they had to fight it all the way to the Supreme Court—was one few know about. In connection with *Behind the Green Door*, they established the right of sexually explicit material to enjoy copyright protection. That made porn films marketable, more lucrative, and led to the porn-film boom of the seventies. It is also the reason that the first thing you see on most porn videos is a stern FBI warning against piracy. Just what J. Edgar Hoover intended, when he founded the Bureau.

JIM MITCHELL

AL: Why have the pirates been so successful when you, as a distributor, ship your prints openly? You take advertisements in *Variety*. Why is it that they've been able to get their duped prints around while you haven't been able to get a legitimate print to the same theater?

MITCHELL: No, I've been able to get a legitimate print to any theater. I haven't had any problems. The pirates just beat us to some theaters.

AL: Why, or how?

MITCHELL: Better sales force. They're covering more territory than we are. They're basically dealing with a lot of people's skim and we're not. Once you're a skimmer, you're a skimmer and skimmers skim together.

AL: So, a crooked theater owner would prefer to buy a pirated print because there'd be no records anywhere?

MITCHELL: That's right.

AL: Getting back to organized pirating, do you think that if the government's attitude changed towards porno that would mitigate the situation in any way?

MITCHELL: Yeah, in fact, that is the single biggest obstacle now. The government's got a lot more pressure on. . . .

AL: There was a robbery about a month ago when two guys dressed as cops broke into a porno theater and threatened to arrest the manager, but what they actually did was run up to the projection booth and steal the print of *Deep Throat*. Now if there were a lot of pirated prints around, it seems they could have bought it a little easier.

MITCHELL: That had to be Bobby DeSalvo's boys going in.

AL: Why do you say that?

MITCHELL: Because DeSalvo's policing *Deep Throat*. There's a million dupes of *Deep Throat*. DeSalvo's trying to control *Deep*

Throat just as he's trying to control *Devil* . . . I've heard of
DeSalvo himself going in. I've seen a theater in San Francisco
burned to the ground that's playing the two pictures, unautho-
rized prints. . . . No one is safe from these shit suckers. They
justify their scavenging someone else's hard work and bleed it
dry, for every penny it's worth, without returning a cent to its
original creator. The pirating will continue until one of two
things happens: (1) the civil courts get behind those whose
rightful property is being misused no matter what the content
and/or (2) the theater owners and exhibitors stand up for their
own future and accept only bona fide distribution of whatever
product their houses play.

—*Screw*, August 1974

Loosely based on *Steppenwolf*, by Herman Hesse, *Behind the Green
Door* is the surreal adventure of a girl's trip into sexual fantasy.
Green Door's production values went beyond other films of the day,
and certainly surpass the crap produced today. But what made it a
hit was the ink given to Marilyn Chambers, when it was revealed
she was the Ivory Snow girl. She showed up at the O'Farrell in
answer to an open-call newspaper ad, and when she read the part
in the questionnaire asking if the performer preferred a sexual or a
nonsexual role, she decided to leave. Chambers was a fair maiden
from Stamford, Connecticut—she had never done anything dirty.

When Chambers turned to leave, there was Artie at the top of the
stairs, near the office, yelling out for her to wait. Marilyn paused and
was soon won over by Jim and Artie's smooth game and hippie
charm. Ten minutes later, she had her shirt off and was posing for
Polaroids. "They were easygoing and honest and on the same wave-
length as I was, and I sensed that right away," Chambers said. Within

a short time, she was hanging off chandeliers, sucking giant black cocks—and taking John Holmes up the ass.

When Marilyn casually mentioned the fact that she was a model whose face happened to grace the cover of every Ivory Soap box in America, the Mitchells must have *plotzed*. They fed that tidbit to the wire services, then sat back while the media went apeshit. Marilyn was jerked from the stores, but the movie was international news.

By 1975, their porn theater chain had expanded to eleven locations, valued at $50 million. One of those theaters, in the straight-laced southern California town of Santa Ana, was the largest-grossing adult venue in the world. Republican Orange County spent more money masturbating than any county in America, but a self-appointed guardian of public morals descended upon the Mitchells. That was Charles Keating, Jr., whose rampaging censorship group, Citizens for Decency Through Law, was riding high. Keating personally took it upon himself to close the Mitchells down, as he also tried with *Screw*. Jim and Artie spent several hundred thousand dollars defending themselves and beat Keating cold in court. Their Santa Ana theater didn't close until 1990, when the Mitchell Brothers lost the lease. Charles Keating, however, was sentenced ten years in prison for the Lincoln Savings & Loan scandal, bilking "decent citizens" out of a billion dollars.

The heyday of the O'Farrell rivaled Times Square. Dancers took showers with patrons, and Artie rented out flashlights to amateur gynecologists who shined the everlovin' light upon perinea in a dark room. The Ultra Room had eight women circulating the stage. A patron could choose from thirty booths, lock himself in, and feed quarters to the hungry slot. As the barrier rose within, Californians could ream out the dancers' spuzz boxes or slobber like hyenas all over their titties. House rules dictated that the dick was to say in the pants—but with the door locked, thousands of peckers sprung forth, draining jism from their hot boiling balls upon the floor. It was a mess to be reckoned with.

It was in this period that Hunter S. Thompson, reporting for the *San Francisco Examiner*, became "night manager" of the O'Farrell. His function was to lend "legitimacy" to the proceedings. In this environment, it became harder to place the Mitchell Brothers in the context of Free Love and 1960s ideals, from which they sprung. Many women at the O'Farrell complained of harassment and violent treatment at the now out-of-control hands of Artie Mitchell. Artie's attitude changed: what was the fun of owning a porn theater if you couldn't grab, suck, and fuck? If you worked for Arite, you were fair game. The Mitchells liked to say that the O'Farrell represented one big family, where the girls loved the Brothers, loved working there. But the family had an uncle whose nieces ran for cover. Artie would take a dancer out, make her his official "girlfriend," ask her to babysit his kids, and then disappear, partying for days on end. When one babysitting girlfriend would storm off, another would take her place.

The inner sanctum was the Mitchells' upstairs office at the O'Farrell, a goodtime place where there was always cold beer, vodka on ice, and a big Wurlitzer rock 'n' roll jukebox. No desks, only a pool table. One or two cronies were always present: Warren Hinckle, a local columnist; Dan O'Neill, a local cartoonist; Ron Turner of Last Gasp Comics; and Thompson, when he was in town.

In a celebration of my monumental weight loss, I was lured to appear onstage at the O'Farrell in 1981. Jim and Artie set up a half-dozen girls for me to fuck. "Hold out till the last one," Artie rasped into my ear. "She's a knockout. Remember, don't come until the last one."

Buck Henry flew in from L.A. in to watch my svelte, handsome figure onstage doing live sex. Buck was repressed and private, never more than a voyeur. Jim and Artie were in the audience, drunk and stoned as usual, hooting and hollering. Hunter Thompson had white powder all over his nose. I fucked five girls in succession, holding my essence for the one who would be the grand finale. I got ready for the sixth girl. Suddenly Artie was beside me, looking like a coked-out leprechaun. "Sorry, Al," he said. "The sixth girl called in sick."

Both Mitchells broke down laughing, like a couple of frat boys who died and went to heaven in the porn business. All of a sudden, a sixth girl did come running out onstage, in a gorilla suit with a dildo strapped to her waist. She'd been paid by Thompson to fuck me in the ass. I ran for my life. I never got to ejaculate, and still feel frustrated twenty-five years later.

The Mitchell Brothers tried to put an innovative safe-sex spin on *Behind the Green Door II,* their big-budget sequel. They hoped America was looking for a film that featured midgets, freaks, and a four-hundred-pound woman, as well as sex with condoms and dental dams. They lost their shirts.

In 1985, Mayor Dianne Feinstein sent two dozen cops to a live appearance by Marilyn Chambers. Chambers was arrested, presumably on charges of "prostitution," but they were quickly dropped. The Mitchells were continually charged with obscenity, but by 1986, after millions in taxpayers' money had been wasted in court, the fiasco ended with no convictions. When a judge tried to smear them in court, referring to the last days of Sodom and Gomorrah, the Mitchells decided to title their next film *Sodom and Gomorrah.* But their eleven-theater chain had shrunk to two rental places.

When I ran into Jim and Artie at the Cannes Film Festival, Artie grabbed hold of my date and began dry-humping her. Conduct unbecoming of a pornographer. But I quickly forgave him because I wanted to dry-hump the woman he was with.

"I always thought I'd like France," Jim told me. "It's too much like America. Do you know what our hotel is costing?" Though they were still millionaires, they worried about their hotel room charge. On his arrival Artie immediately announced he was a "pornographer," taking delight in *epater le bourgeois*. But Jim became uneasy about his smut reputation, and talked only of making mainstream films. Artie stayed lost in a haze of vodka and Columbian reefer. Their empire was crumbling. The Brothers planned to break up their business—Jim would stay with the theater, Artie would go on a recovery hiatus in Mexico.

The breakup had the appearance of going smoothly, but the separation of Siamese twins always involves blood. Rather than Cain and Abel, I thought of the original Siamese twins, Chang and Eng. Chang died of a stroke in the middle of the night. He was the sickly one who drank too much. When Eng woke up beside him and found that his brother was dead, he died of fright, right there in the bed.

The last time I saw the Mitchells was in January 1991, a month before the shooting. They received an award from the Adult Video Association, and came together to the black-tie event in Los Angeles. A whacked-out Artie Mitchell got up and mumbled incoherently into the mike. Then Jim nudged Artie out of the way and began screaming at someone in the audience. In the days before he died, Artie left rambling, snarling messages on Jim's answering machine, promising mayhem to Jim and his new girlfriend if the breakup of the Mitchell Brothers' corporation wasn't handled right. "I'll fuck you both up," Artie vowed.

"I think Artie wanted it to happen," said their friend, Richard Lackey, speaking of the shooting. "Jim just pulled the trigger, but they were so close, it was really suicide."

• • •

Four months after posting a half-million in bail for the murder of his brother, Jim hosted a huge wake party for Artie at the O'Farrell. The "Artie Fund" was established, and still raises funds for the San Francisco Fire Department Cliff and Surf Rescue Team. Civic donations provide good public-relations spin, and help keep heat off the O'Farrell, still open today. Among the hundred letters urging compassion when Jim Mitchell was sentenced was one from then–San Francisco mayor, Frank Jordan. Jim was sentenced to six years for manslaughter and served only three at San Quentin; he was out by 1997.

I should have set up a fire department donation fund at *Screw*.

Melvin Van Peebles

Around 1960, while studying for a degree in astronomy in Holland, Peebles recalled, the Museum of France saw his short films and declared him a genius:

PEEBLES: So I got to France and they kissed me on both cheeks saying we're so glad you could come. So I stood on the shore with two wet cheeks and nothing, man. And I decided right then and there I was going to make it or die trying. So I went back to the oldest profession in the world. A lot of cats come over there, especially if they're a brother and look halfway decent, and they're a rarity, they can pick themselves up a countess. Gigiloing is pretty together. Pimping is pretty much out. There are certain factions that have that sewed up. But I devised a little system of going around with very poor shopgirls. Because if you go around with a countess or a baroness, she doesn't work all day and she's got nothing to do but take you out on a leash—she's got to show you her friends, you've got to go out on a yacht, you've got to go to St. Tropez and all that shit. You don't get any work done. . . .

SCREW: You said one of your favorite reviews of *Sweet Sweet-back's Baadasssss Song* was the one Al Goldstein did in *Screw*. Why was that?

PEEBLES: He gave me a nice, offensive, authentic review. That's where it's at. . . . Al's a schmuck. That's my kind of people. It's not only the review itself, but the flavor of the review. . . . You got to remember that everybody refused to review this film. *Life*, *Look*, the *Daily News* never reviewed it. Hell, I made $5 million before three white people in America had ever seen the film.

—*Screw*, November 1971

CHAPTER 20

Larry Flynt

Flynt and I were friends before *Hustler* started in 1974. He would fly me down to Columbus, Ohio, for his orgies. He owned topless clubs. There'd be twenty dancers and sixteen distributors there, guys he was priming for national distribution when his *Hustler* newsletter went glossy. Althea Flynt would make sure the girls stayed clean, because some of them were smelly. The dancers were local farm girls, not too smart, so Althea would wash down their assholes herself. There was a big Jacuzzi in the hotel, with the distributors invited. The girls would promote these Dr. Columbo–brand vibrators Flynt was selling. He'd get them all sexed up on the vibrators, then they'd start sucking dicks of the distributors. That's how this fucking hillbilly from Lickskillet, Kentucky, got national distribution.

Larry poached my editors over the years, which didn't bother me: I have always considered my employees to be like Kleenex—meant to be used and discarded. I felt less generous about Flynt shanghaiing my lawyers, such as Herald Price Fahringer and Paul Cambria, since decent legal help is both hard to find and critical to my survival.

Throughout the seventies and early eighties *Hustler* stole shamelessly from *Screw*, becoming a colorized redneck imitator. Flynt was a thief, and admitted it during his *Midnight Blue* interview. Our "Smut from the Past" became their "Porn from the Past," my "ShitList" became their "Asshole of the Month." If you wanted to know what satirical pieces would run in *Hustler*, you only needed to look back a few months at *Screw*.

Two instances of Flynt's plagiarism may have contributed to his troubles. During America's two-hundredth birthday celebration, *Hustler* carried a two-page illustration that depicted Henry Kissinger, Gerald Ford, and Nelson Rockefeller gang-raping the Statue of Liberty. Called "Bicentennial Ball," it was supposed to be a comment on government abuse of power. Oddly enough, the year before, *Screw* ran an identical centerfold illustration, by Richard Jaccoma, depicting Kissinger, Ford, and Rockefeller gang-raping the Statue of Liberty—called "Bicentennial Ball."

For *Hustler*'s trouble in copying us, the Cleveland D.A. saw fit to press obscenity charges against *Hustler*. These charges were dropped, but Larry's hometown of Cincinnati picked up the charges and convicted Larry of obscenity there. A series of cases followed, leading to Larry's fateful day in the unlikely locale of Lawrenceville, Georgia, in 1978, where Fahringer headed Flynt's defense.

When Larry returned from lunch to the courtroom, two bullets were fired that left him paralyzed for life. One hit Flynt's local attorney, a gray-haired gent in a blue suit, who resembled Fahringer. Fahringer was ten feet away. The assassin was probably gunning for Flynt *and* Fahringer, not the local lawyer, who did recover. The prosecutor suggested that Fahringer leave town ASAP. I flew to Flynt's bedside within twenty-four hours for moral support. It could have just as easily been me. Larry's initial argument was that the shooter was a CIA operative.

A deranged white supremacist was accused in the Flynt shooting. Conspiracy buffs suspected Flynt's recent offer of a million dollars for new information on the JFK assassination may have prompted the shooting. Others saw the markings of a teamster hit, because Flynt started his own distribution company for *Hustler*, a big no-no in the magazine biz. But the shooting was apparently the result of a Klan serial killer who objected to seeing a black cock and a blonde woman in a *Hustler* pictorial. He had already shot a number of blacks, wounding Vernon Jordan, but said he was sorry for shooting Larry.

More amusing, Flynt's hard-up staff "borrowed" our Campari ad for their Jerry Falwell parody. We'd been running a version of the 1981 Campari liquor campaign, which used a double entendre focusing on the drinker's "first time."

"Al Goldstein Talks about His First Time" made me out to be a faggot. In *Hustler*'s twist, they had Moral Majority founder Jerry Falwell talking about the first time he fucked his mother in an outhouse, where she attracted more flies than the shit.

Falwell's reaction was priceless. He said *Hustler* had attacked him from "the very pits of hell. . . . I have never been as angry as I was at that moment. I somehow felt that in all of my life I had never believed that human beings could do something like this."

Falwell called his lawyer and simply ordered: "Get him." The lawsuit was for $45 million, and raised the question as to whether someone could be sued for inflicting emotional distress upon a public figure. Falwell was initially awarded two hundred thousand dollars for his outhouse experience, but Fahringer was able to have that knocked out on appeal. It was a four-year battle, right up to the Supreme Court, with Flynt emerging victorious, as well as staunching defamation suits every time a pompous celebrity was parodied.

Albert Speer

Over the years, Al Goldstein—and a succession of *Screw* managing editors—tried on numerous occasions to get Albert Speer to grant *Screw* an interview. Needless to say, Speer refused. Just before his death, however, on September 1, 1981, an intense period of personal reassessment forced Speer to decide that the complete story of Nazi Germany had not been told. Through intermediaries, he actually took the initiative to contact Al Goldstein's office in New York. Speer asserted that he had decided it was time to do an interview "of a sexual nature," partially in preparation for a longer work on sexuality and the Nazi movement, to be published posthumously. The sole restriction was that the interview was not to be published until ninety days after his death.

Speer rose from a minor architectural post in the Nazi party to become Hitler's right-hand man and minister of armaments. Almost single-handedly, he reorganized the German war machine—to the point, some experts say, of prolonging WWII by a full two years. His designs for Nuremberg's mass Nazi rallies were blueprints for megalomania. He had said of his intimacy with the German *Fueher*: "If Hitler had a friend, I was that friend."

On August 15, 1981, Al Goldstein flew to Germany to speak with Speer at his country home outside Heidelberg. Al offered to provide a German translator for the interview; but Speer, who had become trilingual during his years in *Spandau* Prison, asserted that he would be just as comfortable speaking in English. Thus, the interview—which took two-and-a-half hours and is twenty thousand words long in complete transcript—was conducted in English.

A Frank Lloyd Wright with a *hakenkruez*, Hitler's grease monkey for the Holocaust, Speer was glib enough to talk his way past the gallows at Nuremberg. He could not, however, talk his way past Al Goldstein. A small excerpt from the text of this historic interview:

AL: I am probably the epitome of everything the Nazis hated: the Jew pornographer who besmirches the pure morals of the white Aryan world. Hitler would have thought of me as the Devil incarnate. So why did you consent to talk to me?

SPEER: Just exactly for that reason: because you are the ultimate product of Germany's defeat.

AL: Thanks.

SPEER: People who first meet me are constantly trying to uncover vestiges of secret anti-Semitism. I suppose it would do no good to assert the truth for the thousandth time—that I do *not* hate Jews. But the reason I've consented to see you is that I realize now how intimately the whole German experience in the Nazi era was tied up in sex. After thinking for almost fifteen years—I'll be out of Spandau [Prison, where Speer was incarcerated for war crimes] for fifteen years on the thirtieth of next month—I have come to realize that all recent German history is a metaphor for sex—an attempt to transform the sex urge into national spirit, probably mistaken. All of it seems wrapped up, somehow, in what the great Semitic philosopher, Sigmund Freud, has called the libido.

AL: Let's talk about that. The way I see it, the early history of the Nazis was made up of a struggle between the homosexual contingent—represented by the SA, also known as the Brownshirts—and the sadomasochistic contingent, represented by the SS. Where did you stand in all of this?

SPEER: Well, off to the side. I am, of course, a confirmed het-
erosexual, and had a normal sex life—or I did before the war.
All of which made me quite the freak amongst the top echelon
of Hitler's administration. There were many raging homosexuals, that is for certain. Especially in the early days, the National
Socialist headquarters looked like some sort of public bath,
there were so many queers strolling about. Pimps, hustlers,
petty thieves, and riff-raff of all types came out of the cold into
the warmth of the SA. What a joke it was to have [Baldur von]
Schirach as the leader of Hitler Youth! He was an outrageous
bisexual, and plucked the cherries from the ranks to be his personal "brownies," as he called them, probably because they
always had his excrement on their faces. [SS Security Chief
Reinhard] Heydrich had a folder on him, in full *Hitler Jugend*
regalia, little peasant cap and *leder hosen*—only these were
pulled down, and he had one blonde boy in front and a pair of
twin girls in back, tonguing him. . . . Disgusting. Add up the
ages of those three beautiful fresh-faced children, and you
wouldn't have come up with more than twenty-five. Then,
Deputy Party Chief Rudolph Hess, of course, whom we used
to call Fraulein Hess; he was homosexual. . . . The most outrageous libertine of all, however, was [*Luftwaffe* Chief] Her-
mann Goering. After the war started, when his heroin
addiction began to overwhelm him, he was never without
scarlet fingernail polish. There are others, of course. Hans
Frank, whom Hitler appointed governor-general of Poland,
and who came off publicly as hating homosexuals—he was a
queer who had his lovers killed immediately after—and sometimes while—he penetrated them.

AL: But all this was stopped by the Blood Purge and the execution of Roehm, on the so-called Night of the Long Knives [June 30, 1934]. Where were you that night?

SPEER: I was in Berlin at that time. And it was definitely a case of the homosexuals being pushed out by the S&M crowd.

AL: You have always strongly denied that Hitler was a homosexual. Have you changed your feelings on that?

SPEER: Well, I think that the urge was present in him. And if you think of German history between 1933 and 1945 as an objectification of the battle within Hitler's psyche, then the Night of the Long Knives becomes his heterosexuality brutally repressing his homosexuality. He told me Roehm and his coterie nauseated him. After the purge, Hitler fell more and more under the sway of [SS Chief Heinrich] Himmler's sort of sadistic cultism. Heydrich had some documents to the effect that for years, Hitler had been a male whore in Vienna, in the first decade of the century. Hitler's biggest hero, the man he modeled himself after, Frederick the Great, was an effeminate homosexual who demanded to be sodomized in the behind by his own ministers. There was always speculation that the Brownshirt Roehm had seduced Hitler in their early years as Nazis. In fact, he may have had Roehm killed out of shame.

AL: Hitler had shame?

SPEER: Certainly. Oh, and one fact about Hitler I can personally testify to was that he only had one testicle.

AL: How did you discover that?

SPEER: I've admitted all along that Hitler and I were very close—in a nonsexual way. He saw himself as my protector in a sense; perhaps because I was so much younger than he. But it was during a weekend I spent with him at Eagle's Nest—his fantastic mountain retreat in the Alps. We were bathing in a natural hot springs—nude, of course, and—

AL: That brings up one thing I definitely must ask: how big was Hitler's penis?

SPEER: It's been so many years I can hardly recall. . . . Mine, I know, was quite a bit larger than Adolph's, which would make his, eight, maybe nine—

AL: Nine inches! Holy Christ, that's twice as big as my own cock, only four inches less than John—

SPEER: Centimeters . . . no, no, centimeters . . .

—*Screw*, December 1981

[The interview goes on to reveal that Hitler's paternal grandfather was a Jew, with an odd derivative of the name Goldstein, putting the grandfather's lineage on track as a lost European grand uncle of *Daily Mirror* photographer, Sam Goldstein—thus, the real reason Speer summoned Al to Germany. "Thank you, oh cousin of *mein Fueher!*" cries Speer.]

CHAPTER 21

Kansas

By 1974, fourteen states allowed *Screw* to be sold, while it was banned in thirty-six. Buckley and I headed *Screw*'s payroll, with official salaries of $1,550 per week each. Our subscription list included 122 college libraries and the Library of Congress. Buckley and I had a Rube Goldberg device connected between our desks to send messages to each other. That's because we were barely talking. *Screw* had become a reflection of my own mammoth ego, expanding girth, and big mouth; my founding partner cut a quiet, more dignified figure, handling the business end.

In 1974, my ex-son Jordan was born. Jordan's birth announcement was a mock *Screw* cover showing Gena nursing him, with these come-on headlines: TALES FROM THE CRIB! THE DIRT ON DIAPERS! BREAST-CRAZY KIDS! WATER SPORTS FOR BEGINNERS! I was a newspaperman at the core.

The tits on a wooden torso of a woman lit up every time my private phone rang. We ran a photo purporting to be of Israeli Prime Minister Golda Meir's old Jewish cunt. Don't ask me where it came from, probably some disgruntled rabbi. Because of the increase in mailed death threats, I got a burglar alarm, bulletproof glass for my office and now wore a bulletproof vest. I wanted to get a bulletproof jockstrap. I got extra death threats for dumping Joe DiMaggio in the "ShitList" toilet. It was a special *fongool* "Fuck You" for hawking Mr. Coffee, which made your coffee taste like piss, and for whoring the Bowery Savings Bank, where the working stiff saw his meager savings ravaged by inflation. One threat arrived on cassette tape, the guy yelling he would strangle me because I was so vile, I was corrupting America, and only a Jew could stoop so low.

Then one afternoon in June somebody knocked on *Screw*'s outside door saying they were delivering food. It was Pavlovian—mention food and my doors open wide. I said, "Let him in." So two ugly goons walked in and pulled out big shiny guns. One put a gun to my head, the other threw people on the floor. I had a shotgun in the office, but didn't go for it because I assumed at first this was another obscenity arrest.

My father now worked in the mailroom at *Screw*, getting things wrong. I fired him once, then rehired him. As seventeen of us lay with our hands on our heads, I remember looking over at my father, thinking here he works for me and we're laying on the floor being stuck up. This never happened at Hearst.

One of them said, "Us guineas are tired of what you been writing about the Family." I'd recently lowered several massage parlors' ratings, for being sleazy and despicable, referring to one as resembling "a Mafia pool hall." Staffers and some hookers and pimps, who'd just dropped by to place ads were piled up together. We were ordered to remove our jewelry and hand over wallets and purses. The goons kept talking about putting silencers on their guns and killing us. I had just become a father two weeks before, and thought about Jordan growing up without me.

But then my thoughts turned to the more immediate matter of protecting the twenty-five-hundred dollar Pulsar watch on my wrist. It was the best thing I owned. I'd been using it to time the intervals between sex scenes when reviewing fuck films. So I slipped the watch under my shirt. Then, when I was dragged up by the hair, a gun jammed against my head, the watch slid down my shirt into my pants leg. I kicked it under a hooker who was lying next to me. Later I told her she could have a year's free advertising in *Screw* for shielding my watch with her body.

One gunman slammed me into the wall, repeating, "You're gonna have to stop writing about us." I anticipated a pistol-whipping. Some of my staffers, who were into masochism, probably would have come in their pants. But not me. I reached into my pants and gave them my last twenty-dollar bill.

We never found out who they were, but they obviously used "the Family" reference as a cover to throw us off track. If it had been real mob-associated renegades, DiB would have had them killed.

I was the October 1974 *Playboy* interview, which gave me a national forum. Outside of New York, we were sold in the biggest cities, but not the towns and hamlets of heartland America. I hadn't been arrested in almost two years, and that was making me nervous. Plenty of libel suits, old convictions to be dealt with, but no *new* obscenity arrests. Where was I failing? So I boasted in *Playboy* that *Screw* would only be getting dirtier and dirtier. I needed the attention of being arrested, the thrill of it, being carried off in handcuffs—that would mean I was still a bug up the ass of the establishment, disturbing the status quo, a gadfly to the state. Acceptance of *Screw* would be the kiss of death.

But locally, the legal experts were still giving me comfort. Long Island Assemblyman Vincent Balletta called *Screw* "dirt, filth, not fit for anybody to read." Sociologist Saul Chaneles said, "It has no place in the marketplace of ideas." Manhattan Criminal Court Judge Joel Tyler wrote that *Screw* "goes substantially beyond the present critical point in compromise between candor and shame at which the community may have arrived."

In 1974, New York Court of Appeals Justice John Gabrielli wrote, "It's hard to conceive how a publication could reach any further lows in attempts to appeal to prurient interests." The U.S. Supreme Court agreed, denying us hearings on several New York obscenity convictions. Four of the Justices were Nixon appointees. *Screw*'s words were unpalatable to the limited minds seated on the bench. We didn't buffer our sex photos with academic bullshit or redeeming social value. A hard-on was its own redeeming value. There was intrinsic value in the very fact that somebody got one. The courts argued, in effect, that a soft cock was more redeeming than a hard cock. As I sat in the courtroom in Albany and heard the old judges refer to fucking as the "ultimate sex activity"—I realized it's them against me. They were old people who didn't fuck anymore. I took their guilty verdict and used it for our subscription ads, placed in the *New York Review of Books*, *Evergreen*, and *Screw*: "Four out of five judges agree—*Screw* is obscene!"

Finally, at the end of the year, in December 1974, Jim Buckley and I were charged in a twelve-count federal indictment for mailing obscene material into Kansas. When the federal marshals barged into my townhouse on East Sixty-first Street with an arrest warrant, saying I was wanted in Wichita, I thought it was a practical joke. Wichita? We don't distribute to Wichita. I couldn't even place the city on my mental map of the U.S. But we were being ordered to stand trial as New York pornographers two thousand miles away, a place where authorities figured we would be most hated.

The federal agents handcuffed me, led me out and bundled me into their car. The doorman across the street gaped at the scene. I was embarrassed—this guy who I joked with, who thought I was a big-shot when I slipped him a copy of *Screw*, was witnessing my public humiliation.

By evening, marshals had Buckley and me in cuffs on planes bound for Kansas. We flew in criminal class, a notch below coach. We were whisked into a Wichita jail before we knew what hit us; all within tweny-four hours, with no chance to talk to our lawyers for intervention.

It would be days before Herald Price Fahringer was able to get us released on bond. We then learned that issues of *Screw*, and our cheap spinoff tabloid, *Smut*, had been mail-ordered by postal officials in Wichita. When they received the mags they'd ordered using false names, they were able to charge us with sending obscene material through the mails. In other words, once we sent them what they asked us to send them, they accused us of sending it to them. But we knew the orders came from high up in the Nixon Administration. I've always believed it was Nixon himself. Legend has it that the aging J. Edgar Hoover's last directive was: "Get Goldstein." This, after our "Is J. Edgar Hoover a Fag?" issue. Within my wide circle of friends, including news hacks and power brokers—who wish to remain anonymous—the Nixon directive was no secret.

Enter Herald Price Fahringer, who would become my leading First Amendment lawyer for decades. It was hard for people to imagine this meticulously manicured attorney who once pronounced, "A neat way about you conveys a neat mind," running around the country defending obscenity cases. Fahringer defended *Deep Throat* and *The Devil in Miss Jones*. "I find much of the material I defend extremely distasteful," he once said. "What bothers me more is that the govern-ment interferes in any fashion with our right to read what we want."

Fahringer grew up poor in small-town Pennsylvania. He originally wanted to be an actor, and once was a member of British character actor Arthur Treacher's traveling theatrical troupe. People would stop him on the street: "Hey, aren't you the guy in the Remington shaver commercial?" He was. Fahringer represented cases that many considered to be the dregs of society—Claus von Bulow, Jean Harris, the killer of Scarsdale Diet doctor Herman Tarnower, jazz drummer Buddy Rich, and after me, that lowest dreg of all, Larry Flynt. He would later represent a coalition of over a hundred Times Square sex establishments when Mayor Guiliani rezoned the area to be rid of them. The cleanup law stipulated that 60 percent of their shelf space be relegated to nonsexual merchandise—and so, Times Square porn stores would now brim over with the Popeye videos dubbed in Spanish and Eric Estrada movies that we see today.

When we were finally sprung on bond, we sat down, went over what was at stake, and worked out our battle plan. Jim and I were looking down the barrel at sixty years' worth of jail time apiece. We were faced with hundreds of thousands of dollars in fines and penalties. Win or lose, we'd have to shell out six figures in legal fees alone. Paul Cambria was also on our team, who would also later represent Flynt, and *Puritan* magazine; Arthur Schwartz was Buckley's personal lawyer.

Up until now, the typical smut peddler in handcuffs would cower like a rat cornered in the glare of a flashlight, and scurry back into their rat hole. Due to ostracism, shame, and cowardice, they would typically go on the lam, cop a plea, or fold up shop. But Buckley and I were used to slugging it out in the tough, but smaller, arena of New York City courts. I also decided to stand and fight because I knew the ultimate sad truth about myself: without *Screw* I'd be back to nothing. Driving a cab. Kansas would become the toughest three-year fight of my life so far.

THE TURNING OF THE SCREW

One of the debacles in Kansas, that repeatedly surfaced in court against *Screw*, was the "angle of dangle" principal. The big threat of obscenity was whether it "appealed to prurient interest." Aside from being dirty, morbid, and offensive, the contents of *Screw* were only deemed criminal if it was sexy enough to, in the words of legalese, "create an erection in a male or a moist vaginal area in a female."

The prosecution, while cross-examining Mr. Average Citizen on the stand, had to determine if *Screw* "went beyond community standards." The defense would extract testimony from offended citizens that *Screw*'s material was, in fact, too grotesque, disgusting or shocking to inspire an erection or moist vaginal area in them. Average citizens would, of course, state that they had most certainly *not* been aroused by *Screw*. Which left the prosecution in the awkward position of extracting confessions from their own expert witnesses—like Fordham University's Father Schroth or NYU Sociology/Law professor, Dr. Ernst van den Haag—that *Screw did* in fact arouse an erection in them. Put in the position of having to admit to a boner on the stand, expert puritans waxed apoplectic. Thus, the prosecution would crumble on the matter of "prurient interest."

At one trial in New York, Buckley and I hired defense attorney Al Gerber, who had defended Lenny Bruce, and had only two losses in twenty-two obscenity cases. In establishing contemporary community standards, he submitted examples of the "new sexual freedom," holding aloft copies of *Playboy, Evergreen Review* and Henry Miller novels for the court to examine. A recess was called so that the three justices could attend that night's performance of the hit musical, *Oh, Calcutta!*

Outside the off-Broadway theater, criminal court judges Lang, Tyler, and Ringel were greeted at the entrance by *New York Post* and Associated Press photographers. They harrumphed some hasty statements, said they'd be back to see the musical one of these days, then tore ass out of there.

The number of judicial man-hours consumed in deciding whether *Screw* was fit for people to read was in the thousands. Meanwhile, courts were clogged with major felony cases where judges were urgently needed.

Jim Buckley was tired of the obscenity lawsuits. He considered *Screw* to be reactionary now, not a reflection of the simple joys of sex he first envisioned as a hippie. He knew that everybody now associated the paper with me, not himself. We'd been having a public feud in *Screw* for several years, writing point and counterpoint editorials. Jim was tired of the endless obscenity trials, sick of pornography. In other words, he suffered from good mental health.

Jim told the *Village Voice*, "Ever since our armed robbery last year, I've been paranoid. When I get in an elevator with another person I go into a sweat. I used to be cool, but now I feel *they're* going to kill me for no reason. After I finish the six porno films I'm working on, I'm heading for Telluride, Colorado, for three months of skiing."

Jim decided he wanted to sell *Screw*. His reasoning had to do with us possibly getting lighter sentences if we didn't own and operate the mag anymore. At this point we'd had *Screw* for six years and our daily battle with the world seemed nonstop. I didn't want to give *Screw* up, so Jim offered to sell out his interest, and in 1975 I bought it for a million dollars. And so, my 50-50 partner, Jim Buckley—a monogamous, repressed Catholic, who once turned down a blowjob from Linda Lovelace—who stepped on the brakes whenever I raced toward destruction—whose cock was bigger than mine—left the building.

That left Dirty Alvin, whose own mother once washed his mouth out with soap for using a four-letter word, as the sole representative of *Screw* magazine. At the office in New York, I started carrying a .38 strapped to my ankle, without a license, and was scared I'd shoot my foot off. I remembered joining the American Civil Liberties Union when I was only fifteen. My father threw me out of the house for six weeks. He thought I was a communist. Friends put me up. I've remained an ACLU member ever since, even though they've said I give freedom of speech a bad name. Buckley would later say that I wasn't the First Amendment's defender—*it* was my defender.

But as an example of how I had won over former enemies, witness this November 3, 1976, letter from the mighty law professor Ernest van den Haag to Judge Theis:

> I continue to regard pornography as harmful, as not protected by the First Amendment and the government entitled to legally punish pornographers. Nonetheless, I am asking you to sentence Al Goldstein to as lenient a penalty as the law permits. In the course of events I have come to know Al quite well, and although we are on opposite sides of the fence, I have come to respect and even to like a person whose views I continue to abhor. . . .
>
> I have found Al utterly honest, reliable, a man of his word and actually generous and kind hearted in all personal matters. . . . I have also found him to have rather self destructive personal problems, perhaps best symbolized by his tendency to eat himself to death. . . . I have come to know his family. I find him to be a good husband and a loving

father. In my personal relations with him I have not only found him to be instinctively fair minded, but also to be sweet natured.

It is my judgment that Al's personality is such that he may not be able to recover from actually serving a term in prison, which might destroy him as well as his family. I am aware of Al's bravado. But I am convinced it defends a basically brittle and tenuously integrated personality that might disintegrate in a prison environment. Thus, I respectfully urge that you find a way of achieving the intention of the law under which he has been convicted without sending Al to prison.

Jim Buckley was still a brave man. He wasn't afraid of going to jail and wanted to take the witness stand. Fahringer put his foot down and said no. Because if Jim took the stand, it would then force *me* to take the stand. And God knows what that might wreak. As the feds were hoping, Fahringer pointed out that a Kansas judge and jury might not be pleased as punch by the fat Jew and short Irish pornographers from New York—the "*Screw* Two," as we were now called. So in all the proceedings neither of us testified.

Buckley and I were nevertheless finally convicted on November 30, 1976. Miraculously, the decision was soon reversed, thanks to two of our lawyers, Arthur Schwartz and Jim Lawing, who shed the spotlight on the government's misconduct. Judge Frank G. Theis ruled the prosecutor had made remarks in his closing arguments that were inflammatory and prejudicial to the jury, declaring a mistrial for government misconduct. But this was just for the time being. A retrial was announced, to begin October 25, 1977, in Kansas City, Kansas.

One precedent that bears mentioning was that of Ralph Ginzburg, publisher of *Eros*. He went to prison in the 1960s. I think he hated me because after he came out of prison, I was making money with *Screw*. He ran a photo essay on female reactions to JFK, breaching the clandestine subject of Kennedy's sex life. He was arrested and prosecuted by Attorney General Robert Kennedy in 1963. *Eros* was not even dirty, it was pretentious "erotica"—they would asterisk four-letter words, didn't show pubic hair, and never delivered. Ginzburg was an excellent, if unethical, copywriter, famous for his full-page ads. He sought mailing privileges from the postmasters of Intercourse and Blue Ball, Pennsylvania, before receiving permission from Middlesex, New Jersey. One of the best jerk-off mags I ever saw was issue #4 of *Eros*, featuring a hot black couple, the very issue that got him arrested. He was convicted of "pandering," for the advertising alone, a whole new concept. The Supreme Court did a close call, 5 to 4 against, bringing into play the "publisher-as-pimp" angle, and Ginzburg served eight months of a five-year sentence in prison.

But I was living in constant fear of spending the rest of my life in prison. The Kansas trial had so far cost me $450,000 in hotel costs, legal fees and transportation. I was sequestered some two thousand miles from my home and place of business, in what the lawyers called the "contrived venue" of Kansas. I couldn't make any plans, buy a new home, think of a school for Jordan. I ballooned up to almost three hundred pounds. The horror of it all haunted my nights till my fat-and-fear-induced sleep apnea got so bad I needed a tracheotomy. Surgeons drilled a breathing hole in my throat and installed a plug, which I could open at bedtime so as not to suffocate in my sleep.

On the bright side, as the case dragged on, I watched the Goldstein curse hone in on our "law-and-order" enemies. Vice President Spiro Agnew had been kicked out of office. Nixon's attorney general, John

Mitchell, was sentenced to prison for his Watergate role, and then Nixon himself was driven out in disgrace in August, 1975.

The Kansas witch-hunt stemmed from a president now out of office, an attorney general in jail, and a deceased gay FBI director. In June of '77 I wrote to Carter's White House counsel Robert Lipschutz—perhaps suffering from a grandiosity that the new president would even be aware of some pornographer's plight:

> The president of the United States takes great pride in distinguishing his performance over that of Richard Nixon. The disparity between his appreciation of the Constitution and Mr. Nixon's attempt to subvert it is dramatic. . . . I would appreciate it very much if you could spend some time looking into the Justice Department's efforts to convict me as publisher of *Screw* for mailing alleged "obscene" materials.

A Justice Department underling wrote back:

> We in the Department, together with the United States attorney in Wichita and his staff, have given careful consideration to the question of whether or not this case should be retried, and we have come to the conclusion that retrial is warranted.

My "Screw You" column was where I still vented my inner self—not the neck-wounded, buttoned-down picture of propriety that people saw in court. From November, 1977: "I say to Jimmy Carter, Washington, the Justice Department, and the whole State of Kansas, FUCK YOU!!! Whether I go to jail or not, *Screw* shall continue."

Round Two. When our new trial began, Dr. Harold Voth, a Menninger Foundation psychiatrist testified that *Screw* appealed to prurient interest because it showed oral sex, which was "abnormal," and that exposure to *Screw* would bring about perverse behavior in Kansans. I felt bad for Dr. Voth's wife, when I considered the cobwebs criss-crossing her uneaten pussy.

Our defense experts declaring *Screw* wasn't obscene included Dr. Walter Menninger, the clinical director of the Topeka State Hospital and the Menninger Foundation—which employed Dr. Voth's unsucked dick. Dr. Wardell Pomeroy, a founder of the Kinsey Institute and coauthor of the Kinsey reports, defined "prurient interest" for our defense: "There are a good number of people who would be aroused by [*Screw's*] pictures," he testified. "But the pictures would appeal to their erotic interest in sex—not their prurient interest. Prurient is appealing to some sick, morbid, or shameful interest." Pomeroy also downgraded his colleague's assessment: "Dr. Voth has very strong views that are not representative of psychiatry nationally or in Topeka. People are sexual beings, and oral sex is one way of expressing that sexuality. We're getting away from the idea that sex is for reproduction only."

Garret Morris, of *Saturday Night Live*, flew in to testify. He had recently posed for *Screw* subscription ads eating watermelon, with the pitch, "What Kind of Nigger Reads *Screw?*" Cries of racism flooded NBC switchboards, after which Morris issued a statement to the *Daily News*: "Did it ever occur to anyone that I *like* watermelon?"

"You're no expert in literature, are you?" the prosecutor, Ben Burgess, asked with condescension. Morris conceded that his college degree was in voice and composition, not literature.

"You have to judge whether I'm an expert," said Garret. "I've done three seasons on *Saturday Night Live*, and I write my own material. [*Screw*] is a good place to steal ideas and humor."

After we had been convicted in November, the press finally raised their voices against the inquisition in personal letters to the court: Gay Talese, Kurt Vonnegut, Jr., Nora Ephron, Lynn Redgrave, Stanley Siegel, Barry Gray, Gael Greene, Nat Lehrman, Hugh Hefner, Gordon Lish, Joseph Papp, Ramsey Clark, Jann Wenner, Howard Smith, Joe Hansen, Dr. Albert Ellis, and my psychiatrist, Dr. Theodore Rubin. Some of these people despised *Screw*, or disliked me personally, but they held a reverence for freedom and felt my going to jail would serve no purpose.

Typical was a two-page letter, excerpted here, sent to Senators Jacob Javits and James Buckley (no relation to our Jim), by William M. Gaines:

> I am the publisher of *MAD Magazine.* . . . In both that capacity and as a private citizen I am extremely concerned about the functioning of our democratic institutions. . . .
>
> It seems to me that if our youth is to respect our institutions and the mechanisms employed to protect them, such tools must be applied with intelligence and fairness. The recent use of the federal apparatus to indict Al Goldstein and Jim Buckley as publishers of *Screw* magazine is a particular example of such lack of fairness.
>
> First, the indictment was brought in the State of Kansas, a jurisdiction whose connection with the affair is less than minimal since the publication has less than ten subscribers in the entire state. . . . Secondly, Messrs. Goldstein and Buckley are publishers of a newspaper which is directed to consenting adults. While it may be distasteful, and represent a political point of view with which many, including myself, strongly disagree, it does constitute an important medium for the dissemination of ideas and information in the entire taboo-filled and controversial arena of sexually oriented material.

In the middle of our retrial in 1977 I was recovering from another tracheotomy operation at home. There had been severe medical complications. The implanted tube had to be changed often and my neck was always bleeding. Federal marshals came to my home, rousted me out of my sickbed and swooped me off to Kansas again, to ensure I'd appear in court for the medical hearing I'd been granted. I coughed out the surgically implanted tube in my throat, and had to be taken to the University of Kansas Medical Center for emergency surgery. Judge Theis called a recess so that everybody could go home for the weekend quail shoot. It was the seventh time Judge Theis had mercifully granted a recess due to my condition. There were no hookers or good times for me in Kansas—no barbecue, raucous music, no Kansas City women and a bottle of Kansas City wine. I called home to talk to my wife and three-year-old son every night, gasping for breath.

Prosecutor Burgess's summation to the jury made my chest expand with patriotic pride, and would have made the best subscription ad yet, had I not been facing prison: *Screw* was "obscene, lewd, offensive, filthy, vile, lascivious, and dirty."

The whole thing went to the jury, and we waited three days and nights. If I lost, it would quite literally have meant the death of me and of *Screw*.

From the *Kansas City Times*, November 18, 1977:

Al Goldstein's obscenity trial in Kansas City, Kansas, ended Thursday with a deadlocked jury, leaving in doubt whether the New York publisher of *Screw* magazine will be tried again. . . . After three days of deliberation in U.S. District Court and 4 votes, the jurors were split 9 to 3 in favor of acquittal. . . . Judge Frank G. Theis declared a mistrial at 4 P.M. after receiving a note from the jury foreman that said simply: "We have a jury who cannot reach a decision."

"The big hang-up was prurient interest," [another juror] Harold Guess, a Kansas City, Kansas, machine operator who was on the jury said. "I voted innocent all the way. The way I saw it, it wasn't obscene."

Again, no one would admit to a hard-on.

I had now spent $650,000 in *Screw*'s defense. At first the government was making second-retrial noises, and there was a possibility that we'd need to go through the entire nightmare for a third time. Burgess offered to dismiss the charges if our corporation, Milky Way Productions, the third defendant in the case, would plead guilty to the twelve-count "conspiracy" indictment. But there was no way we were going to plead guilty—we would not accept a black mark on *Screw*. I did consider pleading guilty on *Smut*, and then folding it. This would result in a mere fine of sixty-thousand dollars. But the prosecutors had been humiliated enough, and decided not to try a third time.

Postal inspectors in Kansas City took out mail subscriptions. Asserting great offense, they brought charges. Nobody who doesn't work for the prosecution ever complained. The Nixonian system of putting people in jail no matter whether they've broken the law goes on. But juries are smarter than the imbeciles who collect government paychecks think they are. . . . If the government is often run by people who have no idea of fairness, you can depend on ordinary people to straighten them out.

—*Philadelphia Daily News* editorial

After the dust settled, I invited the jurors who'd held out for our freedom to New York at *Screw*'s expense for a victory celebration at Plato's Retreat. Five of them came. They were indeed a hung jury.

From now on, *Screw* felt obliged to give another *pornectomy* to its out-of-town edition, substituting a few more soft- for hard-core photos. But as I learned when we first started *Screw*—people were starving to look at nakedness, and the American government would never be able to stop them again.

RUSS MEYER

SCREW: You actually started in the fifties, didn't you, with a movie called *The Immoral Mr. Teas*, which was probably the showed naked people on public screens.

MEYER: Well, that came out in 1959. It was the first film dealing with voyeurism. A character in the film was a voyeur. He had these hallucinations about the three key women—the dental nurse and the waitress and the receptionist. And he saw them without clothes, but in a kind of abstract manner.

SCREW: And that film pretty much set the tone for most of the sex films for the next ten years?

MEYER: I would say more like three years. I know I duplicated myself half a dozen times. I consider some four of my films contributed some important changes of technique and ideas in the "nudie" movies—

SCREW: At that time the films were dubbed "Nudie Cutie."

MEYER: Yeah. Until about '63.

SCREW: *The Immortal Mr. Teas* was probably tamer than most R-rated films today—

MEYER: It is an R-rated film today. It apparently still plays in the South, and is particularly successful in Mississippi, which is one of our more backward states as far as freedom on the screen.

SCREW: One of your early ones, which ran forever in Los Angeles, was a thing called *Lorna*. It had a definite plot. A woman who had exceedingly large breasts.

MEYER: Yes, a monstrous search took place. She was a showgirl, Lorna Maitland, from Las Vegas. She came to my house and unleashed herself—opened her blouse. We had already selected a girl for the part, but when I saw her, I immediately paid the other girl off. Lorna was spectacular. Hollywood would have dubbed her melon-breasted.

SCREW: Where is she now?

MEYER: I have no idea. They usually just disappear. The men kind of hang around in films, but the women either marry or just fade away.

SCREW: After *Vixen*, in 1968, you accomplished something very unusual for somebody involved in the sex field. You got a contract from Twentieth Century Fox. Your first film for them was what a lot of us consider a classic—*Beyond the Valley of the Dolls*. Some people say it may perhaps be the worst film ever made. And therein lies its real value. . . .

MEYER: As a rule when I finish a film, I get five good reviews. Usually in some place like Monroe, Louisiana, or Carpentria, California, some film buff will dig what I do. But by and large the criticisms are good hatchet jobs. Particularly coming into New York it's like coming into the jaws of death.

SCREW: Where do you find them, Russ?

MEYER: Arduous searches. I hire a casting director and he sifts through the multitudes. It's not easy to find the right girls. You know, ones that can't pronounce their names and still be reliable and won't cut out on a production midway or run off with some character.

SCREW: Some feminists might say Russ Meyer is the ultimate male chauvinist . . . that all he ever has in his pictures are big-breasted women. . . . I've never seen a moderately chested woman in your pictures except when she was playing the ingénue role.

MEYER: It's hard to find a big-breasted ingénue.

SCREW: How do you answer these charges? Would you say that you are a chauvinist?

MEYER: Oh, I admit to most anything now. Years before I was quite defensive about these things. Now I admit to almost any indiscretion. There's not nearly enough public outcry about what I do. On only three occasions have I had any confrontation with the feminists. The most recent was in San Antonio at Trinity College. But they are always extremely polite and little points are made.

—*Screw*, January 1977, by Alex Bennett

CHAPTER 22

Feminists

At some point in the 1970s, the people who ran the women's movement were faced with a choice. They could remain allied to civil libertarians, liberals, and lefties who inhabited a smaller side of American culture. This would mean they would have had to put up with smut and loose morals and a few STDs that came with the territory. Or they could accept the offer of the mainstream right wing, and buy into the American nightmare by advocating censorship, thought control, and good old American morality. The temptation to be accepted was just too great for the feminists. They turned neo-facist.

This decision was first highlighted by an incident concerning Hugh Hefner and a national abortion task force run by feminists. Hefner wanted to contribute toward defending physicians and patients who ran into legal trouble when aborting a fetus (this was right before Wade vs. Roe). The first year the feminists accepted Hef's money; the second year they accepted it, then had second thoughts and sent it back. They issued a high-and-mighty statement: Hef's money was tainted, it was an attempt to buy them off.

In refusing the money, such feminists made a decision that continued to haunt them and their movement right into the ground. The ladies who headed up the women's movement showed no forethought in aligning with right-wing conservatives, helping to push their antiporn censorship through city councils from Minneapolis to Indianapolis to Suffolk County. They made their choice, and now their sisters are suffering for it, and the bombs are flattening their political gains straight back into the Age of the Rusty Coat Hanger.

All the spokeswomen for the women's movement were writers. Where were the typists, secretaries, nurses, and teachers? These were not feminists, but writers in search of a movement, hitchhikers looking for a vehicle. Andrea Dworkin represented the furthest extreme in radical antiporn feminism. She was also hideous, and made Ron Jeremy look like Miss America. As such, she was too easy to ridicule, and since I have outlived her—the pitter-patter of Dworkin's elephant hooves boomed across the earth from 1946 to 2005—I will now give her the stage:

> With pornography a woman can still be sold after the beatings, the rapes, the pain, the humiliation, have killed her. . . . The women trapped in the pictures continue to be perceived as the free speech of the pimps who exploit them. No judge seems willing to look such a woman, three dimensional and breathing, in the face and tell her that the pimp's use of her is his constitutionally protected right of speech. . . . Keeping these women silent in courts of law is the main strategy of the free speech lawyers who defend the pornography industry. . . . the challenges to civil rights law have been abstract arguments about speech, as if women's lives are abstract.

Dworkin's belief that consenting women before the camera were never consenting, presumes that women are incapable of free will.

(Explain that to Honeysuckle Divine.) Dworkin's "porn equals rape" equation, a ludicrous assertion in mainstream porn, *did* take effect in law. An Indianapolis antiporn ordinance—supposedly protecting women and children—defined porn as "sexual subordination of women," rendering porn actionable as a civil rights violation. Antiporn fanatics Phyllis Schlafly, Andrea Dworkin, and Minnesota law professor Catherine MacKinnon, conceived the ordinance and tried to take it national. Gloria Steinem and *Ms.* crowned the ordinance a legislative masterpiece. Before spreading to other cities, it was reversed by the Supreme Court in 1986.

I had the honor of debating the widely misunderstood Andrea Dworkin several times. The first time we walked out onstage together, Dworkin spit on the floor before me. I wiggled my tongue between my fingers, taunting, "You'll never get any of this!" But imagine the fireworks Andrea and I could have ignited, two oversized sex hogs, chowing down on each other's genitals like rabid dogs.

There are statements made by Dworkin I would heartily endorse, like: "I want a twenty-four-hour truce during which there is no rape." I would extend this truce to forever. Dworkin's take on prostitution:

> Men of the Right and men of the Left have an undying allegiance to prostitution as such, regardless of their theoretical relationship to marriage. . . . The old pornography industry was a right-wing industry: secret money, secret sin, secret sex, secret promiscuity, secret buying and selling of women, secret profit. . . . The new pornography is a left-wing industry: promoted especially by the boys of the sixties as simple pleasure, lusty fun, public sex, the whore brought out of the bourgeois home into the streets for the democratic consumption of all men.

Prostitutes aside, I only like strong women—women with a career, a sense of themselves. I never wanted women who were merely children, because then I'm responsible for them. I always lived on the precipice of insanity and psychosis, and sometimes when I put my head down to go to sleep, I can't believe that I got through the day in one piece. How could I take care of another human being? When you have some dumb 40-IQ chick who's fucked up on Quaaludes, you may as well hang her up like a ham hock. Call in Ron Jeremy.

I want to be perceived not just as a sensitive mind or bright person, but as a stiff cock and good fuck. Women who object to being sex objects are foolish. They should take it for what it is, and realize that men who have been conditioned to objectify women are merely responding like Pavlovian dogs.

I have often stated that I am appalled by and unalterably opposed to those who violate the sexual sanctity of minors. As a parent and human being, I totally agree with all Supreme Court rulings that kiddie porn is *not* protected by the Constitutional guarantees of a free press. Any child porn being made is produced by twisted individuals in an underground network, far from the mainstream, and I support rigorous laws to prosecute anyone who has anything to do with it.

In debates, I've stated my views of male-female relations, and my belief that biology trumps politics. Men are simple. They get aroused, hard, and pop. Women have a labyrinth of internal complications that men don't have. But we all suffer; men get carved up by lawyers lying in the cut, waiting for one extramarital slip of the pecker to ruin our lives. I'm outraged and shocked at the number of women in this society who use sex as a form of physical extortion. I watch the History Channel. Take wildebeests or bull seals—the male has his harem behind him and any other male that approaches he will try to kill. We're animals, it's natural for males to have a harem, but not let his harem have a harem. I've seen it demonstrated—the boys play differently from girls on the playground, and I enjoyed watching Jordan be more aggressive. Boys and girls are not the same. Feminists changed that, and new conventions of society forced handcuffs on us.

Feminism in its rare sex-positive persona was exemplified by the writer Germaine Greer, author of *The Female Eunuch*, and editor of the British underground rag *Oz*. She accompanied me to the world's first sex film festival in Amsterdam in 1971, the Wet Dream Film Fest. A frequent contributor to early *Screw*, she called us "counter-revolutionary" because we were into "the whole tits and ass thing." She wrote a masturbation essay, "Lady Love Your Cunt" ("because nobody else is going to") in 1971. She endeared herself to sexual liberators, at least the men, with her theory that genitalia, when displayed publicly, would lead to equality between the sexes. And so, this founding mother of modern feminism posed for a centerfold in the Dutch publication *Suck* with buttocks raised skyward, her black-bushed vage and anus splayed, and her lovely face peering from between her knees. And she looked sensational.

PLAYBOY MANSION

When I had my L.A. apartment, I would go to Spago and spend nights with Hefner. Of course, I think he's a great man, and an amazing host. There were a bunch of alter cockers hanging around—Tony Curtis, Robert Culp, Robert Blake, James Cahn. There was rarely sex. Hefner deceives himself into thinking those girls really like him, when they're all paid house niggers. Tony Curtis told me this story: He was at some urinal, and this guy keeps looking at him while he's pissing. Looking at his dick. Tony asks, "Are you cruising me?" The guy says, "No, I just wanna look at your cock knowing that you fucked Marilyn Monroe."

I only did coke to get laid, when I was at Hefner's. I remember fucking two playmates, they were sisters, and the only way I could get at their pussies was through two hundred dollars of coke. Coke was the key to many a pert playmate's spuzz box. Then they would slip away to other guests who had more coke, gone for the night. The girls didn't want me because I didn't make movies. Adam Rifkin, a producer, put Hef and Ron Jeremy in some of his films. The deal was Ron Jeremy would get Adam laid, and Adam would put Ronnie in mainstream movies.

My L.A. girlfriend became Toni, a shrink who wrote several books. I used to take her to S&M clubs and hang her upside down. I had sex with her on the pool table in Hefner's game room. She was pretty, sexy, smart, and got stoned with me. I loved eating her analytical pussy. Then she dumped me because I wouldn't buy her a Rolex, and thereafter denied having dated me.

Larry Flynt dug up pictures of Hef in a 69 with one of his playmates, and asked me to run them. I wouldn't, I felt a loyalty to Hef. But I was impressed by the size of his dick. I brought Flynt and Hef together, like Henry Kissinger, and had Flynt hand over the photos to Hef. But Flynt kept copies, of course. Jordan used to do magic tricks for Hefner and his kids, but then one night Hef wouldn't let Jordan into the movie room. So I wrote Hefner a nasty letter, ending our friendship, as I seem to do with everyone. I said my son was smarter than his daughter. We never spoke again. *Hustler* ended up running the pix of Hef.

Bob Guccione of *Penthouse*, the publisher I've always respected the most, the kindest to me, disappeared. Like me, he must be humiliated that he went bankrupt.

CIGARS

Cigars are living and breathing instruments of pleasure that start from Mother Nature, and through the hands of human beings are rolled into fine-tasting pleasures. At the Upmann factory in Havana, I watched wizened craftsmen with years of experience create works of art called the Montecristo Churchill, the Montecristo A, and my personal favorite, the Montecristo No. #2. I also love the Junior Ultimate and Cuban Trinidads. Before I went into bankruptcy, I had ten thousand cigars.

I saw cigar smoking as power, part of my image because it manifested success. I even did several porn films with a cigar in my mouth. I always liked smoking a Cuban because, every time I lit one up, I knew I was annoying the State Department. I purchased George Burns's humidor at Sothebys for twelve thousand dollars, and also bought Milton Berle's humidor and Red Auerbach's. I had almost a hundred humidors, the most expensive being a Washington Monument for thirty grand. After Bill Cosby sold his show to syndication for $88 million, I loved that he would knock on my door to bum cigars. I also had a satellite dish and he wanted a wire from my dish to his home so he wouldn't have to pay for TV. I said, "If I do that, you have to watch what I watch. And I don't watch porn, just the History Channel."

I opened a cigar store in Pompano Beach in 1997—a cigar bar and gun shop called Goldstein's Glamour Guns—with topless dancers selling cigars behind the counter. But I hated seeing the cigars get sold and leave my store. But I only lost fifty grand on the store. When I was homeless I would go to J&R Cigars. You could get a hundred cigars for a hundred dollars, but because Lou Rothman knew me, they would take 20 percent off. I'd smoke these eighty-cent cigars, but I didn't care, I kept the habit going. I'd be sitting on a park bench, and someone would scold, "Put that cigar out!"

"But I'm outside," I would protest.

STATEN ISLAND FERRY

In February 2002, I was convicted on six counts of misdemeanor harassment, and sentenced to sixty days on Rikers Island for chewing out one of my last secretaries, Jennifer Lozinski. She resigned after eleven weeks, and I accused her of stealing cash from the company. I left a now notorious message on her answering machine: "I'll take you down, cunt." I called her "the smelly cunt from hell" in *Screw*, listing her phone and address.

I didn't anticipate how horrible Rikers Island would be . . . the overwhelming stink of impoverishment, hopelessness and defeat, rats and roaches, the ceaseless farting of third-world criminals. Rikers is the vilest place in America, much worse than the last time I was there in my early thirties. Now I'm sixty-six, with diabetes, on a dozen medications. So they put me in the methadone center. I'm with fifty *schvartzas*, all of them doing methadone in the bathroom. I'm with the Bloods, the Crips, I'm the only white person, the oldest there. Handcuffed all the time. There's no diabetic food. Breakfast, lunch, and dinner is the same—pieces of bread and jelly. Like a third-world country, everything at Rikers was broken—the toilets, the sinks, the copying machines. Nothing to do but stare at space. It's filthy, there are cockroaches, everyone hates you, it's a fuckin' horror.

Some corrections officers asked me for my autograph. But the twenty-year-old gangbangers had no idea who I was. I'm not some

Mafia guy who can do time standing on my head. Theoretically, you're allowed to have visitors, but they wouldn't let anyone visit. I'm not talkin' theory, I'm talkin' truth. Even my supporters within the NYPD were unable to sneak in pastrami sandwiches, and some tried.

I could see *Penthouse, Playboy,* and *Hustler,* but they wouldn't let me have *Screw.* They confiscated *Newsweek* and *Time.* They gave me *Cigar Aficionado* just to aggravate me since I couldn't have cigars, and *Time Out,* the restaurant issue, since I wasn't allowed edible food. They played mind games, determined to break me.

Once in the medical ward, I was denied permission to use a bathroom for seven hours. So I shit my pants. Then I refused to take a shower. "If I am to be in hell, I want to smell like hell," I told my guards. After receiving an involuntary injection, I began hallucinating, seeing double, and hearing voices. Doctors, if that's what they were, performed surgery on me, against my will. They forced a catheter up my leg. They wouldn't refill my diabetic prescription and they switched my antidepressant to Zoloft, which I don't take. They injected insulin in my arm, which I don't take. Now I knew what it was like to be in the hands of Dr. Mengele. One correction officer said I would leave in a pine box.

MAI LIN

AL: So, you met John Holmes's fourteen-and-a-half-inch cock in your first film. Let's talk about that. Did you get into a deep throat when you sucked his dick?

MAI: Well, I sucked on it, but I couldn't take it in all the way. He was very gentle; very nice to me.

AL: Mai, how do you feel about sucking and fucking in front of a camera? Does it turn you on sexually?

MAI: I'm an actress. But, under the right circumstances . . . sure, it turns me on. I remember the first time I fucked John Holmes, when I was doing some loops. I kept my eyes closed most of the time because I just kept coming and coming, and in a funny way, I was embarrassed about how much I liked it. You know . . . being fucked like that in front of the whole film crew.

DEAN [MAI'S HUSBAND]: She loosened up really quickly, though. After John Holmes was finished with her, she was still so turned on, she fucked and sucked off the whole crew. Then, when she finished with the crew . . . must have been about ten guys . . . she came to me and said, "Fuck me, baby. I need you to fuck me now."

—*Screw*, April 1981

Making It as a Mick

To gain the confidence of Irish persons, it's necessary to understand their proud and unique ethnic heritage. This is not hard at all to do, since this heritage is identical in every pertinent detail with every other European ethnic group in America. In the Old Country, that is, the Irish were largely short, fat, violently religious and father-dominated peasants with a viciously homicidal hatred of all foreigners. In this country they tend to be fat, short, deeply sentimental and mother-dominated hardhats with passionate allegiances to patriotic organizations like the Elks, the American Nazi Party, Ku Klux Klan, and so on. Anyone at all familiar with any American ethnic minority—Hunkies, Polacks, Wops, Hebes, Swedes, Serbo-Croatians, etc.—should have no trouble at all understanding the proud and unique Irish heritage.

In passing for Irish, your paramount goals are (a) to avoid the men as much as possible, and (b) to screw the women. Both are best achieved through idle conversation on a stool at the Blarney Stone. You should be wearing a super-thick wool turtleneck, with the smell of the Irish sheep still in it (Alsatian dogshit is an acceptable substitute), bland corduroy "breeches," and a handsome briar pipe (which need never be lit). . . . Inform whoever's at the next stool that he's your oldest, dearest friend in the whole wide world. Recall your blessed *mither* to him, God rest her soul, and her terrible trouble breech-birthing you in the pat-tatty patch after a three-day labor. . . . Recall your youthful poverty, your family of twelve, the little cottage in Boston reeking of corned beef and cabbage, the grand old times you had. Pick a nasty fight with the first person who tells you to shut your bloody gob. . . .

There's one wonderful thing about Irish girls: they're all white. From there on, it goes straight downhill. . . . It's *absolutely* necessary to put on a rubber any time you have knowledge of an Irish woman. Besides the obvious considerations of sanitary prophylaxis, these Irish girls, like all other Catholic pussy, are chronic baby-mongers. Contraception should never be left up to such nun-haunted individuals: The irrepressible fertility of the Irish race *will* ooze out of its women, no matter what. I knew an Irish girl once whose intrauterine coil *disappeared* for two weeks, until she woke up with it lying on her pillow next to her *ear!*

—*Screw*, March 1978, by Dean Latimer

TWENTY-FIRST CENTURY PORN

The state-of-the-art porno film, for me, still remains in the 1970s. I hate pornography today. There are three hundred films a week, all shot on video, the girls are bored, the guys are on Viagra. The best films were shot in my era, the 1970s. Gloria Leonard, Seka, and Annette Haven practically made a political statement, Make Love Not War, Let's Fuck Not Fight. The girls were beautiful, no plastic on them, and they gave a shit. They did a few films a year; today's girls do a few a week. And how can that slut-hippo Ron Jeremy be an object of desire? Ugliness rules?

The films of today are an insult, they're meaningless product. There's no tension or surprise, no human characterization. The men are Viagra sluggers who come on set with "redi-wood;" anal is *de rigueur*, the girls assholes "gape" open; they do double anals, get pounded like Omaha Beach, choke down drug-hardened cocks, gurgle semen, perform multiple cock-swallowing gymnastics, and then are discharged upon like a female toilet. Is this to be my legacy? I never dreamed I'd ever say such a thing, but is there no taste? Assembly-line bleached blondes with nipple pinkenings and pre-paid tit jobs on the installment plan pay back their companies with interest. It's all business. It's only a matter of moments before MIT offers a degree in pornography.

GEORGINA SPELVIN

AL: How do you approach your film roles? The big praise you're getting is for your acting, not for your cocksucking.

GEORGINA: No. I'm not a very good cocksucker, but I *am* a good actress. Every role I've ever gotten has dealt with things that have been foreign to my experience so I simply try to make them part of my experience in order to portray the role convincingly. If I have to learn to twirl the baton, I'll do the best I can to learn it.

Al: Do you work with Stanislavski's method?

GEORGINA: I have my own method. I'm a great seeker of approval. My whole life I've danced on my tippy toes or done somersaults to get attention. I simply try to present what the director has in his head. Cutting film is the greatest experience for an actress because you realize better what they want from you. What makes a film great is the proper combination of all the ingredients, like a good meal—you could have the greatest roast beef but if the Yorkshire pudding comes out like a piece of cardboard, where are you? . . . By the way, I think the sexiest movie in the world is *Wuthering Heights*.

AL: Did you ever have to audition for fuck films?

GEORGINA: I have to say that in fuck films, I have never *ever* been propositioned or told that I have to blow somebody to get a part. The fuck film people are the straightest, nicest, most up-front people that I have ever worked for in my life, and that includes the mercantile industry, commercials, training films, industrials. Trying to get into [legitimate] films for fifteen years, I ran the gauntlet of casting couches. I got tired of having to fuck the receptionist in order to get to screw the second assistant director in order to blow the first assistant cameraman in order to meet somebody to maybe get a walk-on.

AL: And for *Miss Jones*?

GEORGINA: For *The Devil in Miss Jones*, I went to see if I could work on production, I was going to do commissary work for them. They were going to shoot it in Pennsylvania, and I love to cook. I'd been running a soup kitchen in my place to stay alive for the last few months. We charged everybody who came in a dollar. Since I was into that bag, I asked, "How about a commissary?" and they said, "Fine." Jerry Damiano was in the office and he asked me to read. I read for him and he said, "We want you to do the lead."

AL: Who would you like to fuck?

GEORGINA: Jacques Cousteau.

—*Screw*, June 1973

STATEN ISLAND FERRY

Watching CNN one night, an old man whose legs were amputated wheeled in and changed the channel over my protest. That was my one fight in Rikers and I yielded to a legless cripple. Well, let the cripple watch his nigger shows, I thought to myself. I fucked Seka and Linda Lovelace. I'm sure the only girls this guy ever fucked were members of his own family.

I prayed for the first time in forty-two years—since being jailed in Cuba and told I would be executed as an American spy. Fahringer's legal assistant, Tricia Dubnow, tried to rescue me. She saw me laying on the floor shaking, puking, crying. She would not leave without me. The guards locked her up for twenty-five hours while trying to bail me out.

Finally, Farhringer was able to get me released on twenty-five-thousand-dollar bail, after nine days at Rikers. I still owed them fifty more days. My passport had been confiscated, and I couldn't travel a radius of more than twenty miles from my Florida home or New York apartment.

Before I went in, I'd boasted to the *New York Times*, "Jail means nothing to me, because freedom means so much to me." I told reporters I was intrigued by the idea of having a big black boyfriend violate my love holes.

The *Times* was waiting when I stumbled out of Rikers. "They won, they broke my spirit," I admitted. It was the first time I ever cried during an interview.

CHAPTER 23

The Goldstein Curse

Goldstein's sad-sack persona inspired sadness and pity rather than anger and envy, a porn dinosaur usurped by fey, arty, tongue-in-cheek pussies who play-act at being sexually liberated . . . a mangy lion in a New York City winter, pasty white, rather than golden, but a lion nonetheless . . . a sad, overweight, diabetic, financially ruined old Jew with a dwindling list of friends and a nearly dried-up sex drive.

—*New Yorker*, profile by Adam Gopnick, July 23, 2001

I paid a thousand dollars to a high-end dating service for ten names. My first date was a woman named Delores Ritter—who turned out to be the cheating wife of a John Gotti hit man. Gotti put a contract out on my life. In a last great act of kindness before he himself was whacked, DiB was able to cool it out.

Free distribution of the *Village Voice* and *New York Press*, which began running the same ads once exclusive to *Screw*, cut deeply into circulation. And *Screw*, once piled high alongside the *New York Post* throughout the city, was now relegated to the back of the newsstand—just like Countrywide Publications, when their time was up. The *demimonde* of men's magazines gave way to burgeoning online porn. Bob Guccione, once worth $200 million, lost *Penthouse*. *Playboy* was down to a fifth of what it once sold, and so was *Hustler*. My final episode of *Midnight Blue*, after twenty-seven years and twelve hundred episodes, was on November 30, 2002. *Screw* ceased publication as such in October 2003, after thirty-five years and eighteen hundred issues. Marshals were summoned for nonpayment of rent. I grabbed one last handful of Cuban cigars and left forever.

Bill Mudie, the quiet, hardworking, master typesetter and production manager at *Screw* for twenty-five years—the longest of any employee—wrote Josh in January, 2005:

> As for Al, who knows how it will end? He certainly made a mess of his life with Rose's help (an attorney and one-time girlfriend who milked me dry and then some over the course of several years). The only time I ever lost my temper there in twenty-five years, I started screaming at her in a blasting roar that was heard fifty feet away in the front offices. I suppose Rose got her revenge by turning Al against me a few months later. In many ways, his definitive, irreversible decline can be traced to her arrival. She insinuated her way into his life and the company. But he did himself in, too, with four residences and nine cars, a sixty-thousand-dollar boat, insane purchases constantly. I was told that he had approximately a hundred credit cards. They were usually being declined. Once he went to buy cornflakes at a supermarket in Florida, and it took four turned-down cards in a row before he decided to pay cash. He was ranting like a madman and blamed Manny [Neuhaus, then–managing editor]. Payroll checks bounced a few times. The rent on the office was behind months, and through it all he kept spending lavishly. . . . a five-

thousand-dollar TV, laptop computers he couldn't even turn on. . . . One day he started screaming at me at on the phone, telling me to leave if I didn't like it. I gently hung up after saying, "Fine," did another hour of work to ship the paper (didn't want to leave Kevin Hein, the art director, a mess) and walked out the door. . . . I felt the way I'd imagine a released prisoner might feel. Free and a bit frightened of what life would be like on the outside. Then, Al showed up for my unemployment hearing a few months later. I sat directly across the table from him. Kind of surreal to smell him reeking of cigars. He started babbling incoherently, and I easily won the case as my lawyer laughed at him, with Al complaining to the judge that he wasn't being respected or taken seriously. . . . and the equally obese black judge couldn't believe her ears when Al kept repeating that his son went to Harvard Law School. It was a nice day for me, to defeat him in court, perhaps for the first time in his life, in 2001.

Right around the time I was losing everything, someone arranged a date with hotel heiress Leona Helmsley, after her husband Harry, who owned the Empire State Building, croaked. She was ugly, old, mean and fat, but I was willing to suck her clit all night. I figured if I made her come, maybe she'd find me an apartment. She found out who I was and immediately canceled.

After I lost my Second Avenue Deli job, I descended to the streets. For a short spell I worked at New York City Bagels on commission, trying to generate big bagel bucks from corporate accounts, like the *New York Review of Books*. For an even shorter spell, I tried my hand doing standup at the Knitting Factory and Joe's Pub, like Jake LaMotta at the end of his career. The MC announced, "People love pornography, but not pornographers. Well, here's a pornographer you can embrace. Ladies and Gentleman, Al Goldstein!"

• • •

Just like Lenny, my life had disintegrated into a morass of trials and personal hell, clouding everything I'd achieved. This came to a head with the Lozinski trial. I told the *New York Post* I'd have my son defend me when he got out of Harvard. But Jordan was offended that his father was a pornographer. Enter Charlie DeStefano. He told me I was a vile, disgusting, pig-mouthed man. I told him I loved having a greasy wop lawyer. He considered me an uncle. When he was nineteen he was a delivery guy, en route to Forty-second Street where he encountered me in some office. "Hey, kid, c'mere," I said, reaching into a bag of condoms, filling his hands. "Fuck away, fuck away."

DeStefano's a criminal lawyer. As an old legal hound myself, I told him I want a fire in your belly when you go to Brooklyn Criminal Court, and I coached him on the First Amendment. DeStefano played along with me.

Jimmy Breslin, *Newsday*, March 24, 2002:

> The old defender moves with a weariness beyond his sixty-six years as he goes between the defense table and the prosecutor's and up to the witness stand. . . . He is one of four people in the last thirty-five years who effectively protected the First Amendment rights of reporters who bring the news to you. The others are Ralph Ginzburg, Larry Flynt, and Lenny Bruce. I know you don't want to meet them, but you owe them . . . Goldstein started in 1968 with authorities enraged over the same things that they now feature in *Sex and the City* and the *Vagina Monolgues* . . . When they mentioned counts against him for something he wrote, I could feel Lenny Bruce sitting on the windowsill in the corner of my office in the old *Herald-Tribune* newspaper. Sitting there in a tee shirt with a Hershey bar and with huge transcripts of all his court cases . . . the district attorney of Manhattan, Frank Hogan . . . had

Bruce arrested and charged with saying bad words during the 1 A.M. show at the Au Go Go club on Bleeker Street.

I saw Lenny Bruce five times. What a hero. I was nothing then, he was Dirty Lenny. He was the truth. I never met him, but became good friends with his mother, Sally Marr, and put her on salary for ten years as a *Screw* advisor. She denied that Lenny was a junkie. I had three dates with his daughter Kitty, and she stood me up each time. This was the closest I could come, wanting just to touch him. Now my life had disintegrated into the same morass of legal troubles as Lenny. But people doubted whether any of my current troubles had anything to do with freedom of speech.

As I did in Wichita, I created a circus at the Lozinski trial. The D.A. would be so blinded by hatred, he would shoot himself in the foot. I requested that terrorists fly a plane into Brooklyn DA Charles Hynes's office, running full-page aerial directions to his building in *Screw*. I said to send him anthrax letters. I taunted Judge Daniel Chun in the press, saying he made a good pork lo mein, but put too much starch in my shirts. I ran the phone numbers of Judge Chun and DA Hynes on the cover of *Screw*. Al "Grandpa Munster" Lewis was my character witness. He was so old I thought he'd die before lunch. "Whaddya think, I fell off a turnip truck and don't know what I'm doing?" he rambled, calling Justice Chun an amateur.

When Jimmy Breslin got a taste of the trial in person, he did a follow-up column: "I support the First Amendment. But I maintain my right to have taste. And [Goldstein's] a slob. . . . [Al's] kind of filth runs through four generations, at least."

I mooned the media in the hallways of the court, and asked the female reporters if I could eat their pussies. DeStefano insisted I take

Valium before my next appearance in court. I arrived wearing prison stripes for my sentencing. The jury was deadlocked, 5–1. By day six, they'd spent two-and-a-half days undecided, and this was a mere misdemeanor trial—the longest misdemeanor trial lawyers at Brooklyn Criminal Court could ever remember. And only .25 percent of misdemeanor cases ever went to trial, which proved how hungry the DA and judge were to nail me. Finally, I was convicted on six misdemeanor counts of harassment, facing two years. I got sixty days at Rikers. Lozinski took *me* down—the first time I was ever defeated.

I was a medical time bomb, with sleep apnea, diabetes, my teeth were falling out; I was like the Phantom of the Opera. And suddenly got chest pains. I was taken to the hospital in handcuffs in a wheelchair by guards. As they strapped me in the gurney in an ambulance, I moaned, "Macho fucks! Don't rape me, don't rape me. Slip the dildo in."

I told documentary filmmaker James Guardino, now shadowing me, "You're a piece of shit. All filmmakers are voyeurs—you live vicariously through me. You're watching a sad old man as his Titanic goes down. When we get old, that's what happens."

James understood where I come from. "Al offends you . . . then picks up the check," he observed. He soldiered on to release *Porn King: The Trials of Al Goldstein.*

Herald Fahringer got me out of Rikers after nine days. Fahringer handled my Lozinski appeal and the conviction was reversed three to nothing. I had been denied a fair trial—having inflamed the anger of the assistant DA to the point where he refused to let the jury draw their own conclusions—by calling our testimony "lies" forty times in his summation. If Herald hadn't gotten this decision reversed, I would have died at Rikers Island.

My court battles could endow an entire law library. Leaf through the annals of *Screw*'s legal history and you'll be amazed by the rogues gallery of public puritans who tried to crush *Screw*—whose lives and careers then went down in flames or disgrace. These figures were branded with the "Goldstein Curse"—a dark omen I bestowed in my weekly *Screw* editorial to the worst violators in my path. It worked like Jewish voodoo.

It began with Mayor Lindsay, who had me arrested nineteen times on charges of second-degree obscenity. Lindsay's presidential aspirations, career, and health plunged after his last term. Nassau County DA Bill Cahn handcuffed me on trumped-up charges, then ended up in federal prison for tax fraud. Staten Island Congressman John Murphy was jailed in the Abscam investigation after he crusaded to get *Midnight Blue* permanently cancelled. Even those who survived the Curse encountered misfortune of some kind. Mayor Guiliani's prostate cancer was announced soon after he received his Goldstein Curse for cleaning up Times Square.

Raving morality figures that aggressively targeted *Screw* included Charles Keating, founder of Citizens for Decent Literature. The same Charles Keating later imprisoned for the billion-dollar Lincoln Savings & Loan scandal. Televangelist Jim Bakker was ruined by fraud and sex scandal a month after I happened to vacation at his Heritage USA Christian theme park. Attorney General Ed Meese resigned over corruption charges after heading the Attorney General's Commission on Pornography. Among Meese's anti-smut Commissioners was Rev. Morton Hill, head of Morality in Media—who dropped dead after a busy career as self-appointed guardian of the public's morals. Also on the Reagan-era Commission was Times Square's most insidious antiporn crusader, Father Bruce Ritter. His number was up when news hit he'd been squandering Covenant House funds on male hustlers and molesting homeless boys in his care.

Corporate raider Carl Icahn bankrupted TWA and lost his chairmanship in 1993. He had been cursed for dismissing my complaints of continual crappy service. In 1996, I beat longtime foe Time Warner Cable of New York in federal court, for scrambling *Midnight Blue*'s cable signal. Even the U.S.S. *Intrepid* on Pier 86 went into bankruptcy, days after canceling a party for *Gadget*—when they found out it was published by Al Goldstein.

I'll never calculate the millions I spent on *Screw*'s defense. A model named Angie Geary filed a $29 million defamation after *Midnight Blue* parodied her 1988 Wasa Crispbread commercial. Marty Garbus handled that suit, costing a cool $1.5 million, but we won—it was eventually thrown out. *Screw*'s parody of the Poppin' Fresh doughboy prompted a $50 million lawsuit from Pillsbury. I owned two shares of General Mills and flew to a stockholder's meeting in Minneapolis dressed as the doughboy, yelling at them for wasting shareholders' money on frivolous lawsuits. There was a court deposition where my lawyer, Ken Norwick, had to question the CEO of Pillsbury on whether he suffered from syphilis (he claimed he didn't). I upped the ante with a new ad: "Nothin' Says Lovin' Like a Jew in the Oven." Once the suit was dismissed, I co-opted the doughboy as *Screw*'s cover logo for a year. Japanese *Screw* followed. The Pillsbury case established the right, once and for all, to satirize trademarked corporate symbols.

Screw prevailed in lawsuits leveled by ambitious DA's trying to make their bones. In the early eighties, I barely escaped ruin after settling a lawsuit from the wife of an assistant DA in Philadelphia. Her phone number somehow slipped by our security check in the ad department. She appeared in the hooker pages "Willing to Suck Nigger Cock Free."

Any major loss could have bankrupted *Screw* on the spot. The god of hypocritical reckoning was watching my back—my attackers lined up one by one, oblivious to each other's defeats, only to get chopped into herring.

But now I no longer exist, I'm a hologram. An old condom somebody popped a load into, then threw away. I always thought I would surely die from the bullets of an assassin. I could have died a martyr like Lenny Bruce. It would have been a better death than dying in humiliation as a bagel salesman—or in a homeless shelter.

Pioneers create their own extinction. Louie B. Mayer was kicked out of Hollywood, they turned their back and he became bitter and angry. During the last years of his life, he waited for Hollywood to apologize and welcome him back. I keep thinking the porn industry is going to come back and apologize, take me back in. But it's not going to happen. When you're past your time, you're past your time. Like Uncle Junior in *The Sopranos*. I desperately miss the taste of pussy.

Jordan came with me once to the AVN awards in Las Vegas. He had just finished at Georgetown University, where one of his courses was "Christian Feminist Theology." It was before he started Harvard. I was there to receive some award, and the the *Miami Herald* later quoted Jordan describing his father:

> What I felt they were acknowledging was his fighting for something he believed was not sinful, was constitutionally protected, that he was willing to go to prison for when others tend to only give lip service to First Amendment protection. . . . Society needs people who push the envelope, and that's his self-appointed role.

Jordan hugged me when I stepped down from the podium. And said
something I've never heard anyone say, before or since:
"I'm proud of you, Dad."

Screw You

A prime example of an unmitigated failure is a turd-encrusted delivery
service called Special Courier, which boasts about its fast, efficient
operation. Several months ago, however, when I had Special Courier
forward a box of magazines from *Screw*'s New York offices to my vacation retreat in Florida, the trip not only took twelve days because of
that odorous delivery service's sheer incompetence, but Special Couri-
eractually had the nerve to send me a bill. In fact, Special Courier's
malevolent service was so awful that it actually made the U.S. Postal
Service look good.

Last week in this space, I revealed the cruel, sadistic truth about an
alleged children's amusement park in Pennsylvania called Sesame
Place, which was such a totally repressive experience that I wondered
if the place weren't being secretly bankrolled by the KKK. However,
space limitations prevented me from expounding on another lump of
drek which is connected with Sesame Place—that is, the hotel that I
stayed at while visiting that putrid amusement park. It's the Hilton
Inn Northeast, 2400 Old Lincoln Highway, Trevose, Pa., and it serves
food that would make your cat puke. What's more, its cataract-laden
bellhops are constantly crashing into one another as their seeing-eye
dogs try to tear each other apart. This place was so incompetent that,
three minutes after I checked out after having been there for two days,
the front desk told a friend of mine who called that I had never even
stayed at the place. In short, the Hilton Inn Northeast is a hotel that
will only give the traveling public poetic justice when a condemned
sign is tacked to its front door.

Speaking of condemned, I've ofttimes wished that fate on the New York Health & Racquet Club, a horrendous rip-off health facility located here in the Big Apple. I've blasted the NYHRC time and again on this page because of the club's complete indifference to the needs and requirements of its members. This vomit-soaked place works much like a pyramid scam—it sells you memberships and then totally ignores you. In fact, in hearings recently held in Washington, the Federal Trade Commission corroborated these charges with a definitiveness and a lucidity that makes the reckless violations off the NYHRC something that the F.B.I. should immediately investigate.

However, as negligent as the owners of the NYHRC obviously are, even more repulsive is that cheap New York pussy Carol Lynley, who has been shamelessly huckstering for this sham outfit. Lynley is no different from the pimps on Eighth Avenue and Forty-second Street who vigorously try to sell the diseased flesh of their syphed-up hookers. I don't know how much she is being paid by the NYHRC, but whatever the sum, it is blood money. Lynley's total lack of respect for the prospective members of this unscrupulous club is equaled only by her total lack of respect for herself. It is truly nauseating to see this blonde bimbo compromise her integrity by offering gross come-ons which suggest that the New York Health & Racquet Club is a bona fide health facility, when in fact it is nothing but a scurrilous consumer rip-off.

(Second part in a series; continued next week)

—*Screw*, Sept. 29, 1980

Acknowledgments

Special Thanks: Peggy Bennett, Charles DeStefano, James Guardino, Penn Jillette, Booble.com, Paul Bresnick, John Oakes, Kenny Law, Peter Bloch, Kenny Lull

Some material in "Fat City" appeared in different form in "Sex in Fat City," *Penthouse*, November 1984, by Al Goldstein

Some material in "Spent" appeared in different form in "The Harder They Fall," *Playboy*, April 1983, by Al Goldstein

Some material in "The Goldstein Curse" appeared differently in *When Sex Was Dirty* by Josh Alan Friedman, Feral House, 2005

Numerous day-to-day dispatches from the *Kansas City Star*, the *Kansas City Times* and the *Wichita Eagle*, all from 1977, helped in documenting *Screw*'s federal obscenity trial.

The Other Hollywood, by Legs McNeil and Jennifer Osborne, Regan-Books, 2005, provided some information on *Deep Throat*.

Passage from "Pornography: Men Possessing Women," by Andrea Dworkin, copyright 1989, Andrea Dworkin Web site

Jim Buckley quoted from *Village Voice*, by Howard Smith and Brian Van der Horst, February 24, 1975

Jordan's quote from "Filthy Rich," by Elinor J. Brecher, *The Miami Herald Sunday Magazine*, August 9, 1998

Some quotes on cigars from "An Interview with Al Goldstein," by Steve Nathan, *Cigar Magazine*, Spring 2005

Some quotes in final chapter from the film documentary *Porn King: The Trials of Al Goldstein*, written and directed by James Guardino, 2005, Lancaster Associates, Inc.

Interview excerpts from *Screw*:

Seka excerpt, #723, January 10, 1983, and from *Screw*, October 22, 1979

Mayor Koch letter, #559, November 19, 1979

Tiny Tim, #657 and #658, October 12 and 19, 1981

Georgina Spelvin, #223 and #224, June 11 and 18, 1973

Russ Meyer, #411, January 17, 1977, by Alex Bennett

Vanessa Del Rio, #587, June 2, 1980

Harvey Fierstein, #742, May 23, 1983

Ron Jeremy, September 11, 1995

Henry Miller, #62, May 11, 1970

Sammy Davis, Jr., #97, January 11, 1971 "What Makes Sammy Come?"

Jack Nicholson, #194, November 20, 1972

Marilyn Chambers, #245, November 12, 1973

Terry Southern, #86, October 26, 1970, by Michael Perkins

Honeysuckle Divine, #266, April 1, 1974, from her diary January 15, 1972

J. P. Donleavy, #362, February 9, 1976

Harry Reems, #272, May 20, 1974, and #391, April 29, 1976

"Fuck of the Irish," by Dean Latimer, #472, March 20, 1978

John Holmes, #329–330, June 30, 1975, "John Holmes: King of the Cocks"

Desiree Cousteau, #581, June 16, 1980

David Allan Coe, #633, April 20, 1981

Melvin Van Peebles, #141, November 15, 1971

"Albert Speer," #669, December 28, 1981

Annette Haven, #324, May 19, 1975

Mai Lin, #631, April 6, 1981

Chuck Traynor, # 588, June 9, 1980

Jim Mitchell, #283, August 5, 1974

John Lennon, #18, June 1969